YACHT RACING

THE AERODYNAMICS OF SAILS
AND
RACING TACTICS

YACHT RACING
THE AERODYNAMICS OF SAILS
AND
RACING TACTICS

BY

DR. MANFRED CURRY

REVISED AND ENLARGED
FIFTH EDITION

FROM THE GERMAN
BY
ROBERT W. ATKINSON
AND
CHARLES E. CURRY, PH. D.

NEW YORK
CHARLES SCRIBNER'S SONS
1948

FIRST PUBLISHED IN ENGLISH 1928

REPRINTED 1930

THIRD EDITION 1933

FOURTH EDITION 1935

FIFTH EDITION 1948

To my Father
CHARLES EMERSON CURRY
who taught me the first principles of yachting.
He died on his yacht during a regatta, 1935.

DR. MANFRED CURRY

PREFACE

I was eighteen years of age when I wrote this book, but the first edition did not appear until 1925. The book was published in German, French, English, and Turkish.

Today, twenty-three years later, I am happy to realize that those who love yachting still use my book, and that it has proved helpful to many yachtsmen, both young and old.

In spite of experience gained in about 1,400 regattas, I have been unable to improve on my racing tactics.* The fact that other yachtsmen have also failed to develop new ideas on this subject suggests that research along this line has been more or less completed.

In boat and sail design, on the other hand, further progress is to be expected. Many of the suggestions made in the first edition of this book — for example, the Marconi rig, the Genoa jib, the parachute spinnaker, the plank or so-called **Park Avenue boom** (used on the cup defender Enterprise), turning masts, arched and adjustable centerboards (employed on the inland scows) — have been generally accepted.

As technical developments cannot be foreseen, several devices suggested in the first edition which have not yet come into general use have again been included in this new edition. It is my belief that some of these — for example, transverse battens and brakes for boats — will ultimately find general acceptance.

In this edition, as in the foregoing ones, I have not discriminated between large and small boats, but the skipper will know whether I am referring to a keel or a centerboard boat.

The fine points of yacht racing are especially apparent in the smaller classes. In the large yachts, they are harder to perceive as they are more deeply hidden. I therefore recommend that the study of regatta sailing be begun in a small boat. A good small-boat sailor will soon understand a large yacht, whereas the skipper of a large yacht may never discover the traits of the sensitive small boat.

* See my book, "Racing Tactics in Questions and Answers." New York, Charles Scribner's Sons, 1932.

The abilities which the racing boat requires of its skipper are not confined, as in other sports, to a circumscribed category; they are not mainly physical, as is the case in almost all other sports. I do not think I am mistaken in saying that, in sailing, head-work comes first, physical prowess second. Of course, I am speaking of the highest development of the sport, regatta sailing. No other sport requires such versatility of talent and accomplishment as sailing a race: logical thinking; clear, quick consideration; presence of mind; courage; endurance, often for hours at a time; keenness of observation; delicacy of feeling. To these may be added as desirable, if not absolutely essential, physical strength, agility, and a certain feeling for equilibrium.

Not least, sailing affords an opportunity for the enjoyment of Nature's beauties. Nowhere else are they displayed more richly than in water and cloud. Never is sea or lake twice the same. At times, the storm lashes the water to froth and urges man to contest with the fiercest of all elements. At other times, the calm or gently rippled surface of the water affords him peace. The breeze or wind which carries the sailor from the shore separates him from the storm and stress of life and brings him nearer to Nature and her treasures of unsuspected beauty.

CHICAGO, ILLINOIS, 1948.   MANFRED CURRY, M.D.

CONTENTS

PART I: THE AERODYNAMICS OF SAILS

PART II: RACING TACTICS

PART I

The Aerodynamics of Sails

The Aerodynamics of Sails

Nature as a Guide to the Construction of a Sail

If we observe the great difference of type in our modern sails, if we listen to the varied opinions on their efficacy, we cannot escape the conclusion that our technical knowledge is too limited to permit one to speak with absolute authority as to the correct and best form of racing sail. When one sees that the same boat, under similar conditions, sometimes sails better than at other times, one comes gradually to the conclusion that, inasmuch as the hull has not changed, the set and form or cut of the sail must be more or less decisive in determining its efficiency. As only *one* form of sail can be correct and not, as is so often held, a different form of sail for every type of boat, we must deal first and foremost with this vital problem. In the following I am adhering to the process of thought developed, step by step, in my observations and experiments on this important subject.

As a starting point, Nature should give us an indication in which direction we should undertake our researches, uninfluenced by current opinions or theories. It is astonishing that it has not been recognized that the sail is, and should be, precisely nothing more nor less than a great *bird's wing*, which moves the slender hull through the water. If we are persuaded that the sail should correspond to the wing of a bird, and that the requisites for both are the same, it behooves us to study this natural sail in all its intrinsic details.

But first we shall ask ourselves, to what extent can we speak of a likeness or similarity in the process of operation of a sail and those of a wing. To answer this question we shall compare the soaring bird and the sailing boat. Both move at a given angle to the wind by means of a certain power, the force called into action by the pressure of the wind, whereby only that component force that acts at right angles to the surface comes into consideration. The other component force parallel to and along the surface in the opposite direction to propagation acts as a retarding factor in the form of surface and form friction and must be overcome. As Nature has endowed the bird with wings of such favorable form that a large pressure is created, called the "up-drive," which enables the bird to hold itself in the air, we must by constructive means, through the form and cut of the sail, endeavor to attain a maximum pressure and at the same time a minimum retarding action or component. The pressure or component force at right angles to the sail can again be resolved into two components, one of which is directed forward — the other component acts at right angles to the lateral plane of the boat

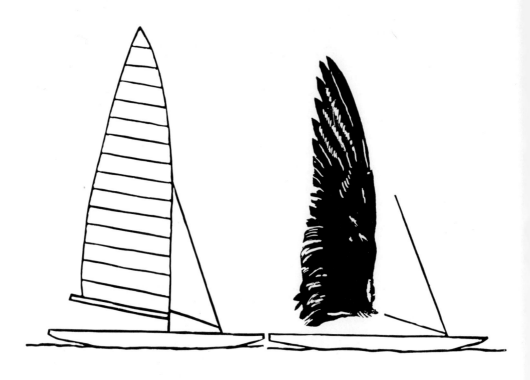

Sail and Bird's Wing.

(cf. Introduction to Part II). How far we may follow the construction of a bird's wing in making a sail, the closer observation of the wing and of its operation will reveal.

It would be a mistake to try to deduce any principles alone from the aeroplane or even birds in flight without a previous study of the bird's wing, because not only would one fail to recognize readily the peculiarities which cannot be utilized for a sail, but also one would fall into the same error, which led aeroplane constructors to depend on large motors instead of improved wing design. Much more instructive is the observation of soaring flight, which has, from the very beginning, followed new paths of research in the development of aeroplane surfaces.

It may also be interesting to study the peculiarities of the free flight of gliders, though this may not be absolutely necessary. The flying of gliders has developed into a sport, and planes have been built which fly for several hours — *without motors.*

We shall first treat of the flight of birds and observe Nature in her minute accuracy. When we observe the various good flyers among birds, we should not commit the error of including the "air acrobats," such as swallows; rather should we direct our observations to those species that conquer the atmosphere by soaring and achieve a great "up-drive" without a stroke of the wings. To these belong the albatross, the gull and the buzzard. How is it possible, we may ask, for them to soar freely in the air — one over land, one over sea, the gull over land and sea; to play with the third dimension without a stroke of the wing? The secret, so long concealed, lies in the wind, which, though it may have only a small velocity near the earth's surface, almost always increases in velocity at greater heights. Another factor is the direction of the wind and — last but not least — the extremely favorable form of the wing, which enables these birds to perform such feats.

Let us state briefly here the physical laws by which the action of the wind on a plane surface is governed and upon which in part the flight of man, on sea and in the air, depends:

1. Whether a plane is moved against the air or whether the air, in the form of wind, blows against the plane, the effect is the same. The requisite air pressure or density, which renders it possible for a bird or aeroplane to float or soar freely in the air, is not obtained until the wing is struck by air that has attained a certain (high) speed. This speed, at which the air becomes dense enough to float the bird or plane, can be attained in two ways. Either the plane moves against the air or the air moves against the plane — the result being the same in either case according to the above principle of relativity. To the former category belong gliding flight as, for instance, the gliding of a bird from the top of a tree to the ground, whereby height, which is essential here, is sacrificed — conversion of potential into kinetic energy; and also the ascent of an aeroplane, the speed of which is accelerated by the propeller until it is borne up by its planes, whereby no initial height need be sacrificed. The work done by the motor is transformed into work against the air, which is in turn imparted to the wings or planes and makes ascent possible. To the second category belongs the bird or glider sailing or soaring against the wind.

2. The pressure or resistance increases as the

Gulls

5

square of the velocity and directly as the area of the surface; for flat surfaces according to the formula:

$$A = 0.13 \cdot F \cdot v^2 \cdot \sin a.$$

That is, a plane surface of one square meter, which, moved at uniform speed in a direction at right angles to its surface, covers in one second a distance of one meter, will develop a resistance of approximately 0.13 kilogram. By this formula we can calculate the resistance A of the air against a surface of F square meters area that is inclined at an angle of opposition a * to its direction of propagation and is moved at a uniform speed of v meters per second against the air.

A second favorable factor for flight is that the wind has not, as is commonly supposed, an exactly horizontal direction, but blows at an angle of about 4° upward.

Finally, the bird is aided by the peculiar action or operation of its wings, a factor of greatest moment in our ensuing investigations.

If we observe gulls against the sun, as they soar along easily over the water, the shadows in their wings show that these are being continually pulled and turned. They are evidently seeking by this means to catch and utilize every puff of wind in its constantly varying direction. And we also observe that birds, under ordinary circumstances, fly upward never *with* the wind, but always *against* it.

The sketches on the next page show the different types and forms of wing of various species of birds in flight and permit of an interesting comparison with the sail.

We observe that there is considerable difference in the length of these wings. The longer the wing, the better soarer is the bird. To the albatross, for example, Nature has given remarkably long, narrow wings — up to a span of nearly ten feet — which, in spite of their small area, have to bear up a comparatively large body, often without any movement of the wings and on the lightest breeze. In spite of the hindrance such long wings may be to the bird in its nest or when they are folded on the body, Nature provides them. She might even make them longer, if a longer lever arm were feasible. At all events, she appears to lay special stress on a large proportion of length to breadth.

Then there is the thickness of the fore edge of the wing, which entirely contradicts all earlier views on air resistance; to this we shall return in our later observations.

All wings have a certain degree of *arching* — slight in those of swift flying birds, greater in those of our slow flyers, which fact should surely demand our further consideration and careful study. And not only birds show an arching in their wings; in the vegetable kingdom also there are to be found winged seeds, such as Zanonia seeds, whose wings are arched, that they may sail off on the wind.

After these general observations let us turn to some phenomena, seldom

---

* I prefer the nomenclature "angle of opposition" to that used in the technique of flying "angle of incidence," as the latter is employed in physics — in the theory of light — to denote the angle, which the direction of the ray makes with the normal to the surface.

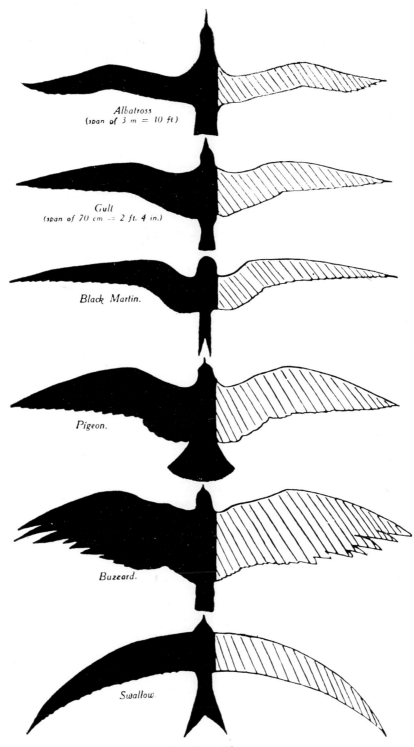

Albatross
(span of 3 m = 10 ft)

Gull
(span of 70 cm = 2 ft. 4 in.)

Black Martin.

Pigeon.

Buzzard.

Swallow.

Our Best Flyers
Turn picture 90° and compare with sail.

Gull's Wing as Seen From Below

observed by sailors, which should illustrate what has just been mentioned and are investigated in part in the treatise "Vogelflug" ("Bird Flight") by Lilienthal, one of the first pioneers in this field.

The striking thing about these phenomena is the greater lifting power of an arched or vaulted surface in comparison to that of a plane surface of the same area. Let us recall a few examples from everyday life, which certainly everybody has noticed but on which few have expended much thought.

An umbrella held horizontally, that is, with its stock upright, will, even in horizontal motion, exercise an upward pull.

The family wash flapping in the wind is lifted, in consequence of its involuntary vaulting or arching, above the horizontal. An accustomed sight to the sailor, so natural that it remains unobserved, is the flapping sail.

Flapping is due to the action of a force that is called forth by the arched surface. The belly of the sail is pulled by this force in the direction of its arching, which manifests itself in a lateral motion. As it is blown out beyond its natural limit, not only the belly but the whole sail is pulled over to the other side, whereupon the same process is repeated. This alternate play, which occurs with great rapidity, gives us the flapping sail. But let it be noted that the shaking of the leech of a drawing sail has another cause, to be discussed later.

A last example: A spoon passed through a cup of coffee or a spoon oar dragged through the water in the direction at right angles to its arching tends to evade the path prescribed and to turn off in the direction of its arching, without offering greater direct resistance to the motion imparted.

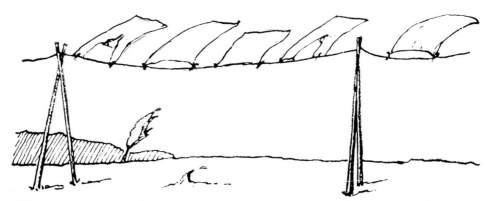

Wash blown above Horizontal in consequence of Arching produced by joint Action of Wind and Gravity.

The accompanying drawings, wherein the forces acting on plane and arched surfaces are represented graphically, give us an explanation for these phenomena. The first measurements on surfaces were made by O. Lilienthal with the primitive apparatus shown in the sketch below.

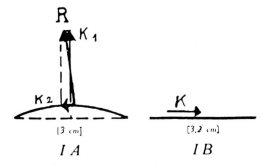

I A   I B

Forces acting on arched and plane Surface.

The parallelogram of forces for the arched surface will certainly be a surprise to the layman. On the plane surface held in a horizontal position appears a force K acting in the direction of the wind (sketch I B), which tends to move the plane in that direction. It is the resultant or sum of two retarding or obstructive forces, that act in one and the same direction. The one is called the form or front resistance, which is called forth by the form of the surface, that is, by the volume of air displaced by it; the other the friction, surface or skin resistance, which is caused by the friction of the air particles that adhere to the sides of the surface.

On the other hand, for the arched surface the resultant force R is directed *upward* (sketch I A), with a tendency * *against* the wind — in the direction of flight.

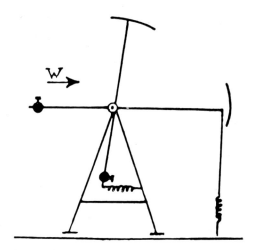

Primitive Apparatus for Measurement of Forces.

It can be resolved into two components, a vertical one K_1 and an horizontal one K_2, the latter directed forward — against the wind; this horizontal component acts in the opposite direction both to the front or form and to the friction resistance and can neutralize both. Hence, a properly arched surface will, in a sufficiently strong wind, both rise and, on the assumption that it is correctly balanced, move forward *against* the wind, as is confirmed by the flight of birds. This forward movement is favored by the upward direction of the wind, if not caused by it — see footnote.

This advantage of arching becomes more pronounced, when the wind hits the plane at an angle from below or when the plane is moved against the wind in an inclined position (cf. drawings II A and II B page 10). The arched surface develops more than double the force of the plane surface in this position.

* This is a moot point, the most recent view being that the forward tendency of this force is due to the upward trend of the wind — of 4° near the surface of the earth.

Curry, Aerodynamics of Sails and Racing Tactics.

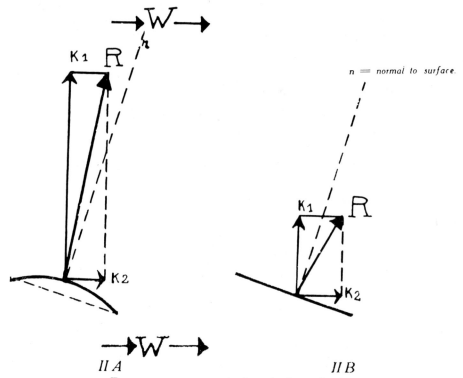

n = normal to surface.

II A   II B

Forces acting on arched and plane Surface.

Now we come to the question as to how much the plane should be arched. To determine the arching, which a bird's wing has in the act of soaring in the wind, one loads its hollow surface with sand until the weight equals half that of the bird. This done, the wing, which naturally must be fresh and untreated, regains the form — a slightly enlarged arching, which it has in the air. The measurement of the wing arching of good flyers shows an average depth of curvature of 1/15, that is 1/15 of the breadth of the wing at the point of deepest arching; of less rapid flyers 1/10 to 1/12. To make the

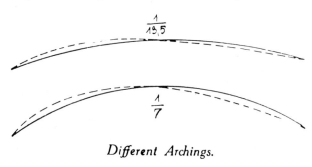

Different Archings.

matter clearer, experience with kites may be recalled. A kite with a flatly stretched surface rises notably badly; also the cord to which it is attached makes an angle with the ground of much less than 90° (see drawing on p. 11). On the other hand, a kite with a loose, bellying surface reaches a much greater height, and its cord forms an angle of almost 90° with the ground, the kite soaring approximately perpendicularly overhead. In favorable cases

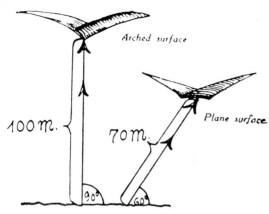

Arched surface

Plane surface

100 m.

70 m.

90°

60°

Experiments with Kites.

the cord may be observed to cross this perpendicular, which means that the kite is then soaring against the wind at a speed greater than the velocity of the wind itself. As the pull of the cord gives us an idea of the magnitude of the force developed by the kite, its inclination determines the *direction* of that force.

The following further experiment with kites is of special interest: Let two kites rise, one having a loose covering, which will be blown out by the wind into an *arched* surface, the other a *stiff arched* surface. To our surprise the latter will soar considerably higher and more perpendicularly than the former; that is, it will exert a greater pull. A comparison here with the boat's sail is of great importance, for thereby it is confirmed that the stiffening of the sail with battens is fully justified.

Drawings III below disclose the *reason* for the different forces developed by the plane and the arched surface in a current of air. Here the flow of the air is represented pictorially. In experiments of recent date the flow of the air is made visible by filling it with smoke, but the flow may even be seen in dusty air exposed to the rays of the sun; the surface is then moved through the air and the flow with its various eddies is recorded photographically.

In the upper drawing we observe that the lines of flow or the air paths (and by air paths we understand the paths of its single particles) are broken and torn asunder by the plane and that eddies are formed. An eddy has motion, that is, kinetic energy, which is developed at the cost of another source of energy. Consequently every eddy, whether in the air or water, means loss of energy to the moving plane.

It is different in the case of arched surfaces; here the lines of flow are not *torn* but *bent;* this is equivalent to a gain of energy: a downward acceleration is imparted to the surface by the air, that is, the surface itself

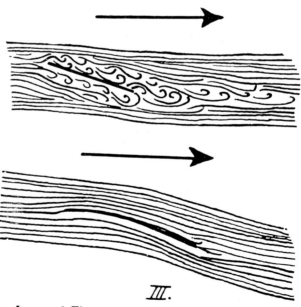

III.

Lines of Flow for arched and plane Surface.

11

is lifted or forced upward to a greater degree. In the case of a plane surface this lifting tendency is more or less paralyzed by the formation of eddies with their capricious effect — arbitrary rotation. The process of eddy formation is the same in water and, truly, this is the principal reason why the sharp-cornered form of the boat's hull has been abandoned for the rounded one in most of our racing types.

The next important factor is the *relation of length to breadth* in the wing. The following experiment should give us an idea of the influence of this relation on the carrying power — the attainment of high pressure: a rectangular plane, whether flat or arched, does by no means behave similarly, when placed, at the same angle of inclination, lengthwise or sidewise to the wind (cf. the drawing below). It develops a higher pressure, when its longer edge (plane II of drawing) is cutting the wind — at one and the same angle of inclination. Moreover, a peculiar humming is distinctly audible from plane I, which is nothing else than the noise produced by the eddies formed on the edge facing the wind, a phenomenon that is less pronounced on plane II. Larger eddies, which contain more energy, that is, revolve faster, arise in the former position of the plane (plane I of drawing). This means that more energy is lost than when the rectangle is held lengthwise to the wind, where, it is true, many eddies form, but these are of both smaller and weaker structure.

With regard to the general form of birds' wings, we can discern the presence, in most of them, of small "taking off" points on their rear edge. These "taking-off" points are the tips of the feathers, beginning, where their rigid portions terminate, by means of

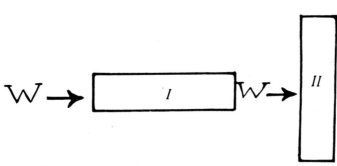

Plane held lengthwise and sidewise to Wind.

which the wings when spread fan-like are stiffened. It is conceivable that these points possess a property similar to that exhibited by such points in the flow or discharge of electricity. The jagged or indented form resulting from these "taking-off" points is characteristic of the wings of all birds and is not alone confined to the rear contour of the wing but also to be traced in the feathers that project laterally. This peculiarity of structure is also observable in the wings of many butterflies, bats and flying squirrels, as also in

Gull Viewed From Above

12

the fins of fish. It is quite possible that the object of these indentations lies in the formation of small, weak eddies instead of the larger, stronger ones, which would otherwise appear on the rear edge of every wing.

Perhaps it is not superfluous to note here a further observation I have made. All birds have little downy feathers on the underside of the wing near the fore edge, that is, just in front of the point or line of its largest curvature. When one blows on the underside of the wing from the rear, these feathers erect themselves. Experiments on models constructed similarly to the wing of a bird, with the greatest curvature in the fore third of the surface, have shown that, when these models are inclined at certain angles to the wind, a large eddy is formed under the fore edge, which in the technique of flying has been given the name of the "ram" or "Aries" eddy. This eddy revolves at its greatest distance from the surface in the direction of the wind, then turns up toward the arched surface and finally passes along it in the opposite direction — that of flight. The flow of the eddy along the surface — in the direction of flight — would, therefore, be obstructed more or less by the downy feathers just mentioned that consequently tend to erect themselves against that current; or, in other words, the bird is facilitated in its flight by this forward driving force thus imparted to its wings.

To ascertain the action of this eddy, I have held various wings horizontally in a wind current, employing the so-called "blizzard" which barbers use for drying the hair. It appears that, in a weak current, the feathers, which are arranged in the form of a large "pocket" on the under side of the wing just behind its fore edge, begin to tremble; in a stronger current they erect themselves at an angle of about 45° to the current. This pocket may even be observed on large birds in flight, it being especially noticeable on gulls as they follow in the wake of a ship, soaring for minutes without a stroke of the wing. The opening of the feather pocket is aided by the anatomical structure of the fore edge of the wing and by these downy feathers projecting from its skin (see first picture on next page); if this sinewy skin S is hit lightly, the pocket P opens automatically. The pressure of the wind, which is brought to bear on the wing of a soaring bird, acts on this sinew and thus might tend to open the pocket.

If we peel off the skin on the fore edge of the wing with a knife, we discover two muscles (see the pictures on next page); the one (1) stretches the skin, thus closing the pocket; the other (2) contracts it, thus releasing the tension and opening the pocket. The second picture shows the position of the muscles in the wing and illustrates their mode of action.

The proof of a forward air current along the wing was established by Gustav Lilienthal in 1913. He fastened little bannerets onto the underside of bird-like planes, which he caused to fly in a circle. The experiment confirmed that the current of air flowed not at all points along the surface from the front to the rear as one might suppose, but, even at a considerable distance from the fore-edge, from the rear toward the front, as indicated in the third drawing. Lilienthal was of the opinion that this current of air is utilized as a forward driving force by the bird. Furthermore, he established the fact that this eddy does not become pronounced till a speed of five meters per second is reached, which is the average minimum speed of birds.

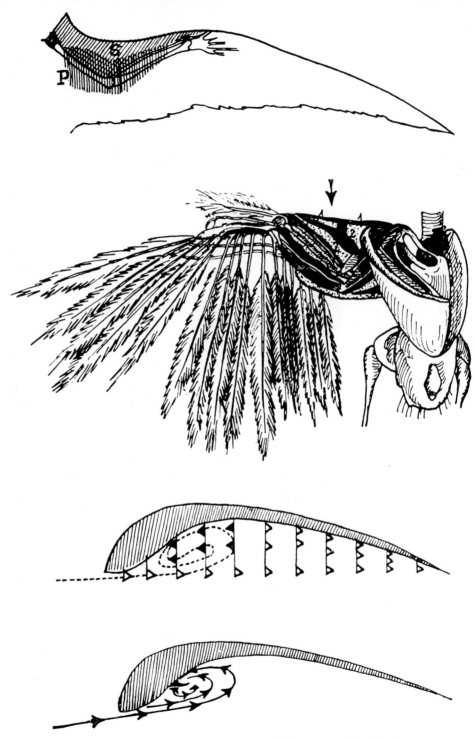

Mechanism of Pocket and Lines of Flow on under Surface of Bird's Wing.

To summarize, my experiments have confirmed that not only do the separate feathers erect themselves, but there is often a regular "pocket" exactly where the principal eddy strikes the wing; further, that this pocket is opened partly by the air current flowing forward along the surface near the fore edge of the wing and partly by the anatomical structure both of pocket and fore edge of wing.

Now the greater the arch of the wing and the smaller the angle of opposition, the larger the eddy produced and the farther back it strikes the wing. Accordingly, the pocket on wings of greater arch is farther back from the fore edge than it is on wings of smaller arch. Nature, in fact, operates

The Pocket Opens by Pressing Thumb on Fore Edge of Wing

so exactly, that in one and the same wing she gives the pocket such a form, that it is developed to the greatest degree and placed farthest back at the point of deepest arching, gradually decreasing in size and approaching the fore edge of the wing as we proceed from the body toward its flatter outer end (cf. the accompanying photographs and those in the chapter on the "Reciprocal Influence of the Sails").

Before I draw from all these considerations those conclusions, which have a bearing on the form of a sail, or attempt to confirm their correctness from the knowledge we possess of the most effective forms of sails, I desire to state briefly the various characteristics of birds' wings, aeroplanes and boat sails. Why one may not adhere *strictly* to the form of a bird's wing, so well planned by Nature, will be discussed later.

In the first place, the wing, even that of the best soarers among birds, is intended not only for soaring, but also for the stroke of the wing, for which the motion of the tip of the wing is more rapid than its portion nearer the body and thus the pressure of the air that is brought to bear on its various parts differ. In order to protect the wing from breaking and also that it may adhere to the body when not in use — when the bird is in its nest — Nature has invested it with great elasticity.

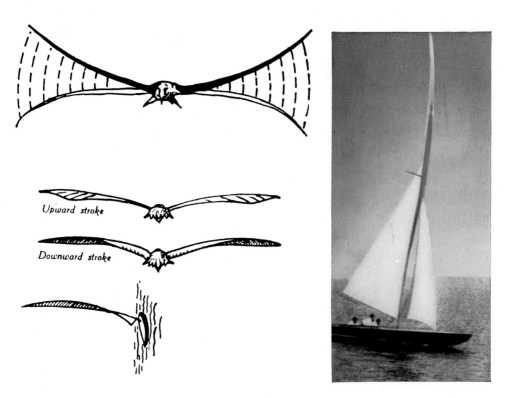

Give and Twist of Wing and Sail

It is not only the whip-like elasticity of the whole wing (cf. the first of the adjacent figures), but also the give of its rear outer portion (see the figures and compare the similarity of wing and sail), when pressure is brought to bear on it, which has led to the false conception that is still stubbornly maintained in most yachting circles, namely, that the upper part of the sail should swing out, that is, that the give of the gaff or of the top of a Marconi mast is a favorable factor. This is a gross error, which has only persisted, because few sailors have taken the pains to look into the matter, thinking it simpler to accept the old, though unproved point of view. We only need to wave a fan or a piece of paper through the air, first with the outer edge giving way to the pressure of the air and then with the edge stiffened so that it cannot give, and we notice at once that the stiff surface offers a greater resistance than the supple one does. Experiments in the wind tunnel have supported this theory.

In the case of the bird the tip of the wing bends upwards on the downward stroke, in order to avoid too great a *strain* on its weakest part and to spare the muscles *expenditure of energy* — necessary in consequence of its long lever arm. Further, however, we must realize that the tip of the wing gives *only on the downward stroke* and that in soaring it always retains its normal form.

The wing of a bird is necessarily of light structure; for Nature to make it stiff and unbending would be, aside from the above considerations, most difficult. But this need not be so with the sail; by means of stays and battens the essential stiffness or rigidity may be achieved without any material increase in weight, which in the case of a boat is of little moment.

The conclusion is that to win *increased power*, the sail should be constructed rigidly, so as to prevent any sagging or giving of its upper and rear portions.

Finally, we should not attempt to follow those lines, which insure the birds longitudinal and lateral stability and play important roles for the bird, but not for the boat. For example, the fore edge of the bird's wing is inclined more and more backward toward its tip, which appears to have led yacht designers, especially the Swedes, to give the mast a considerable rake aft. This backward inclination of the wing has the single purpose of insuring the bird the necessary longitudinal stability. It is marked with swallows, which have a special claim on it on account of their acrobatic air stunts. The give of the tip of the wing answers the same purpose. Aeroplanes rigged with such wings proved especially stable, but they lacked the greater carrying capacity.

It is also surprising that arching has an unfavorable influence on stability; wherefore aeroplane builders are accustomed to avoid extreme arching. This might suggest that the sail could be cut with a somewhat larger belly.

In other respects the sail should correspond to Nature.

To the limit consistent with stability the relation of length to breadth shown in bird's wings should be followed in designing sails. As yet this limit is far from having been reached, for the center of gravity even of our Marconi sails lies, with few exceptions, not much higher than that of gaff rigged sails.

A thick opposing surface to the wind is not harmful. Therefore a thick mast may be used, if by some means the transition from mast to sail can be effected in the form of a *uniform* curve (cf. the streamlining of the mast on p. 75).

The modern device of inserting battens in a sail, and letting them project slightly aft — out of the pockets reminds one of the "taking-off" points of the bird's wing, and they may possess a small advantage.

The S-shaped contour of the fore edge of the wing, from the point where the wing projects from the body, deserves notice and is evidently to be accounted for by its junction with the body and the action of the muscles. More important is the fact that the wing presents a remarkably smooth surface to the wind, over which it can glide with minimum friction. The advantage gained in stiffening the sail by inserting as many battens as possible is confirmed empirically, especially on the wind.

Tiny Sailors of Animal Kingdom

Finally, it may interest the yachtsman to know that there are sea animals that actually sail, a species of jelly fish (siphonphora). Although they are old Phoenicians compared to our luxurious yachts, it is amusing to observe how they can tack and jib, reciprocally blanket one another and even, one may imagine, a regatta. I had an opportunity to watch these animals, which sail the Mediterranean to the number of millions, off the Italian and African coasts, day after day, and to study their manner of life.

When we observe the animal closely, we can imagine that we have a little model boat before us. Its body can be compared best to that of the scow. Of a finger's length, the flat body, which lies almost entirely on the water, is rounded off evenly fore and aft. Under the water the animal possesses a number of feelers, which are used to capture food as well as to steer, and even, when held lengthwise, to serve as centerboards. The sail consists of a transparent, arched membrane, which crosses the body diagonally, and, in tacking, arches itself in the direction of the wind — to leeward.

These little fairy sailors, with their bluish, shimmering wings, proceed in great squad-

Sailing Jelly Fish

rons over the endless surface of the water. In the wake of one another, abreast one another, mutually blanketing one another, these miniature navigators beat against the wind in long tacks. And when in their midst one looks at them from a skiff, one might imagine oneself a judge in a small-boat regatta; an uncommonly amusing sight! Only that, in a storm, no judges' boat comes to the rescue of the overturned, and the poor helpless creatures soon lie keel up, blowing hither and thither on the water — dead. These animals know what fate awaits them and they avoid sea paths dangerous to them, often fleeing to the shelter of islands, where one may find hundreds collected behind protecting rocks, some with flapping sails, apparently anchored, others maneuvering desperately in order to remain protected from wind and wave. If they do not succeed and are caught by a wave and overturned or driven ashore, then boat and rigging are lost, and they dry up in a few minutes on the hot strand.

More Exact Examination of the Sail

Experiments With Down

Having established the general principles described above and in order to become acquainted with the sail in operation and to observe the wind currents and eddies on its surface, I performed the following experiments:

I fastened a bit of down, as light and dry as possible, on a hair or thin thread of about half a meter length, attached at the other end to a pole or fishing rod. With this simple device I was able to investigate the wind currents on the greater part of the sail. I wish to mention here that the first time I groped about various sails with the down, not only did I find all existing theories more or less contradicted, but I found myself up against questions, which caused me much brain cudgelling. If I now simply record these experiments without elucidating the various questions at issue, they will, I fear, not be much clearer to the reader — in part at least — than they were to me at the time, but I am, nevertheless, doing so, because I want to present the experiments as such collectively, in order to be able to refer to them in our further enquiries.

The experiments give more positive results when performed in a strong wind. And we begin them with the boat *on the wind*.

We hold the down close under the boom (see region a of sketch on next page), moving it slowly along that spar toward the mast, and we notice the following: Toward the after part of the sail the down flutters under the boom, almost directly aft, in extreme cases with a slight tendency toward the lee; *this divergence becomes more pronounced as we approach the mast;* the air current forms a constantly increasing angle with the boom, becoming nearly 90° at the mast. A remarkable phenomenon, inexplicable at first sight! In order to eliminate any possible influence of the mast or the jib, we repeat the experiment under the jib, and we obtain the same results. Why should the air current on the imaginary boundary between the windward and the leeward side of the sail tend more toward the perpendicular to the plane of the sail as we approach its luff?

The second experiment deals with the windward side of the mainsail and the luff of both sails. According as the boat is lying higher or freer on the wind, the current changes its direction somewhat in the mainsail but it is directed *forward* almost always in its fore quarter, that is, just forward of the belly, and aft, toward the stern, in its other three quarters (see regions b of sketch). The current in the after part of the sail quite near the sail itself, i. e., to a distance of about 20 inches from it, flows also parallel to its surface.

A further peculiarity is the deflection of the down from the horizontal. As we approach the upper or lower part of the sail, the greater becomes the tendency of the air current to be directed upward or downward as the case may be (see regions b of sketch). This tendency is especially pronounced in the currents that are directed forward — toward the luff of the sail — to a less degree in those directed aft.

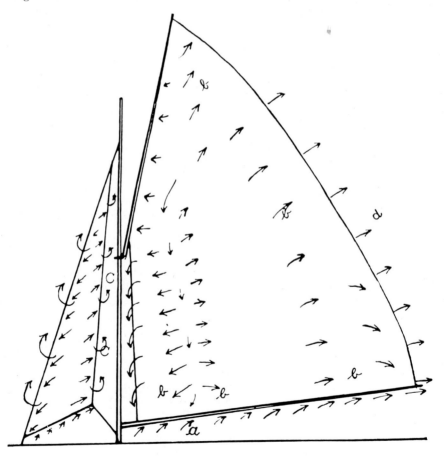

Lines of Flow on windward Side of Sail.

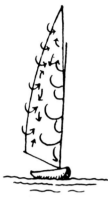

Now as to the *luff* of the sail: here the current, which is directed forward, passes swiftly around the luff and, in the case of the mainsail, toward the lee between sail and mast. There is nothing extraordinary here in the behavior of this air current except its accelerated speed, which appears to be caused by a certain suction effect produced near the luff of the sail on its leeward side. This indicates that it would be advantageous to intercept this current by closing the slit between sail and mast, which can be easily accomplished in the Marconi rig by running the sail in a groove on the mast.

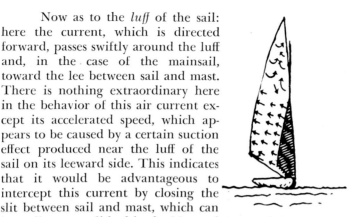

Lines of Flow in Lee without Jib.

Lines of Flow in Lee with Jib.

Now let us pass the down along and close to the *leech* of the jib and the mainsail (see regions c and d of sketch). In the case of the jib the down is blown toward the lee, with a certain acceleration around the leech and in the lee of the jib forward. But this is not the case with the mainsail. The down retains the direction it has along the sail, i. e., it is blown directly aft. In order to obviate any possible influence of the jib on the mainsail, which, indeed, one might easily suspect, especially as the wind is partly thrown off the jib onto the lee of the mainsail, the experiment is repeated without the jib. But no difference is apparent in the behavior of the current as it passes off the leech of the mainsail.

Next, we investigate the currents along the mast with the down on the *windward side* of the mainsail: just abaft the mast we discover a strong eddy, which either carries the down forward toward the mast — compare with the bird's wing — or causes it to fly in all directions. Directly *next to the mast* the down is driven forward around the mast toward the jib. Consequently, this current, which is directed forward, is utilized again by the jib, especially when there is no slit between mainsail and mast.

Now we proceed to our last experiment, exploring the *lee* of the mainsail, first with the jib and then without it. We find that the lines of flow of the air currents assume a most irregular form, when no jib is set (cf. the above sketch). Toward the luff of the mainsail we discover a large eddy at the mast, which, seen from above, on the port tack, turns clockwise at high speed first away from the sail — at right angles to it — then parallel to it toward the stern and finally onto the sail and along it back to the mast. If we let our down grope along farther aft, we encounter at certain points small eddies, which either drive the down *against the sail* or cause it to flutter forward — toward the mast: often it is pressed against the sail as though it were stuck there. Other small eddies may be detected near the leech.

Investigating the same regions with the jib set, which is trimmed close as we are on the wind, we find an entirely different disposition of the currents (cf. the above sketch). The down, except, in the immediate neighborhood of the mast, where it reveals small eddies of indefinite direction, has

21

a tendency to be drawn from the mainsail or to be blown aft parallel to it, as on the windward side of the sail. It is thus apparent that the jib has a powerful influence on the behavior of the wind currents in the lee of the mainsail; whether of favorable or unfavorable nature has hitherto only been surmised. It may, however, be supposed that the pressure as well as the suction, with which we shall deal more particularly later, undergo a material change from the wind off the jib.

THE DISTRIBUTION OF PRESSURE

In order to understand the phenomena revealed in the experiments with the down, a more exact knowledge of the resistance of the air and of the laws of aerodynamics is indispensable, and on this account I shall be obliged to recall a few fundamental principles, explaining their application to the technique of flying. But in order to avoid a repetition of these principles and my observations thereon in the treatment of surfaces in general — the arched planes that concern us in our investigations on sails — I shall proceed at once to the investigations and the application of the principles in question to arched surfaces in reference to the experiments I made on tin sails in the aerodynamic laboratory at Dessau, for which I am indebted to the courtesy of Professor Junkers; a more exact account of these experiments is given in a later chapter.

Chamber With Wind Tunnel and Measuring Apparatus at Dessau

The determination of the pressure on a surface — that is, in the case of aeroplanes the so-called "lift" and "resistance" of the air to which the wings are subjected and of sail boats the driving force and resistance — is investigated as to its amount and direction in the "wind tunnel."

Let it be understood that in the treatment of sails, when the angle at which the wind strikes the sail, the so-called angle of "opposition," is spoken of, not the angle which is formed by the sail and the actual direction of the wind is meant but that angle at which the current of air, in sailing parlance the so-called "apparent" wind, actually falls on the sail. The direction of this apparent wind is indicated by the pennant and it alone is to be considered in the determination of the driving force. The greater the speed of the boat the more will the apparent wind deviate in direction from that of the actual wind. This is especially pronounced in the case of ice boats, which, due to their high

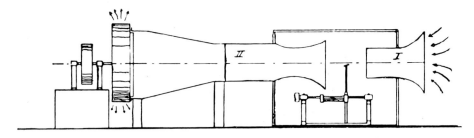

Sketch of Wind Tunnel.

speed, have such a small angle of opposition to the wind, when running with the wind abeam, that they have to be sailed with their sheets close-hauled, and for this reason can cover a distance *before the wind much more quickly* on a zig-zag course than on one dead before the wind.

The *wind tunnel* is represented in the picture on the foregoing page; it consists of a room, into which the air enters through a large funnel on one side. The current of air is generated by a ventilator fan and streams across the room, leaving it through another funnel on the opposite side, which leads it away.

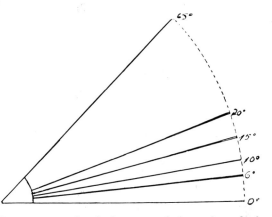

Formerly the ventilator was put at the outer opening of the first funnel and the air current forced into it; but later, in order to produce a more uniform current, the fan was placed at the outer end of the second funnel and the air *sucked* through the tunnel (see above sketch). In order to free the air sucked into the room of its eddies and to insure a uniform, parallel flow of the current, the funnel through which the air is sucked is provided with cell-like divisions similar to those of a grating. The plane to be investigated is made fast to a stand in the position desired; the latter is placed between the two funnels, which extend so far into the room that their inner openings are only 4 to 6 feet apart. The velocity of the current can be adjusted to vary from one to thirty-five meters per second. The plane is affixed to the stand, the air resistance of which is deducted from the measurements, and is connected with an instrument that registers the momentary pressures, the resultant as well as the two component pressures, for the various angles of inclination of the plane — in angles, as indicated in the above drawing. If it is desired to ascertain both the total pressure that a plane develops (I use the word "develop," because the pressure depends not only on the speed of the wind but also on the form, arching etc., of the plane) and the distribution of the pressure at the various points of the plane itself, this is effected in the following manner: Holes are bored in the plane or wing in question at those points for which measurements of pressure are desired.

All except one are then closed with plastilina. Then a measuring instrument is applied to the one hole still open; this exactly fills the opening with its receiving surface. When the current of air is flowing, this instrument registers the pressure at that particular point on the surface, and thus, one after another, the pressures at the other various holes in the plane are recorded. When this measuring apparatus is placed with its recording disc on the surface opposed to the wind, the positive pressure of the wind at that point is recorded. But when the recording disc is affixed to the opposite side of the surface, on the side turned away from the wind, the negative pressure or suction is ascertained. By means of this ingenious device, first employed by Eiffel, builder of the Eiffel Tower, a great secret was disclosed in the technique of flying. But also the yachtsman is confronted with a phenomenon that seemed entirely incredible at first thought. This negative pressure, namely the *suction effect in the lee* of the sail, amounts to from *three to four times the positive pressure on its windward surface*. In other words, *we yachtsmen sail, properly speaking, not by means of the pressure, which arises from the impact of the wind on the sail, but chiefly by means of the "suck," which acts on the leeward side of it*. A sail boat is sucked not driven forward. This fact should give the yachtsman quite a new feeling in the handling of his sails.

The difference in pressure on the two sides of a plane was first suspected by aviators. In fact, it was a great surprise to the pilot who, purposely or involuntarily, having dropped abruptly in his flight, found the upper wing covering of his plane torn into shreds, when he again assumed a horizontal course; the negative pressure had done this, while the positive pressure had *not pressed* in the under covering. Of late this has been taken into account and the covering of the upper surface of a plane is generally given double the strength of that of the under surface.

From Eiffel's notes and the many data supplied by recent research on this subject I have calculated the positive pressure, the driving force on the windward side of the sail, for two rigs, and have drawn the curves of equal pressure, the so-called "isobars" (see the diagrams on page 26 and 27). The pressure in question, in terms of unit pressure kg/m² (kilograms to the square meter), is inserted on the curve or isobar. This enables us to follow the change in pressure throughout the sail according to its position to the wind or to the course sailed; of these I have reproduced here the curves for three such courses, namely on the wind, wind abeam and before the wind.

On the wind the main pressure lies in the fore third of the sail, but it decreases as we approach the mast, which has a detrimental blanketing effect upon that part of the sail. The pressure also decreases, but more gradually, toward the leech, finally vanishing at the isobar or close to it; beyond this *it becomes negative*, that is, opposite to its previous direction. Herein lies *the reason for the shivering of the leech, so disagreeable to the sailor*, which to my knowledge has never been explained; it can, as we know, be corrected by the use of short battens in the leech.

With the wind abeam the pressure increases toward the mast, where it reaches a maximum. The negative pressure (on the windward side) on the leech has decreased to a minimum of almost nil. The isobars bend also more toward the end of the gaff, which they would do on the wind, were it not for the unfavorable effect produced by the sagging off of the gaff to leeward.

Before the wind, the curves look quite natural; the wind strikes the center of the sail with great force and glides off with diminishing pressure toward the sides. The negative pressure (on the windward side) of the leech has vanished. (The sail never shivers in this position.)

Diagram B I represents graphically the pressure (to windward) and the suction (in lee) and thus their relation to each other at any given point or distance from the mast (see page 26). The length of the perpendicular from any point on the plane — abscissae axis of diagram — to the curve gives the amount of pressure or suction at that point of the sail — the lower curve the pressure on its windward side, the upper one the suction on its leeward surface; let it be emphasized, however, that this distance or quantity has nothing to do with the *extent of action of the suction. To obtain the total pressure or resultant driving* force at any point of the sail the positive pressure on its windward side (represented by the lower curve) is added to the negative pressure or suction on its leeward surface (given by the upper curve).* The curves of the diagram represent the pressure and suction in cross-sections of the sail parallel to the mast.

Diagram B II represents graphically the same quantities, pressure and suction, with the wind abeam and B III those before the wind; the latter is the *only* course on which the pressure is approximately equal to the suction.

A comparison of the isobars for the gaff rig with those for the high Marconi sail is extremely instructive (cf. the diagrams on p. 26 with those on p. 27), as it confirms the enormous superiority of the latter on the wind. The isobars of high value (3 and $4\frac{1}{2}$ kg/m²) are much longer and those of negative pressure at the leech smaller in value in the Marconi rig. With the wind abeam, on the other hand, the isobars of the gaff rig are apparently the more favorable. Although they are shorter, they are of higher value (up to 5 kg/m²) and, moreover, include a smaller area of negative pressure at the leech than those of the Marconi sail do. It is interesting to compare the curves for the two rigs in respect to suction for wind abeam. In the gaff rig the suction is considerably greater, because, as I may say in advance, the large eddies in the lee, which appear at greater angles of opposition, have not yet begun to form. The high sail shows, on the other hand, decided eddy formations. Before the wind the two rigs are about alike with regard to both pressure and suction.

One conclusion to be drawn from these two systems of curves is that the foot of the sail in both rigs should be cut as *high* as possible toward its out-board end, causing the boom to *rise sharply* aft. The sails of our modern racing boats, especially the smaller ones, are in fact cut according to this principle. This reduces the surface of negative pressure on the windward side of the sail along its foot, that is the lower leech, which, most likely, is still greater than indicated in the diagrams on account of the 4° upward tendency of the wind.

For the diagrams on p. 28, curves from Eiffel's work "La resistance de l'aire et l'aviation, Expériences effectuées au laboratoire du Champ-de-Mars," Dunod et Pinat 1910, Paris, have been applied to sails; they give the isobars for a flat

* The actual "driving" force is the vertical component of this quantity (see next chapter).

Curry, Aerodynamics of Sails and Racing Tactics.

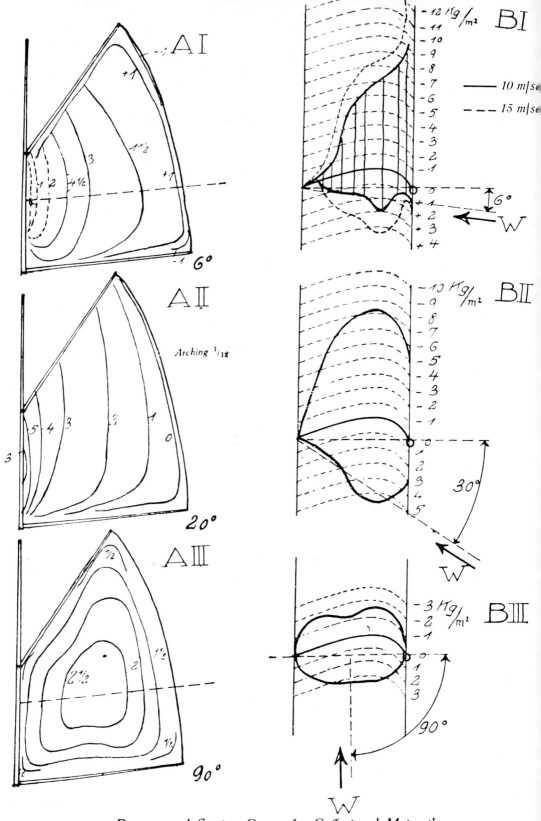

Pressure and Suction Curves for Gaff rigged Mainsail.

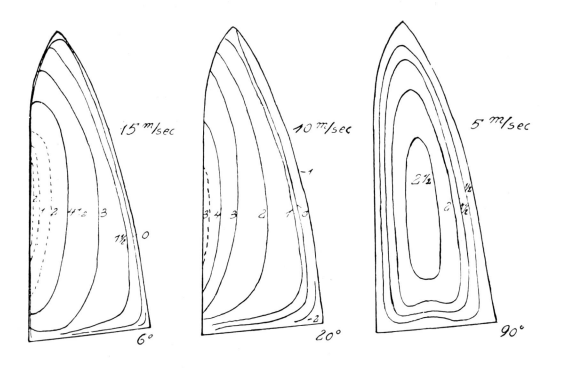

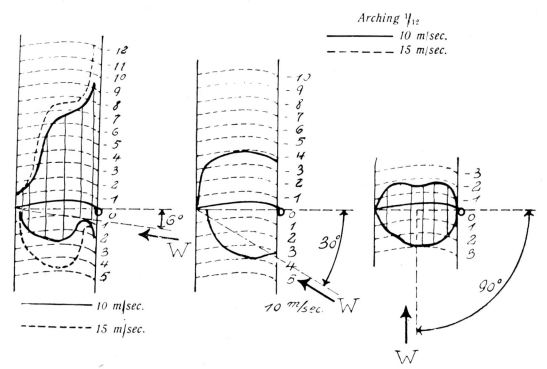

Pressure and Suction Curves for Marconi Mainsail.

surface and the pressure and suction curves for various arched surfaces.

More important, of course, than the pressure are the suction curves, which, however, I have reproduced here (see the last three diagrams) for only one angle of opposition on the wind — on account of their great differentiation and varying form due to the smallest difference in the arching (bellying) of the sail. These suction curves are so irregular in form, so unstable, that they cannot be regarded as exact.

The following statement may be made with regard to the *suction* curves — the distribution of suction over the sail (cf. diagrams on page 29) : To windward the greatest negative pressure is concentrated along the luff, the

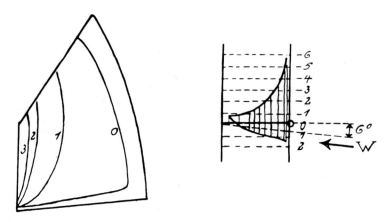

Isobars on Windward Side of Flat Gaff Sail and Pressure and Suction Curves on Wind.

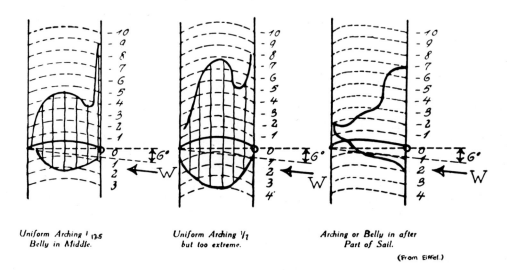

Uniform Arching ¹⁄₁₃.₅
Belly in Middle.

Uniform Arching ¹⁄₇
but too extreme.

Arching or Belly in after
Part of Sail.

(From Eiffel.)

Pressure and Suction Curves on Marconi Sail on the Wind, 10 m/sec.

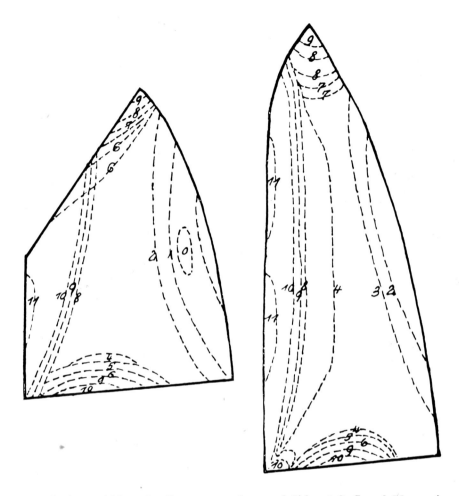

*Isobars of Negative Pressure on Leeward Side of Gaff and Marconi
Sail on Wind, 10 m/sec.*

foot and the head of the sail, whereby we may observe, along the last only
in the case of a light breeze, when the gaff does not swing off too far
to leeward. It is evident from these two diagrams as also from the foregoing cross-sectional ones that the leech is subjected to a relatively so small
negative pressure (suction), that this may at times be partly or entirely overcome by the negative or under pressure that acts in the opposite direction
on the windward side of the sail, which gives rise to the characteristic shivering
or shaking of the leech.

With the wind abeam the suction travels from the luff toward the head
and foot of the sail. Before the wind it is more or less uniformly distributed,
increasing perhaps somewhat toward the head and foot. On the gaff rigged
sail there is a region a short distance from the leech and about half way up
the sail, where the *negative pressure in lee is nil.* This diminution in suc-

tion is apparently due to an eddy that rebounds against the sail and thus disturbs the suction in this region. This phenomenon will be investigated later.

THE ARCHING

We are confronted with the questions: Shall a sail be arched? If so, how deeply? and where shall the greatest arching be?

There is no more doubt today as to the answer to the first question. About seventy years ago the famous American schooner yacht "America" had great success on a visit to England; it was attributed by the English chiefly to her sails, which were cut much flatter than the English yacht sails of those days. Accordingly, the English began to make their sails flatter, but they went to the other extreme, cutting them much too flat. For many years yacht sail manufacture tended in this direction all over Europe, until a change was brought about by the visit of the German "Sonder" boats to Marblehead. They were beaten and their defeat was attributed to the more bellied sails of the American boats. From that date more bellied sails were adopted in Germany. At present most yachtsmen are convinced of the superiority of strongly arched sails but few are able to offer an explanation for their conviction.

The next question is, how deep should this belly be? Let us first summarize the conclusions reached by experience:

The lighter the wind the greater must be the arching. This is confirmed by Nature in that the wings of slow flying birds are of greater arching than those of the fast flyers.

Moreover, it is an empirical fact that even with the same wind — of the same velocity — the sail should have different archings on the various points of sailing, if a maximum pressure is to be attained. The system of curves on the next page taken from Eiffel's work cited above furnishes us with data on the pressures developed on four differently arched, rigid surfaces. These curves, formed by uniting the points, which are measured for the various angles of opposition, are called "polar" curves. Inasmuch as a rigid sail, that is, one stiffened with battens, develops, as we have observed above, about 20% more pressure than a flexible sail that is bellied out by the wind, we can utilize Eiffel's curves, which have been drawn from the measurements on tin wings, in their essential points for our modern sails. These curves, on which the different angles of opposition are inserted, that is, the different angles which the surface presents to the direction of the wind, or, in other words, the angles, at which the wind strikes it, give the magnitude and direction of the force K developed by the sail; that is, the straight lines drawn from the lower right hand corner 0,0 of the quadrangle of the diagram to the given points on the curve give us the magnitude and the direction of this force. This resultant force K can be resolved into two components, which are denoted by K_y and K_x. These two components, which in the case of birds and aeroplanes are termed "up-drive" and resistance and in yacht sails "side-drive" and resistance respectively, are determined as follows: K_y, the up- or side-drive, by the distance of the point in question of the curve, corresponding to the given angle of opposition, from the horizontal line

Polar Curves for various Archings.

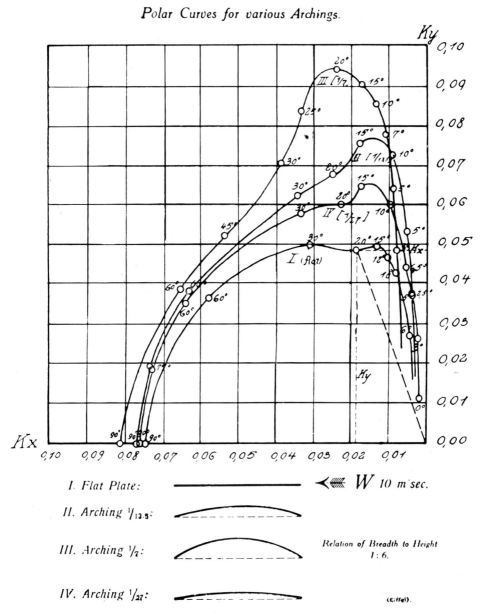

I. Flat Plate: ——————————— ◄≪≪ *W* 10 m sec.

II. Arching 1/13.5: ⌒ — · — · —

III. Arching 1/7: ⌒ — · · — · · —   Relation of Breadth to Height
1 : 6.

IV. Arching 1/27: ⌒ — — · — — ·   (Eiffel).

0,0 — K_x, of the quadrangle and K_x, the resistance, by the distance of that point from the vertical through the point 0,0.

For a sail the most favorable curve is that which, on the one hand, attains the greatest height and, at the same time, runs closest to the vertical through the point 0,0 of the quadrangle. But it is not always easy to determine the most favorable relation between these two components or distances; for example, K_y can be very large and still the surface may be subjected to a

31

large resistance K_x, which is naturally not propitious. This relation K_y/K_x does not play such an important role with the wind abeam or before the wind. Here the magnitude and not the direction of the resultant pressure K is the decisive factor, inasmuch as the resistance K_x acts less or not at all in the direction opposite to that of the course.

A comparison of the various curves leads to the following observations: A flat sail, the curve of which is represented by curve I of the diagram, develops a very small pressure. This is especially true for all angles of opposition up to 15 or 20°, for which the pressure is about half that developed by the three arched surfaces; the flat sail is, therefore, inferior on all points of sailing, that is, for all angles of opposition.

The most favorable of the three arched surfaces is apparently that for which the arching is 1:7 — depth to width (Curve III). Still this holds only for the larger angles of opposition, that is, especially for the wind abeam. For the smaller angles its resistance is somewhat large; here the surface of smaller arch (Curve II), 1:13½, is to be preferred, in spite of its somewhat lower pressure. In general, one may conclude that the arching should correspond approximately to that of surface II, except in the case of stronger winds, where a weather helm or the stability of the boat has to be taken into account.

The last and most difficult question to answer is: Where should the bellying be deepest — forward, in the middle or aft? My own experiments have confirmed what has been verified by experience, namely, that the position of the belly, whether forward or aft, is of little moment, and that under ordinary circumstances the sail is just as effective with the belly farther aft, near the leech. The general opinion of sailors tends to the conclusion that it is most advantageous to have the belly in the fore third of the sail, behind the mast. The construction of the bird's wing appears, indeed to confirm this view, but still we should not forget that the bird has no mast in front of its wing; and the wind strikes the bird's wing at a somewhat smaller angle than it does the sail of a boat.

An English yachtsman, prominent also as an aeroplane designer, made experiments on variously bellied sails in 1921 and 1922 and came to the conclusion by simple experimental tests that a uniform arching over the whole sail produced the best result or, at least, a hardly less favorable one than when the belly lay in its fore third.

It is easy to imagine that the mast might counteract the favorable effect of the belly if it lay in the fore third of the sail, and it is certain that the belly, if too *far forward*, directly behind the mast, is harmful under all circumstances. Personally, I have obtained the best results with the belly about in the middle. Aerodynamic measurements on the wings of aeroplanes at such angles of opposition as concern us here have confirmed that a shift in position of the greatest arching under the most favorable circumstances can improve the wing only inappreciably. Therefore it is the size, not the position, of the arching that is the decisive factor. The system of polar curves given on page 33 may confirm my opinion, but every one should draw his own conclusions therefrom.

In order to determine the most favorable effect, that is, the most favorable relation between side pressure and resistance, we cannot simply divide

Polar Lines for different Archings of Surface.

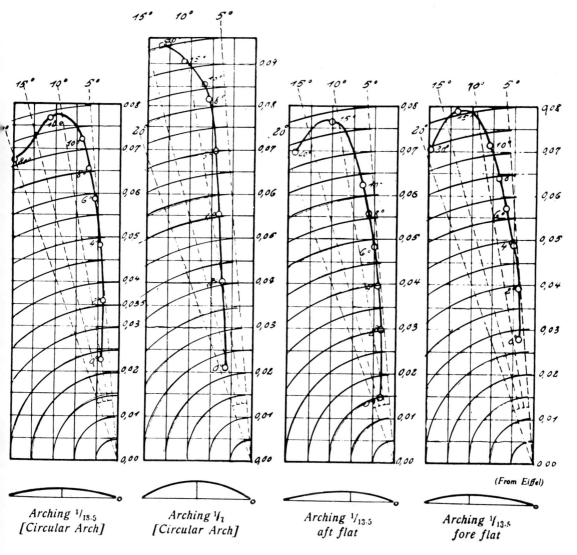

| Arching $\frac{1}{13.5}$ [Circular Arch] | Arching $\frac{1}{7}$ [Circular Arch] | Arching $\frac{1}{13.5}$ aft flat | Arching $\frac{1}{13.5}$ fore flat |

(From Eiffel)

the one by the other, the former by the latter, as determined by measurement from the curve, that is, we cannot, as is generally assumed, maintain that this quotient $\dfrac{\text{up-pressure}}{\text{resistance}} = \dfrac{\text{side pressure}}{\text{resistance}}$ as such or, more correctly, its maximum value will correspond to the most favorable form of sail. We must take into account the fact that, as the angle of opposition increases, *the resistance does not act unfavorably to the same degree as the up- or side-pressure acts favorably,* and for this reason it is evident we cannot employ

33

the given quotient in this simple form — without any corresponding correction — for the determination of the maximum, that is, the most favorable arching sought. Not until we know *how* the values of the pressure and resistance actually vary with increasing angle of opposition is an exact comparison of these two quantities possible. According to Eiffel the resistance W is represented by a parabolic curve, that is, it is a function of the second order of the angle of opposition and its value thus small in comparison to that of the pressure, which for small angles — from 0° to 10° — is approximately proportional to the angle itself. The difference becomes more pronounced and the whole matter more comprehensible, when we realize that in sailing the (side) pressure plays a still more important role or, rather, that it acts far more favorably than the resistance does unfavorably, as the latter is approximately nil on all courses from wind abeam to before the wind. Thus, the relation of resistance to side pressure (driving force), indicated in the diagrams by the broken (polar) lines, which plays so important a part in the technique of flying, has little significance in sailing. Therefore, the non-mathematical reader need not bother himself further about these broken lines that radiate from the common center 0,0.

We will be surprised to find how small the archings of our sails really are, should we take the trouble to measure them. In Germany only the small centerboard boats — the 15 qm² and 22 qm² racers — have dared to adopt the correct arching; *all* yacht sails are arched much too little. Measurements of the sail arch of Sonder boats and the 8 m R-yachts, which can be made simple by stretching a cord on the windward side of the sail from the luff to the leech and then measuring the greatest depth, show archings of from 1/25 to 1/35 instead of from 1/13 to 1/15.

Any desired arching may be obtained by the use of battens inserted in pockets in the sail and extending from leech to luff; the greater the tension under which they are bound into the pockets, the greater the arching. In this manner one may adjust the driving power developed by a sail. In a strong wind, for example, where the stability of the boat plays an important role, the sail, especially in its upper part, should set as flat as possible; this is accomplished by loosening the battens. Also, one may regulate the *position* of the belly by planing the battens thinner, where greater arching is desired.

Practice has shown that in a heavy wind a flatter sail is better than a strongly bellied one. The reason for this is that in strong gusts or flaws one must luff up and let the sail shake, in order to diminish the driving force, whereas the resistance, which is greater in a strongly bellied sail, can not be reduced by this maneuver.

RELATION OF LENGTH TO BREADTH

Let us now consider how the pressure in the sail is affected by the proportion of its height to breadth. With birds, we have noted, the average proportion of the wing's length to breadth is 3:1. How much length is valued by Nature is shown by the wing of the albatross, where the proportion of length to breadth is 5:1.

The albatross, a bird weighing 25 to 35 pounds, has a wing spreading surface of only about 8½ square feet. It flies without a stroke of the wing off the water, is able with a minimum speed of about 50 feet a second to

An Albatross

soar without exertion and attains a speed of about 100 feet per second, that is, approximately 68 miles an hour. It enlarges or diminishes its carrying surface according to the momentary strength of the wind by spreading out its feathers more or less; in other words, it utilizes this reserve carrying power to attain greater altitude when needed, also expending it when the wind lets up. Or it gains speed in gliding or sailing with the wind, without sacrificing height, and transforms afresh this increased speed, upon turning against the wind, into greater height. And it performs all these feats with its cutting surface at an angle to the wind, in most cases, of about 3° *downward* — and in spite of this negative angle it soars forward! Wind direction 4° upward, minus 3° wing direction downward, gives an angle of opposition of 1° for the wing. Should not all this put the yachtsman to thinking? Let us get at the root of the matter.

Eiffel has investigated exhaustively the relation of length to breadth. He was the first to establish the surprising fact that a square plate (that is, relation of length to breadth 1:1) develops the greatest pressure not, as was formerly assumed, at an angle of opposition of 90°, i. e., when the wind strikes the plate at right angles, but in an inclined position, at an angle of 38°. It is interesting to note that at this angle the positive pressure amounts to only *one-half* that at 90°, but that the suction has *increased threefold,* which combined give a larger total driving force. This would appear noteworthy in the case of the sloop rig, inasmuch as this rig corresponds to a relation of length to breadth of generally 1:1, seldom 1½:1. An angle of opposition of 38° is identical to the wind abeam and accordingly the sloop rig should be the most effective on this course, which practice has confirmed. Moreover, *longer and narrower plates* of the same area do not develop as great a driving force at this angle of opposition, but at *smaller angles decidedly larger values* are attained than with the square plate at the same angles of opposition.

The most favorable proportion of length to breadth for the smaller angles of opposition is, according to Eiffel, about 6:1. A greater extreme, for example

9:1, is scarcely more favorable. And even from 3:1 to 6:1 the driving force increases relatively slowly. The greatest increment in the driving force resulting from a lengthening of the surface is, therefore, reached, for smaller angles of opposition, at the proportion of about 3:1. This means that, on the wind, a sail, whose height to breadth is 3:1, develops *decidedly* more driving force than one of the proportion 1:1 or even 2:1 does, but that, in consideration of the question of stability, it would not be advisable to cut the sail much higher, for example, in the proportion 4:1 or 5:1, because the increment in the driving force would then be only *slight*.

The following simple experiment demonstrates how important it is for the full development of the driving force to employ comparatively long, narrow surfaces and not low, broad ones, in other words, to give the Marconi rig the preference: If one clips an insect's wings, for example, those of the dragon fly, half off parallel to the body, the insect cannot raise itself from the ground, but, if one cuts off the same amount of surface at right angles to the body, so that they remain just as long but only half as broad, the carrying power is hardly diminished.

Before we proceed to the application of the above facts to boat sails, let us seek the reason for this remarkable behavior of the driving force, investigating variously shaped surfaces. The abnormal variation of this force must apparently be attributed to marked changes in the suction. My investigations of the leeward side of the sail with down, as also the assumption that various eddies are formed there, led me to look into this matter more thoroughly. For this purpose I examined planes of various proportions of length to breadth for different angles of opposition in *flowing water* or rather, what is identical, I observed the behavior of such planes moved at uniform velocities through standing water.

Hydrodynamic Experiments

As a medium for my hydrodynamic experiments I colored the water in a reservoir with blue ink and then scattered flour or

Sketches of Eddies.

Hydrodynamic Experiments.

I. Eddies formed on plate held at right angles to direction of flow (90°). Formation zone 4 times breadth of plate.
II. Eddies formed at angle of opposition of about 60° Formation zone shorter. A stationary and a detachable eddy.
III. Eddies formed on mainsail of correct arching high on wind.
IV. Eddies formed on mainsail of uniform arching in wind.
V. Eddies formed on jib and mainsail on wind (10"). Compare with experiments with down.

sawdust thinly over its surface. When flat or arched tin plates were moved through the water, the slightest movements of the different parts of the water became visible in the form of the moving particles of flour. The pictures that appeared are represented in the sketches on page 36.

It is well known that water behaves like air (except with respect to density), when bodies are moved through it. Upon examining these sketches one recognizes the similarity of the currents in the water to those of the air on the sail, and the formation of many obscure eddies such as we had anticipated is revealed. We have seen on page 11 that with only a slight inclination of the plate to the current no marked eddy formation appears. This holds true up to about 20°, provided the fore edge of the plate is without the mast. Beyond this point — at greater angles of inclination than 20° — two large eddies form, a larger one on the fore edge of the plate, which, remaining stationary with regard to the plate, moves along with it, and a smaller one on its rear edge, which detaches itself from the plate at short intervals (see sketch II).

It is apparent that the negative pressure is diminished materially upon the appearance of the eddies; this is also experienced in sailing, being manifested by a sudden diminution of the pressure, when the sail is trimmed in close and the boat is swung off on a freer course without the sheets being eased. The greatest pressure being developed in a Marconi rig at angles of opposition of the sail to the wind smaller than 20 degrees. The same *sudden* change in pressure is experienced, but in this case an increment, when we suddenly run higher on the wind — from a course with the wind abeam to one on the wind with sails trimmed close. At this moment the large eddy formed on the freer course diminishes at once in size or may disappear entirely, especially in the case, where the jib is set and drawing. Let us imagine a boat sailing high on the wind. As she bears off gradually, the highest attainable pressure will be reached *just before* the eddy is formed; it is now an empirical fact that *this critical moment is reached sooner with a high, narrow sail than with a low, broad one*, in fact, 10 to 15° sooner with the Marconi than with the gaff rigged sail (cf. also p. 38). It is thus obvious that the high, narrow sail develops its greatest driving force higher on the wind than the gaff sail, the latter being better with the wind abeam. Consequently, the superiority of the high sail over the gaff rig on the wind lies in the development of its greater suction power, which is indirectly proportional to the breadth of the sail; whereas its disadvantage is to be sought in the earlier appearance of the harmful eddy, whereby its suction power is greatly weakened. Of the variation in the driving force arising from different relations of length to breadth of the sail about 80% can be ascribed to suction and, at most, 20% to change in pressure — positive pressure on its windward surface.

The two systems of curves A and B on the following pages give the total pressure — on both sides of the sail — for the Marconi sail and the gaff rig of the same area, on various points of sailing. The curves of system A represent only the total amount of pressure without regard to its direction, curve H that for the high rig and curve G for the gaff sail at the various angles of opposition.

Variation of Pressure according to Relation of Length to Breadth.
System of Curves A.

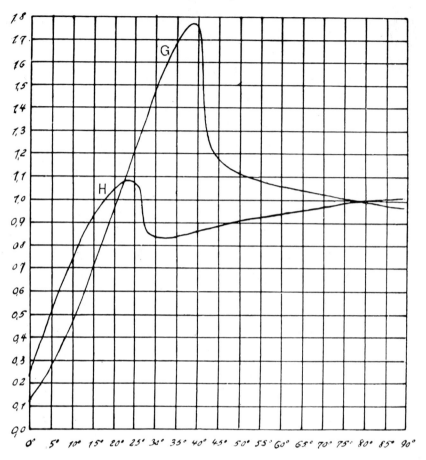

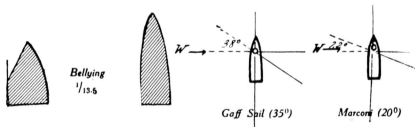

Bellying ¹/₁₃.₅

Gaff Sail (35⁰)

Marconi (20⁰)

The curves of system B represent the *polar curves* for the high rig and the gaff rig and consequently give us both the total pressure and its components the driving force and the resistance, for both sails — curve I for the gaff and curve II for the Marconi rig at the various angles of opposition.

On comparing these curves, we observe the great difference in the driving force developed by the two rigs, which we may briefly summarize as follows:

Direction of Action of Forces for different Relations of Length to Breadth.
System of Curves B.

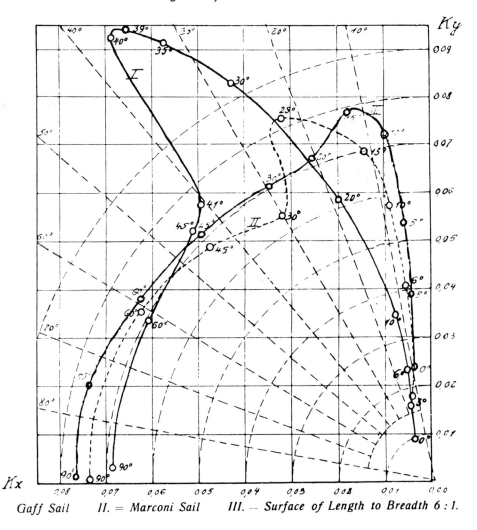

I. Gaff Sail   II. = Marconi Sail   III. -- Surface of Length to Breadth 6 : 1.

With the high rig one can sail higher on the wind, i. e. the Marconi sail develops the same driving force at a smaller angle — higher on the wind — or a greater force for the same angle of opposition. It retains this superiority over the gaff rig, in fact, up to an angle of 25°. From the curves of system A we see that the total pressures for the two rigs are related to each other as follows for the given angles of opposition:

	Marconi		Gaff
At 6°	0.55		0.31
10°	0.75		0.48
15°	0.93		0.70
20°	1.05		0.96
23°	1.10	=	1.10
25°	1.10		1.19
38°	0.87		1.78
80°	1.00	=	1.00
90°	1.02		0.98

Furthermore, the resultant pressure in the narrow sail *inclines more toward the vertical* of the diagram B, that is, its horizontal component or resistance is much smaller than that of the broader gaff rigged sail, as is evident from the curves of system B.

In the above table we find the answer to a question that every observant sailor has probably put to himself, the answer to which is dictated more by feeling than by an actual knowledge of facts: At what angle should the mainsail be carried with the wind abeam? Some sailors let it off considerably; others trim closer. I myself used to be of the opinion that a mainsail trimmed closer than customary developed more drive, but after I had discarded the gaff rig for the Marconi, I changed my opinion quite unexpectedly and joined those that advocated the counsel to "pay out the main sheet as much as possible."

That here again feeling and practical experience had indicated the *correct* path in advance of theory, is confirmed from an examination of the two systems of curves.

As a matter of fact, the lower gaff rigged sail must be trimmed about *15° closer* with the wind abeam than the high sail because the maximum drive for the former is reached at an angle of about 38°, for the latter at about 22° (cf. the system of curves A). It follows, therefore, that a gaff rigged boat can often cover a leg before the wind quicker by sailing it in zigzags — with the *wind on the beam,* first on the one quarter and then on the other, than by *running down dead before the wind* to the mark; but seldom anything is gained by this maneuver with the high Marconi sail. We may recall how often it occurs in racing that boats running with the wind *abeam* overhaul a whole field of boats that are sailing dead before the wind, and thus cause a great commotion. Many will have noticed that the lower, gaff sail is extremely difficult to manage with the wind abeam, that one must constantly change the position of the sail, and that it is on this point of sailing that even the best skipper with his repeated commands to "pay off" and "haul in" is taxed to the utmost. *The reason for this is that it is no easy matter to keep the sail under the maximum drive, as this is confined to only a few degrees.* With the high rig the curve of maximum drive is flatter, that is, it is extended over more degrees (from about 20° to 27°), and for this reason the skipper is not obliged to trouble himself so much about the proper position of his sail (with the wind abeam). Although the gaff-rigged boat is faster on this point of sailing, she is not so much faster as is indicated by the above systems of curves; the reason for this is that her sail is seldom kept under the highest driving pressure, which, as we have observed, is most difficult and requires a certain amount of feeling and long experience. Furthermore, in the Marconi rig of more recent date the mainsail is unproportionately large compared to the jib, although it is customary to set a large ballooner with the wind abeam. We may also observe that the narrow mainsail with its shorter boom tends less to turn the boat into the wind, that is, to give her a weather helm. Before the wind the two rigs are of about equal value.

From these observations the following *facts* may be established:

1. The high sail, in consequence of its better qualities to windward, where it develops about a third greater pressure than the low (gaff) sail, is superior to the latter. As the beat to windward is generally decisive in a race, there is little doubt as to its superiority.

2. The proportion of height to breadth should be at least 3:1.

3. With the wind abeam the ordinary gaff sail is more difficult to handle, but, if properly tended, it develops about a third more pressure than the Marconi sail does.

4. The gaff sail has to be hauled in about 15° closer than the high sail with the wind abeam.

5. In consideration of the direction of the forces acting on the sail *in their transmission to the boat,* a gaff sail should be carried at an angle of opposition of about 35° with the wind abeam, the high sail at about 20°.

6. Before the wind the gaff rigged boat should, in most cases, sail a somewhat zigzag course, whereas the Marconi-rigged boat should seldom deviate from the direct course.

The Center of Pressure

With the changes in relation of length to breadth of a plane, not only do the pressure and its distribution change, but the center of pressure does as well, shifting either toward the fore edge, that is opposed to the wind, or toward the rear edge, where the wind passes off the plane.

The shift of the center of pressure is represented by a curve, whose abscissae give the inclinations of the plane to the wind and ordinates determine the distances of that center from its fore edge and the latter are expressed in fractions of the breadth of the plane.

The curves of system I show the shift of the center of pressure

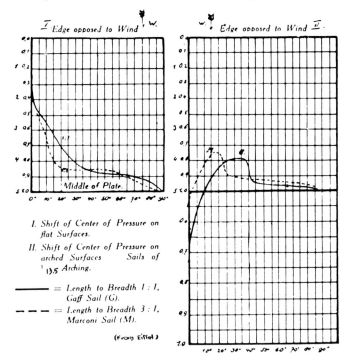

I. Shift of Center of Pressure on flat Surfaces.

II. Shift of Center of Pressure on arched Surfaces Sails of ¹⁄₁₃.₅ Arching.

——— = Length to Breadth 1 : 1, Gaff Sail (G).

- - - - = Length to Breadth 3 : 1, Marconi Sail (M).

(From Eiffel)

Shift of Center of Pressure.

Curry, Aerodynamics of Sails.

41

on two rectangular flat plates, the one with a relation of length to breadth of 3:1; and the other of 1:1; the former is represented by the broken curve the latter by the ordinary one.

System II represents the corresponding curves for *arched* surfaces of the same relations of length to breadth. Inasmuch as system I relates to flat surfaces and system II to arched ones, we may, therefore, apply the former to our centerboards and the latter to our sails.

The two curves of system I, where only the upper half of the plate is represented in the drawing, because the center of pressure lies between the middle of the plate and its fore edge, show that *for the smaller angles of opposition the center of pressure lies farther from the fore edge on a rectangular plate with a relation of length to breadth of 3:1 than on one with a relation of length to breadth of 1:1.*

The curve of system II marked M represents the shift of the center of pressure on a high (Marconi) sail; the curve marked G that on a broad, low (gaff) sail. These curves show that the center of pressure on the high sail for the small angles of opposition — that concern us on a beat to windward — lies farther forward, nearer its luff, than on the low, gaff rigged sail. For the larger angles of opposition it is just the reverse. This is important for the yachtsman, because in changing the rig of his boat from the gaff to the high rig, he must take into account this shift in the center of pressure due to the different relations of length to breadth of the two sails. Here he has to bear in mind three facts:

I. The center of pressure is shifted farther forward on the Marconi sail, because the *sail* itself on account of its height is concentrated farther forward (shift of the center of pressure with regard to the boat — her lateral plane).

II. The center of pressure on the sail itself lies somewhat farther forward, as we have seen above (shift of center of pressure due to form of sail — relation of its length to breadth).

III. A further comparison of the two systems of curves reveals, however, the fact that for small angles of opposition the center of pressure lies farther aft on the arched than on the flat sail; it thus follows that the position of the center of pressure depends on the arching of the sail, especially on the wind, to the effect that the greater the arching the *farther aft* will the center of pressure lie. As the Marconi sail *generally has a much greater arching* in comparison to its breadth than the gaff sail has, the shift of the center of pressure of the latter toward the luff due to points I and II may be entirely counteracted by that of the former aft, arising from its greater arching — point III.

The general conclusion is therefore that a high sail, with the *same* mast step as that of the gaff rig, will tend to affect the helm of the boat — giving her a lee helm — surprisingly little, perhaps not at all.

Now let us examine the transmission of the pressure on the sail to the centerboard. If we should rig a boat in such a manner, that the center of effort of her sail (-plan) lies in the center of gravity (effort) of her lateral plane, the boat would have such a *weather helm* that even in a moderate breeze she would be quite unmanageable. It thus happens that most boats have a weather helm, and many a designer has been greatly surprised in his first productions on finding his theoretical calculations on this point upset in practice.

This tendency to luff is explained by the fact that the center of pressure of a plane surface, in this case the centerboard, lies a considerable distance farther forward than that of an arched surface, here the sail (cf. also the two systems of curves on page 41). Inasmuch as any tendency to luff or bear off is to be ascribed to the relative position of these two centers, we must endeavor to balance the forces acting in them. In general, we should be guided by the *rule that the center of effort of the sail should lie in front of the center of the lateral plane,* and that the former, according to the form of the hull and the rigging, should have a lead of from 0 to 15% of the water line length over the latter.

Nevertheless, one may notice that many yachts that have a weather helm on the wind beat to windward better than others that are accurately balanced. This is, generally, the case with the former, when the rudder is attached directly to the fin. Here the blade of the rudder of the boat makes an angle with the surface of the fin and thus, similar to the arched surface, develops, as we have seen above, a strong pressure — pressure on the one side and suction on the other — in the direction of the arch (cf. chapter on "New Forms for Centerboard and Rudder"). A further favorable factor arising from the pressure developed on these two surfaces (fin and rudder) is that the boat will show less tendency to luff with increasing speed than in the case, where the rudder is hung quite free farther aft. The reason for this is likewise to be sought in the bent or arched surface, inasmuch as its center of pressure and thus that of the lateral plane of the boat lies farther aft. It follows, therefore, that the relatively small resistance called forth by the slightest weather helm in steering will produce a great pressure in the blade of the rudder, tending to counteract any inclination to luff. This alone accounts for the use of the relatively narrow rudder blade with its great efficiency when attached to the fin, in spite of its shorter distance from the center of the lateral plane — its smaller lever arm.

THE OUTLINE OF THE SAIL

By the outline of the sail is meant the sail's contour or silhouette. Let us assume that we wish to cut a sail of the most advantageous form. We know the most favorable arching and position of the belly; also the proper relation of length to breadth. But we still have to determine what form we should give the luff and the leech; in other words, should the mast be straight or bent, moreover vertical or inclined? and should the leech be cut straight or rounded.

We should here also be guided by the form or contour of a bird's wing as much as possible, but we must not forget that the latter is constructed with due regard to the mechanical process, to the beating of the wing, and to the habit of folding the wings on the body when not in use.

We notice that Nature gives most wings a backward slope; swallows' wings are an extreme in this point. But the more the bird tends toward a quiet soarer, like the gull, the more are the wings placed at right angles to the body. We came to the conclusion in our former observations on birds that no advantage was gained with regard to power by a backward slope of the wing, but that this property of the bird's wing served only to insure the *stability* of the flyer. It is remarkable, too, how Nature endeavors to avoid corners and apparently gives curved lines the preference — to straight ones.

We can learn here also from aviators, whose attention was first drawn to this subject. In 1922 at the Aerodynamic Laboratory at Göttingen experiments were made with models, the results of which are given in another chapter (see also chapter on "Experiments in the Aerodynamic Laboratory of Professor Junkers"). In the accompanying table are recorded the various values *per unit surface area* at different angles of opposition, between 6° and 15°, for the forces acting against the direction of flight (the resistance) and for those acting perpendicular thereto (the up-drive). The six surfaces investigated are represented in the drawing on the next page. They are of varying form, but all have the same surface area.

Wings	Up-drive	Resistance	$\dfrac{\text{Up-drive}}{\text{Resistance}}$	Angle of Opposition
1	73.4	4.72	15.55	
2	80.4	4.38	18.36	
3	75.9	4 64	16.36	6°
4	77.0	4.66	16.52	
5	85 0	4.81	17.67	
6	83.5	4 12	20.26	
1	93.9	7 23	12.98	
2	99.2	6.80	14.60	
3	95.0	6.97	13.63	
4	97 5	6.95	14.03	8.7°
5	105.0	7.32	14.34	
6	103.0	6.35	16.22	
1	109.5	10 2	10.74	
2	113.0	9.4	12.02	
3	112.5	9.93	11.33	
4	115.7	9.7	11.93	11.7°
5	116.0	10.10	11.50	
6	111.0	9.9	11.21	
1	115.6	13 8	8.38	
2	116.0	14.2	8.16	
3	121.0	13.2	9.15	
4	124.0	13.4	9.25	14.7°
5	117.0	15 2	7.69	
6	108.5	15.7	6.91	

From these values we infer the following: Wings 1 and 5 are relatively poor at every angle. Wing 6 is remarkably good for the smaller angles. Wherein lies the advantage? In the peculiar way in which the fore edge of the wing — that opposed to the wind — is inclined backward or because the wing itself is pointed? One may exclude the former, I think, because wing 5 is also inclined backward, but, in spite of this, is *inferior* to all the others. Therefore, we may assume that the superiority of wing 6 is to be ascribed to its greater length or to the fact that it is pointed, which would indicate a "Huari" * rig or, better, a Marconi sail.

For the larger angles of opposition, 11.7° to 14.7° the wings numbered 2, 3 and 4 are by far the best. If we are contemplating beating to windward with the wind striking the sail at an angle of 10° to 12°, then wings 2 and 4 should be the most advantageous.

* A mainsail with a short hoist or luff on mast and a very long gaff that runs almost parallel to the mast and projects high above it.

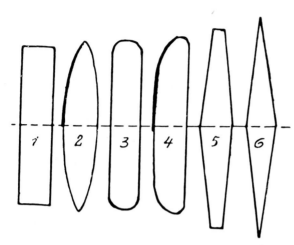

But let it be recalled that, for reasons given in the chapter on "Arching," the efficiency of the surface is not exactly expressed by the value of the quotient $\frac{\text{up-drive}}{\text{resistance}}$, since, especially for larger values of opposition, the retarding effect produced by the resistance as such is much less than that indicated by the resistance curve, whereas the up-drive or pressure becomes more and more the decisive factor as the angle of opposition increases. This higher evaluation of the pressure as

Wings of different Shape but same Surface Area.

compared to the resistance is still more pronounced for *sails*, as here the retarding forces — the resistance — due to the position of the sail to the boat play a still more inferior role. With reference to our sails, we may, in view of these measurements, establish the following principles:

I. The Marconi mast, that is, the luff of the sail, may either be slightly and uniformly curved from top to bottom or, what is better and more practical, on account of the simpler method of staying the mast, run straight up from the deck for at least two-thirds of its length and then bent back gradually more and more toward the top. A uniform curvature for the luff is indispensable with sails that have to be reefed frequently.

II. For a Marconi sail, a perfectly straight mast from top to bottom is, however, in spite of the few theoretical advantages of the curved mast, preferable to the latter on account of the difficulties encountered in staying it properly; but any pronounced *inclination aft or so-called "rake" of the mast should be avoided.*

III. The form of the leech is determined more or less indirectly by the principle that, in order to avoid unnecessary weight, as large a sail as possible should be bent on the shortest serviceable spars. Therefore, we are justified in giving the leech as great an outward arching as compatible — with the use of transverse battens.

POSITION OF THE SAIL

Regarding the position of the sail little need be said. When we speak of the position of the sail, we must indicate whether we mean *the position of the sail with respect to the wind or with respect to the boat.*

In respect to the wind, as we conclude from the polar curves, the most effective position of the sail differs for the various forms of sail, as the one develops its maximum pressure sooner, the other later. Besides, on the wind, the principal thing is not always the maximum pressure but the closeness that can be attained to the wind. As we have already observed, the most favorable angle between the current of air, i. e., the apparent wind — the direction of the wind as indicated by the pennant * — and the sail is to be ascertained from the polar curves.

On the wind, that is, in beating to windward, one may assume for most sails an *average* angle of opposition of about 10°. The upper part of the sail in this case, especially with the gaff rig, forms an angle of only 3° to 4° with the pennant in consequence of its sagging out, while the boom is hauled in at an angle of about 15° to the apparent wind. One should, naturally, not forget that in a strong wind, in consequence of the sagging out of the upper part of the sail, the angle between the gaff and the pennant becomes smaller, so that the pennant may even be blowing in the direction of the gaff.

On a freer course the angle of opposition may be somewhat larger i. e., the wind may fall somewhat fuller on the sail; in fact, the most favorable angle of opposition depends upon the maximum pressure, which is to be ascertained from the polar curve for the particular sail. The practical possibility of trimming a sail *closer to the wind is,* therefore, *dependent entirely on the form of the sail,* its arching and relation of length to breadth, whereby, as we have already observed, the *sagging out* of the upper part of the sail has, under all circumstances, an unfavorable influence on its efficiency.

In the latter case — *the position of the sail with regard to the boat,* the position of the sail on the wind depends on the hull of the boat and its speed, which is, in turn, dependent on the lines of the hull. It is, therefore, possible to trim the sail closer on a racer than on a slower boat (cruiser), because the drift to leeward of the former is less on account of her greater speed. Inasmuch as the speed increases with the strength of the wind, the closer trimming of the sail is also dependent on the strength of the wind.

We may, therefore, formulate certain general rules for trimming sails:

The more the wind increases the closer may the sail be trimmed. Naturally only feeling can decide the limit to which a sail may be trimmed to advantage, it being quite impossible to be guided by any exact rule; whereas, as already mentioned, the *position of the sail to the wind* may be ascertained exactly from the polar curve for the particular sail. For reasons of stability, the resistance of the rudder and the facility in steering, which is dependent on the speed, the angle between sail and boat must be increased, that is, the sheet eased, if the wind becomes too strong. Just when this easing of the sheet is advisable depends on the stability of the boat. And, as we well know, the waves play an important part here on account of their retarding effect. In general, the sail may be trimmed gradually closer and closer on smaller boats up to a wind velocity of 2 to 3 meters (about 6½ to 10 feet) per second, on larger boats or yachts up to one of about 5 to 7 meters (about 16 to 24 feet) per second. As the wind increases beyond these velocities, the sheets must be gradually eased, more and more.

* The direction of the apparent wind is that which determines the position of the sail; this wind is the resultant of the real wind and that created by the speed of the boat. It is determined in magnitude and direction, as the resultant of these two components, by the parallelogram of forces (cf. the drawing on next page). We see from the drawing that the apparent wind falls on the sail, in the first place, at a sharper angle and, secondly, with greater force.

I wish to call attention here to a fact that ought to interest every yachtsman. We all know from experience that the wind veers from the quarter in every puff, and that, consequently, it is possible to run higher on the wind in the flaws. How is this to be explained? Although much has been written on this subject, the explanation is quite simple. Through the accelerated velocity of the wind in the flaw the apparent wind, the direction of which is indicated by the pennant — the resultant of the real wind and that created by the speed of the boat — is deflected less from the direction of the real wind. This is due to the fact that the velocity of the wind has increased more than the speed of the boat; for example, the former may have doubled, while the latter has increased hardly appreciably.

The *accelerated velocity* of the real wind in the puff thus causes the pennant to tend more in its direction than the *speed of the boat* can influence it to blow in that of the wind created by her speed. Consequently, the pennant streams off more to leeward, that is, the wind strikes the sail at a greater angle. The apparent wind thus has a tendency to veer from the quarter in a flaw, although the direction of the (real) wind has not changed a single degree. The appended sketch will serve to illustrate graphically the above.

Let the line OM represent strength and direction of real wind and the line AM, BM, CM or DM distance of course sailed in unit time and direction of same.

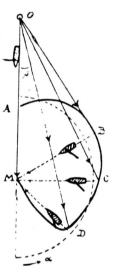

Then MA, MB, MD or Md will represent strength and direction of wind created by speed of boat and *a* angle of direction of that wind to real wind. And hence the line OA, OB, OC or OD strength and direction of apparent wind.

Position A is before the wind; position B on the wind.

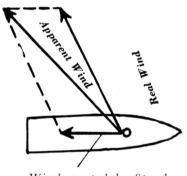

Wind created by Speed of Boat

The curve ABCDM is purely empirical and not directly calculable varying according to the particular characteristics of boat and rigging.

Here we are interested only in the change in the direction of the apparent wind, when the real wind increases in strength. Suppose, for example, the wind blows twice as hard; then we must double OM; but the distance covered by the boat will not be anything like twice as great, because the resistance of the air and water increases, not as the speed, but as the square of the speed. Therefore, the wind created by the speed of the boat will be much *less* than twice as strong as that represented by the quantity MA, MB, MC or MD. Hence, the corresponding angle of opposition (MOB, MOC or MOD) becomes smaller; that is, the wind veers more from the quarter as it increases and the boat can thus run higher on the wind. From this fact it becomes clear how much superior the boat that can run higher on the wind on a beat to windward must be to one that cannot point so high, although the latter may travel faster.

A summary of these results in the following concrete form may be of interest:

A boat

that *points high on the wind*	that *does not point so high*
(1) Is slower.	(1) Travels faster.
(2) Works up more to windward and hence has the shorter course.	(2) Falls more to leeward and hence has the longer course.
(3) Her speed to velocity of wind smaller, hence apparent wind *more quarterly.*	(3) Her speed to velocity of wind greater, hence apparent wind *less quarterly.*
(4) In strong wind heels less and hence drifts less to leeward.	(4) In strong wind heels more and hence drifts more to leeward.
(5) In strong wind less pressure on rudder and hence speed less retarded.	(5) In strong wind more pressure on rudder, blade more horizontal and hence greater lifting and less steering effect, i. e., retarding forces greater.
(6) Shows tendency to drift to leeward in light airs.	(6) Drifts to leeward less in light airs.

Inasmuch as it is only the *apparent* wind which operates on the sail, the following property peculiar to the wind should be treated under this head.

On account of the friction of the air on the water and boat, the velocity of the real wind increases as we ascend above the surface of the water, or, in other words, the wind is weaker in the neighborhood of the boom than in that of the gaff. This retardation of the wind near the water may amount to 30 per cent. This means that, according to our above considerations, the apparent wind in the upper part of the sail may be expected to veer more from the quarter than in its lower portion. Some yachtsmen contend that this fact justifies the sagging out of the gaff; but, granting that a *small* sagging out is advantageous, the actual amount, even with the Marconi rig under the most favorable circumstances, is *too* great, as the *difference* in the direction of the wind due to its greater velocity in the upper part of the sail amounts, at the most, to from 3° to 5°, and many gaff sails sag out in a strong wind as much as 30° to 40°.

On the other hand, it is advisable to tip the boat somewhat in light airs to bring about the desired sagging out of the upper part of the sail. This sagging out is not, however, a direct result of the tipping, but an indirect one due to the stretching property or elasticity of the duck.

RECIPROCAL INFLUENCE OF THE SAILS

The relation of the sails to one another has not as yet been treated, at least with regard to the favorable influence they can exert. As this subject should be of greatest moment to the yachtsman, it would be interesting and instructive, if one could give exact information about the influence of the mainsail on the jib, and vice versa; if one could determine definitely the correct size and form of the jib and ascertain just how far it should reach abaft the luff of the mainsail.

I must admit that I have only lately succeeded in bringing these questions nearer to a solution. The first and most serious obstacle to a clear understanding of this subject presented itself to me in this manner: If, as we have found, the chief driving power of the sail is to be ascribed to suction, then why does not the wind off the jib nullify this suction in the mainsail? If, on the one hand, the greater driving power of the suction is established and, on the other hand, it has been confirmed by experience that the jib is decidedly advantageous, then where does the fallacy lie?

We know that a boat with a jib is superior to a cat-rigged boat of the same sail area. This has been proved by re-rigging the same boat, as well as by comparing her with other boats of different rig; in fact, a sloop-rigged boat with a total sail area of 25 square meters (about 30 square yards) is known not to be inferior to a cat-rigged boat with a sail area of 30 square meters (about 36 square yards). Also we may often have been

surprised to note, how much slower a boat moves the *moment* the jib ceases to draw, this being especially marked with the wind abeam.

For the solution of these questions a discovery, which has been made in the technique of flying, is of great significance. It led to the construction of the Handley-Page and the Lachmann aeroplanes. Both inventors

Longitudinal Section of Wing of Handley-Page and Lachmann Aeroplane.

succeeded in attaining greater carrying p o w e r by means of a *s m a l l, narrow, auxiliary plane in front* of the main carrying surface. Especially for the somewhat larger angles of opposition to the wind, 10° to 15°, the greater efficiency of these planes

appears in a most striking manner.

May not we yachtsmen maintain that this innovation is nothing new to us, that we have, in fact, already benefited from its great advantages instinctively? What the technique of flying has only lately discovered for the plane in horizontal position, has been the common property of all mariners for years — the jib. The Handley-Page gains greater carrying power by using the little fore "sail" to throw air onto the main plane, whereas Lachmann simply makes a small narrow slit in the main carrying surface a short distance from and parallel to its fore edge, thus dividing it into a smaller fore and a larger rear wing (cf. the sketches on page 49). The slit passes from below diag-

Eagle's Wing With "Pocket" on Under Surface

onally upward through the surface toward its rear, becoming narrower and narrower, so that here, as in the Handley-Page, the air is conducted as through a funnel onto the upper surface of the main wing. How ingenious and valuable this device of the air conducting fore wing really is may not appear at first sight; it was, at least, the case with me, when my attention was first called to the Lachmann slit. Not until I had succeeded in identifying Nature as the inventor of this recently adopted innovation in the technique of flying could I reconcile my theories of sailing to it.

As in thousands of other cases, man does not invent; he only observes casually that Nature presents in her creations the most ingenious mastery of a certain problem. The *bird* possesses on the fore edge of its main wing a narrow, tiny wing, which acts as a conducting surface in throwing the air onto the main wing. Although in our small birds this fore wing is, if at all, only slightly developed, many of the larger birds of prey, such as the eagles, possess it to a marked degree. This conducting wing on the fore edge of the main wing, which we may imagine as replacing the thumb of the hand, projects somewhat beyond the latter, as shown in the photograph on this page. Hitherto no explanation has been offered for the function played by this small conducting wing, nor has even any attempt been made to attribute any function whatever to it. In the insect world, in the case of the June bug for example, the stationary fore or so-called protecting wing appears to possess an air guiding function. With most flying insects the fore wings are also smaller and, curiously enough, always overlap the hind wings somewhat.

But all these facts apparently contradict the suction theory, and up to date (1923) the technique of flying has failed to arrive at any definite conclusion with regard to these peculiar phenomena. In order to facilitate the understanding of the problem, let us briefly *review* the manner of action of the suction.

We know that the suction developed on the leeward side of the sail is to be attributed to the partial vacuum that actually exists there. The sail is pulled or sucked into this space, while the various currents of air in the neighborhood are naturally drawn into it from all sides and tend to fill it and thus to reduce the negative pressure. We also know that a current of air arises only in consequence of difference in density of the atmosphere. The wind itself is, in fact, caused by the tendency of the atmosphere to adjust all inequalities in density, which are due principally to differences in temperature.

The suction on the sail acts, as may be confirmed, *close to* its surface and we should not allow ourselves to be misled by the diagrams already presented — the curves, the absissae of which represent the pressure and suction on the sail. These curves give the values of pressure in question *on the sail itself, not the ex tent of action* of that pressure or suction.

Further, we know that the formation of eddies, which unfortunately most of our present sails tend to promote, has an unfavorable effect on the development of the pressure. When we discover large eddies in the lee of the sail, not only on but off the wind, we may assume that at the beginning of their formation as they recede from the sail, they develop a strong suction, that is, that they act favorably, but *Eagle's Wing With Small Projecting Fore Wing*

51

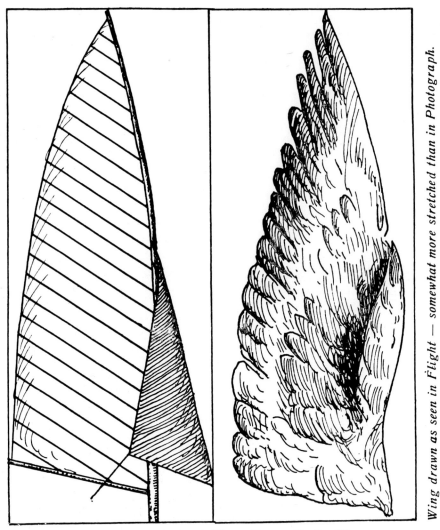

Similarity of Sails of Sloop Rig to Bird's Wing.

that in their final stage, as they turn back toward the sail, the suction is disturbed and the development of the negative pressure in the sail is thereby retarded, that is, that the eddies then act unfavorably. This agrees with actual observation, namely, that when the largest eddies are formed — and these appear, when the sail is at right angles to the wind, that is, when the boat is running dead before it — a sail with holes pierced in it at certain points draws just as well as the original sail — without the holes — because the eddies on their return to the sail are repelled or dissolved by the currents of air streaming through the holes from its windward surface.

The next thought in order is: On the assumption that eddies have already formed, could one reduce their unfavorable influence on the suction

52

by intercepting them in their final stage — on their return to the sail? We can easily imagine that, could we *prevent* the air currents *from streaming* into *the partial vacuum* produced by the eddies as they recede from the sail, then the sail would develop a correspondingly greater suction or pull due to its increased effort to fill out that space.

That the suction is increased, when an eddy is intercepted on its return flow, is confirmed by the experiments of Prof. Fr. Ahlborn with submerged plates. My experiments, previously described, were limited to the determination of the eddies formed on the edges of plates, which, only partly submerged in water, were moved through it, and these cannot, therefore, serve for acquiring an exact knowledge of the subject. As we are dealing here with a sail, a surface that is surrounded *on all sides* by the medium, we can study the complete process in water only on *entirely submerged* surfaces.

By means of a camera, which moved along with the plate in the water, Prof. Ahlborn photographed the currents formed by a rectangular plate of relation of length to breadth of 3:1. A study of the photographs revealed the following:

I. On the longer sides, which correspond to the luff and leech of the sail, the large eddies formed along the edges, those already observed by us, describe two large ellipse-like paths and finally unite to form the so-called "return" or "back" current (see sketch A on next page). With the plate placed at right angles to the current, this return current hits it exactly in the middle. The less the plate is inclined to the current, the more the center of this back current shifts toward the rear of the plate and the more the eddy on its fore edge increases and that on its rear edge decreases in size. This return current hits the back of the plate at exactly the same distance from its rear edge as the dividing line of the current on the front of the plate is distant from its fore edge (see sketch C, which presents the same view as seen from above, as sketch A, it is drawn only on a larger scale to facilitate examination).

II. Eddies are also formed on the two shorter sides of the plate, which correspond to the head and foot of the sail, the upper one turning downward and the lower one upward (cf. sketch B). These eddies are considerably weaker than those formed on the longer sides of the plate, but they are larger or, rather, they extend to a greater distance from it. Their combined back current unites with that of the eddies formed on the longer edges, and the two thus united form the common back current N.

It is this "return current," which causes paper and other light objects to be sucked along behind the last car of a moving train or blows the hair of those sitting behind the windshield of an automobile forward into their faces. Similarly, the pacemaker on a motorcycle is enabled to "suck" along in his wake the cyclist directly behind him. The former, in fact, makes use of a broad plate made fast to rear of his motorcycle at right angles to the direction of motion, which has the effect of increasing the suction to such a degree that the cyclist following him is able to attain a speed of 75 miles or more an hour.

Lines of Flow on Plate and Sail.

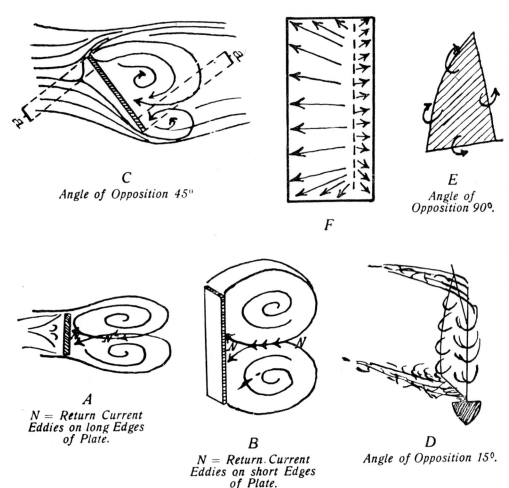

C
Angle of Opposition 45°

F

E
*Angle of
Opposition 90°.*

A
*N = Return Current
Eddies on long Edges
of Plate.*

B
*N = Return. Current
Eddies on short Edges
of Plate.*

D
Angle of Opposition 15°.

III. With the plate inclined to the current, the relation of these four
principal eddies to one another is quite different. The less the
plate is inclined to the current, that is, the smaller the angle of
opposition at which the current strikes it, the more pronounced are
the eddies formed on its longer edges; that is, these stronger eddies,
on their return to the region of negative pressure on the leeward
side of the plate, suppress more and more and thus finally destroy
the weaker eddies streaming from its upper and lower shorter edges,
so that:

IV. at an angle of opposition of 50° the latter are so completely torn
asunder that they cannot return to the plate; in fact, before they have
begun to return, they are intercepted by the outward currents of the
larger eddies and thus, being detached from the plate, flow off from
its edges in the form of long drawn out spirals, the so-called "pigtail

eddies" (cf. sketch D). The formation of these spirals becomes so marked at angles of 20° to 25°, that they actually drag portions of the stronger eddies from the longer edges of the plate along with them on their course.

Now if our conclusion concerning the harmfulness of the return current or "back drive" of the eddy is correct, then, *the moment the upper and under eddies of the plate cease to strike back onto it, but, in the form of spirals, are detached from it, an increase in the suction, and hence in the total pressure or effect must occur*. This is actually the case.

The total pressure on a rectangular plate attains its maximum at an angle of opposition of about 20° to 30°, depending on its relation of length to breadth, and not, as one might expect, when the current strikes it at right angles — at an angle of opposition of 90°.

Accordingly, upon measuring the pressure at various points on the back of the plate, when it is inclined at small angles of opposition, we should expect to find the suction along its *shorter edges,* from which the "pig-tail" eddies are detached, appreciably increased. This also proves to be the case, as confirmed both by Eiffel and by the suction curves of the diagrams for the leeward side of the sail. On a further inspection of these curves, especially of those for the gaff sail, we note that there is a certain zone of zero pressure which is confined to that region, where the return or back current of the eddies hit the sail.

It thus follows that every return current, that is, the back drive of every eddy, is detrimental, and that the interception of every such current is equivalent to an increase in the pressure (suction).

We can now return to the reciprocal influence of the sails.

Let us examine the approximate course of the current as represented in the two drawings A and B on pages 56 and 57. These lines of flow may be determined on the sail itself with down or, on surfaces similar to sails, which one moves through water, by the method already employed in the chapter on "Hydrodynamic Experiments."

Drawing A represents the cross-section of a catboat's sail on the wind. Due to the action of the eddies the drawing shows two systems of forces, the one those of suction, which act favorably, and the other the reactionary or retarding forces.

If we now imagine the same mainsail in the same relative position to the wind, but with jib set and drawing, the stream lines undergo a decided change (see drawing B). With reference to this drawing let us recall the experiments with the down: The eddies have practically vanished; the wind flows in the lee of the mainsail straight toward the rear; this is to be ascribed to the wind off the jib, which is directed aft over the mainsail. If we hold the down at a distance of one or two meters from the sail — in the lee, we can detect the remnants of eddies that have been intercepted by this back wind; in other words, the *return flow of the eddies is blocked from reaching the mainsail by the current of air off the jib flowing directly across its path.* Thus we perceive that, when the jib is correctly trimmed, the *beginning* of the eddy, flowing off in the direction of the suck close to the sail, is *not* materially influenced by the wind off the jib; whereas its *return* current is *intercepted* or, at least, thrust aside and carried off toward the leech of the mainsail; or, in the more scientific terms of the technique of flight, due to the device

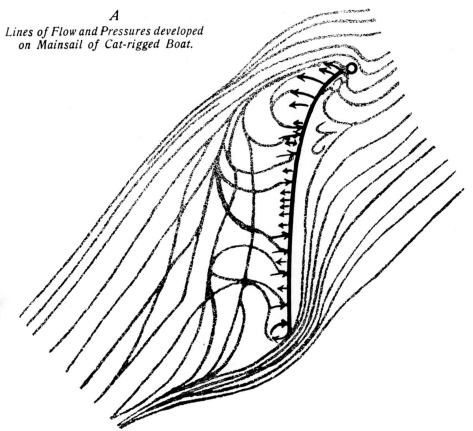

A
*Lines of Flow and Pressures developed
on Mainsail of Cat-rigged Boat.*

of the funnel, which causes a contraction of the air between jib and mainsail, the velocity of the current in the lee of the mainsail is accelerated. As the rider of a motorcycle, running at high speed, is unable to describe a sharp curve, so this current of air, being accelerated, will not be deflected from its path by the partial vacuum immediately in the lee of the mainsail and thus not be drawn into it. Consequently, the sail will be sucked into this space with increased force. Or, in physical terms, the greater the velocity of this current of air, the less the atmospheric pressure and hence the greater the negative pressure developed. Compare also the *modus operandi* of the Flettner rotor.

It is thus proved that the efficiency of the mainsail is increased by the use of a jib.

But we can learn still more from these drawings. The wind, which strikes the luff of the mainsail, especially on a somewhat freer course, and tends to pass forward around the mast to lee, is partly intercepted by the current off the jib and partly thrown onto the jib. This is one of the reasons why the jib develops a disproportionately *large driving force* to its area. Every yachtsman knows how important the correct handling of this sail is; also that, on a reach, a boat sails to a great extent with the jib. Furthermore, the wind passing from the mainsail around the mast onto the jib produces an increased drive not only where it strikes it, in its after-third, but also in its fore-portion by imparting to the current of air that strikes this sail a component more from the quarter. This is confirmed by the empirical fact that the *jib can be carried at a much larger angle to the wind than the mainsail.* And this explains my statement why the *jib develops a greater drive in proportion to its area than normal.* We thus see that the two sails are influenced to a great extent by each other, the *driving force of the mainsail being increased by the presence of the jib and that of the jib by the mainsail.* It is, moreover, interesting to examine and compare the approximate curves for the pressure to windward and for the suction in the lee of the jib and mainsail at various angles of opposition (cf. the systems of curves on the next page; the dotted lines show the proportionate amounts of pressure and suction).

The almost *abnormal suction of the jib* at the angle of opposition of 18° is most striking. The obvious explanation for this is that the return current in the lee of the jib is also somewhat influenced, that is, checked on its return by the accelerated speed, at which the air is forced through the funnel-like passage between jib and mainsail; in other words, it is not easy for the air at the high speed, at which it is pressed through the funnel-like slit between the two sails, to be deflected from its path toward the region of the partial

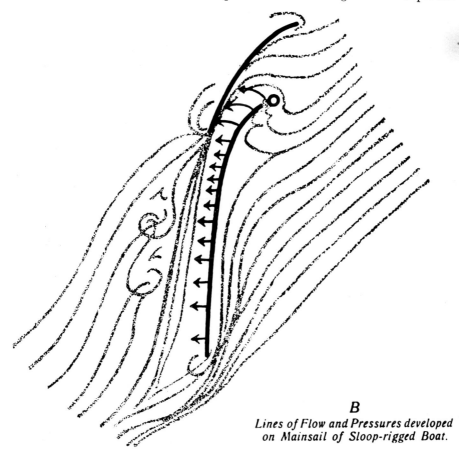

B
Lines of Flow and Pressures developed on Mainsail of Sloop-rigged Boat.

Curry. Aerodynamics of Sails.

vacuum in the lee of the jib. Furthermore, the customary proportion of length to breadth in the jib is favorable to such behavior.

Now we understand the direct advantage of the *jib* and also its *indirect advantage* in increasing the suction of the mainsail. Moreover, we know why a cat-boat is apt to have a *weather helm* and why a sloop-rigged boat of the *same relation of center of effort* — center of gravity of the combined sail area — *to center of gravity of the lateral plane does not.* It is alone the greater driving force developed by the jib, which has enabled us to obviate this mistake — of the weather helm.

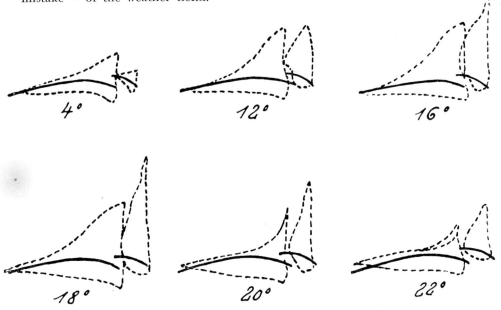

I. Distribution of Pressure on Jib and Mainsail for different Angles of Opposition.

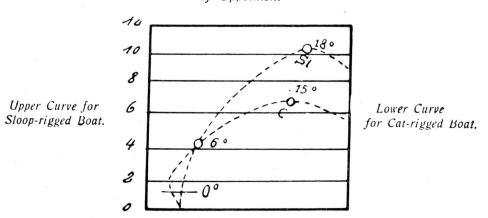

Upper Curve for Sloop-rigged Boat.

Lower Curve for Cat-rigged Boat.

II. Curves of Pressure developed by Sloop- and Cat-rigged Boat of same Sail Area.

58

We are enabled from all this knowledge to determine to a certain degree of accuracy the most advantageous form of jib. However this has been pretty well established, though more or less unconsciously, by practice.

For beating to windward the jib should be cut according to the following principles:

I. The jib must *operate so* that its back wind does *not flow* into the region of partial vacuum in the lee of the mainsail, but, at the same time, prevents any influx of air, especially from the return currents of the eddies, into that region by its own flow, which should be directed somewhat away from the mainsail, unless transverse battens are supplied.

II. The jib must not be cut too full — with too large a belly, because it would not fulfill conditions I. We know also from experience that it is quite impossible to beat to windward properly with a jib that is cut too full.

III. The jib should reach well abaft the luff of the mainsail, that the stability and hence efficiency of the lines of flow may be insured. The *extent* of the overlap depends first on the *beam of the boat* and secondly on the *breadth of the mainsail*, and it should *amount to about a quarter of the length of the boom.*

IV. The jib should reach as high up — the mast, as possible, that its favorable influence may extend along the *entire* luff of the mainsail. One might recommend having the fore triangle of the sail area meas-

Like a Bird's Wing
30 sq-meter Swedish Cruiser

ured for two jibs: a *high,* narrow jib that can be set well aft on deck for light airs and a *lower,* broader one farther forward for strong winds, this latter for reasons of stability and to reduce that sagging of the luff of the jib, which is so difficult to correct, when the wind increases.

V. The foot of the jib should ascend toward the leech, that it may not hinder the advantageous formation and detachment of the "pig-tail" eddies along the boom, which increases the suction of the mainsail. Every yachtsman knows that one beats to windward badly with a low-cut jib. Its unfavorable effect may also be proved empirically by hoisting the main boom 8 to 12 inches higher than usual, so that the foot of the jib now lies lower than the boom.

VI. The distance between the throat of the jib and the mast should not be too large. At greater distances the wind off the jib does not flow parallel to the mainsail, but "spills" *onto it.* Furthermore, the shorter the distance between the throat of the jib and the mast, the steeper the luff of the jib and hence the more horizontal its direction of drive.

If the distance between the throat of the jib and the mast is short, one may trim the jib closer, and by thus narrowing the slit accelerate the velocity of the air current and hence increase the funnel effect (see drawings C and D on page 65).

Explanation of the Experiments With Down

The reader will understand now the currents revealed on the sail by the down, and I shall call attention only to the following:

I. Immediately under the boom, the down is blown toward the lee at a larger angle to the boom increasing as the mast is approached. This is *caused* by an increase in the suction, the maximum negative pressure lying just abaft the mast. With the wind abeam this maximum suction shifts more toward the middle of the boom.

II. The direction of the air currents on the windward side of the sail coincide with those of the currents of water on the rectangular plate (see drawing F on page 54). The direction of the battens and even the seams of the sail should be made to correspond as nearly as possible to that of these air currents.

III. The best proof of the intensity of the suction is the great velocity with which the down when brought near the narrow slit between the mainsail and mast is sucked through it. The acceleration of the air current that pulls the down toward the lee is thus confirmed; and the same phenomenon can be observed on the luff of the jib.

IV. That the down on the leech of the jib is sucked strongly toward the lee and even blown forward on the leeward side of the sail is accounted for by the *large* suction, which is active on the leech of the jib (see drawings on page 58). On the other hand, the fact that the down is blown directly aft along the leech of the mainsail is to be explained by the little development of suction in that region.

We have already explained how the jib influences the flow of the currents in the lee of the mainsail.

Every yachtsman can carry out the experiments with down for himself and it will be easier for him to form an idea of the various currents acting on the sails by so doing.

The Lead or Direction of the Jib Sheet

As it must be our endeavour to have the slit between the jib and mainsail from the foot to the head of the former of as uniform breadth as possible, we are confronted with the question: How is the jib to be trimmed that it may conform to the sagging out of the mainsail caused by the gaff? If we wish to remain true to our theories and trim the jib not only below but above in such a manner that it will make an angle of opposition to the wind of 10° less than the mainsail does, the upper part of the jib will then have to be trimmed at an angle of about 35°, in as much as the gaff makes an angle of about 25° with the keel of the boat (cf. drawing B). The jib should, therefore, be given exactly the same twist throughout that the mainsail has.

On comparing the direction of the wind, which is indicated in drawing B by an arrow, with the position of the sails, we are confronted with the surprising fact that both sails, but especially the jib, show *negative angles of opposition* to the wind in their upper parts. In other words, the wind would appear to fall on the leeward side of the jib and to press it over to windward; that is, the jib should be expected to flap in the wind. But this is not the case. Many will surely recollect this strange phenomenon as confirmed by experience. Actual measurements, which I made on sails, gave negative values of opposition of from 5° to 16°. But this result need not astonish us especially, for in Nature itself we may observe the same process. We know that the wing of a bird shows a similar twist toward its outer end and that the wind that falls on this portion strikes it also at a negative angle of opposition — of from 3° to 5° — that is, the current is directed onto the upper instead of the lower surface of the wing. How is it then possible that both wing and sail,

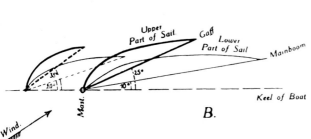

61

in spite of this negative angle of opposition, should show a pressure on the under or windward surface respectively? The reason is the following: The air current that strikes the inner part of the wing or the lower portion of the sail is partly transformed into eddies; the rest streams out toward the end of the wing or *upward* over the sail, following the twist of the surface. This latter current is so strong that it exerts sufficient pressure on the outer or upper surface respectively to more than counterbalance the pressure that is brought to act on it — in the opposite direction — by the current that strikes the wing or sail from the other side, to the effect that the sail retains its arching and continues to draw without flapping.

But let us return to our subject. How can we bring it about that the slit between the jib and mainsail assume the same size or breadth from below to the head of the jib, or, what is equivalent, where should the *reeving eye or the outrigger for the jib sheet* be fastened to the deck? It is obvious that we can obtain the desired twist or sagging out of the upper part of the jib by stretching its foot more than its leech. If, as is customary, the jib sheet — in its prolongation — halves the angle at the clew of the jib (cf. drawing A), then the same tension will be brought to bear on both leech and foot of the jib and, as a result, its upper part will throw its back wind onto the lee of the mainsail. I, therefore, propose the simple rule for the direction of the jib sheet, that, namely, it make a *right angle with the luff* of the sail. Hereby the tension is greater on the foot and less on the leech, and the twist of the upper part of the jib will thus be made to conform more to that of the mainsail. I may observe that the relative tension on the foot and the leech of the jib, which determines its twist, is not affected by the inclination of its luff, whether it is more or less steep. On the other hand, we may not assume the perpendicular to the luff of the jib to be an exact or the most favorable solution for the direction or lead of its sheet, should the relation of length of foot to that of leech of the jib not be a normal one, as in the case of a broad balloon jib; for here the two lines may coincide or even change their relative position to each other. The above rule may, therefore, be expressed better in the form: The lead of the jib sheet should be such that its direction forms an angle of 10° to 20° with the line that halves the angle at the clew on the upper half of that line (cf. drawing A).

The Advantages of Transverse Battens[*]

The Importance of the "Slot-Effect" Demonstrated by a Simple Experiment

Practice has proved that in light airs a strongly arched sail is superior, while in heavy winds a somewhat flatter sail is preferred. This is confirmed by nature in that the wings of slow flying birds show greater arching than those of the fast flyers. For this reason most of the International 6-, 8-, 10- and 12-meter boats have several sets of sails, either cut flat or strongly bellied. Just before the race a decision is made as to which sail is to be used in the prevailing wind. The question arises — Why not use a sail with a changeable arch?

Curry, Aerodynamics of Sails and Racing Tactics.

[*] This article was inserted later—in new edition.

The author's 22 sq-meter Racer "Aera," winner of several championships.
(Note 14 transverse battens)

Must we go as far as China or Egypt to learn what a sail should look like? The Chinese junk uses a sail with long battens. Would the natives of China use this seemingly complicated system if they were not aware of a decided advantage, *i.e.,* the increased speed of their boats? Must we be reminded of the fact that a kite with a rigid surface flies one-third higher than the one with a canvas surface which is bellied by the pressure of the wind?

I used long battens (wooden battens extending from the leech of the mainsail to the mast) on my boat, a 22-Square-meter racer, in 1922. Since this time the batten sail has progressed in Germany from one class to another and has now made its way into the larger classes, in spite of the strong opposition with which it was met by the cruising fraternity. Today, almost all small boats and very many of the larger yachts use transverse battens.

The German Racing Association decided, at the request of the Cruising Clubs, to bar long battens for all types of cruising boats. In a later meeting of the Association the same people who had been fighting the battens asked that this restriction be dropped for cruising boats. Why? Because a boat with a batten mainsail is faster and because a batten sail is cheaper, and lasts longer. It is also cheaper to have two sets of battens rather than two sets of sails.

Long battens that extend from the leech to the luff serve the following purpose: They give the sail the uniform arching desired, and produce a somewhat rigid surface; * they also admit of a change in the arching at will, as demanded by the prevailing circumstances. For example, the "belly" may be brought to lie in the fore-third of the sail by planing the battens thinner in that part; they are thereby rendered more pliable and bend more easily toward their fore ends, the flexible canvas assuming the same curves as the battens.

The arching should, as we know, depend on the strength of the wind. This may, to a certain degree, be regulated in two ways: The greater the tension under which the battens are inserted and made fast in the pockets, the greater the arching of the sail. The same results may be achieved by the use of several sets of battens of different thickness or size. In a light wind thin flexible battens are used, these being inserted in the pockets under greater tension; in a stiff breeze a set of thicker and less pliable ones are inserted under correspondingly less tension.

To be able to appreciate the superiority of the batten sail and to understand the great aerodynamic advantage involved we must first be familiar with the heart of every sail system. In my opinion, the success of a yacht stands or falls on the correct "slot effect" of her sails.

The new theory of sailing has revealed the fact that the suction in the lee of the sail is from two to three times as great as the pressure on the windward side. Thus, we sail with suction rather than with pressure. When close hauled, the wind passes from forward aft between the jib and the mainsail. A thorough study of the air currents on sails has taught us that with the correct relative position of the two sails a greatly increased driving force can be obtained. By forming a slot similar to a valve with a broad opening at the front and a narrow outlet at the back, the movement of the air is accelerated. This accelerated air increases the suction of the mainsail ** and thus the speed of the boat. To produce this effect only a small overlap of the jib is essential. The most efficient valve effect is created by the most highly accelerated air current — and this again is obtained with a very narrow slot.

* This is 20% more efficient.
** Amounting to more than 30% for the entire sail system.

64

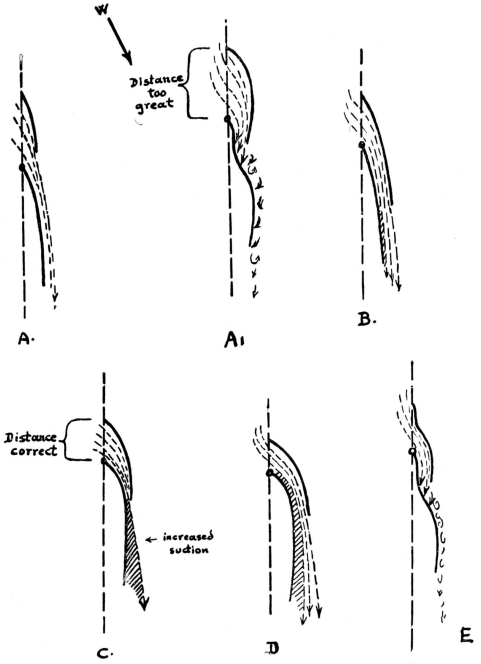

Efficient valve effect can be obtained only with batten-sails.

A. Old fashioned rig. Jib has long base. No overlap of jib. No valve effect.

A1. If distance of foot of jib to mast is long and overlapping jib used, the wind of the jib is spilt onto the mainsail. No valve effect.

B. Large overlapping jib and wide slot. Small valve effect.

C. Most effective rig. Smaller overlapping jib with narrow slot and mainsail with transverse battens. Strong valve effect.

D. In very strong winds the slot must be widened to avoid healing of boat and to increase forward drive.

E. If battens are removed both sails luff.

A highly efficient slot-effect with a very narrow valve can only be produced with a mainsail stiffened by long battens. Any other sail will be back-winded near its luff by the wind off the jib. Sails without these battens offer only two alternatives: Either the after leech of the jib must be held far away from the mainsail, thus forming a very broad slot, or the mainsail must be cut very flat. In both cases the result is a rather ineffective valve. I have become so accustomed to battens that a mainsail of a small boat without them reminds me of an umbrella without ribs.

Inasmuch as wind tunnel experiments on airplane wings and metal sails have suggested a very pronounced arch — draft, as we call it in sails — why, in practice have we preferred flat sails? The reason for this is very simple.

Before the discovery of the overlapping jib for beating to windward the normal rig used was about as shown in Diagram A. When introducing the overlapping jib universally, we took special care to avoid any interference of the two sails which manifested itself by the so-called back-wind on the mainsail (A1). To obtain a satisfactory result we used outriggers for sheets (Diagram B). As happens with any new device, there are always more people willing to bar and forbid an improvement rather than to adopt it and try to improve it. So outriggers were forbidden in all countries! However, in this instance the adverse ruling resulted in a good effect. Unable to use outriggers, we either had to give up our big jibs or trim the sheets of these jibs to the deck. But a surprise was in store for us. *The boats were faster than before!* Some other radical change in the rig must have occurred in the meantime which changed the entire air currents. This was the use of long battens. Diagram C shows approximately the most efficient rig. Note the very narrow slot which is made possible only by applying battens. We are now able to use a strongly arched sail, as Nature and aerodynamics taught us years ago.

While, without battens, this sail would be pressed in at its luff by the back-wind off the jib, we now force it to remain in this position and to create the highly efficient and much desired slot. The interesting feature is that the front part of both sails now operates with a *negative angle of incidence* to the wind, and while the luff of the jib when pointing high would tend to flutter (Diagram E), it is now drawing full through the air being pressed on it by the mainsail.

If we take the battens out of the mainsail on a beat to windward, not only half of the mainsail falls in and begins to flap, but — and this is the most interesting fact — *the jib falls in*. The rigid mainsail compresses the air between it and the jib so as to force the jib to draw — in other words, the compressed air is powerful enough to overcome the pressure on the leeward side of the jib caused by the negative angle of incidence. The bird's wing operates with the same negative angle of incidence, *i.e.*, the air current strikes the front part of the bird's wing on the upper side, as in the case of the mainsail and the jib in similar circumstances. There is no doubt that, if the bird's wing were not of rigid construction, the front part of the wing would fall in and the efficiency of the wing would be so impaired that the bird would be unable to fly. And this is the type of sail that is being used by most of us!

With a more efficient rig we are able to reduce the size of the sail as well as its cost. The greatest efficiency, however, is dependent upon several features; *viz.,*

66

1. The correct arching of the mainsail
2. "   "   cut of the jib
3. "   "   distance of the foot of the jib to the mast (Diagram C)
4. "   "   lead of the jib sheet
5. "   "   amount of overlap.

And why are we not copying nature more closely; why are we not making progress; why are we not using sails with long transverse battens? — Because of rules! Must we continue to do things the old way just because we have been doing them that way? Why are things ruled out before they have been tried?

It seemed impossible to convince yachtmen of the value of the overlapping jib for beating to windward through the publication of articles until I beat the six meter boats on the Mediterranean by using the first overlapping jib at Genoa (Italy) and until the Swedish boat *"Maybe"* beat the American six meters by using these large jibs.

May I now explain by means of a simple experiment, which anyone can try, why I am convinced that the batten sail is the sail of the future?

Take a piece of somewhat stiff paper (heavy writing paper which is to be cut down to half the size), fold it in the middle (Drawing I, page 68) and cut one side into the form of a sail (Drawing II). Now bend this side with your fingers so as to give it the arched form of a rigid batten sail. So that the sail will swing more easily, cut several very small slots, one above the other, in the fold of the paper which represents the luff of the sail (Drawing II). Now hold part A horizontally in front of your lips (Drawing III) and blow along the *upper side* of A. You will notice the astonishing fact that, although blowing towards what would be the lee side of the sail, the sail will move upwards and towards the air current, as in Drawing IV. Naturally, you can hold the paper vertically as would be the case in the sail. But holding it horizontally (as shown in Drawing III) will give you a still better proof of the force of the suction which even lifts the weight of the paper — representing the sail — and which would in this position hang down (Drawings III and IV).

If you blow on the lower side of A, which, relative to the curvature of the sail, would be the windward side, the sail will only be lifted up to the horizontal. (See Drawing VI.)

These experiments prove: 1. The correctness of the suction theory as well as the greater and more favorable force of the suction compared with the pressure. 2. The advantage of a rigid surface held in form artificially (by battens). 3. The favorable effect of the off-wind of the jib (now produced by blowing more or less strongly) which accelerates the air current in the lee of the mainsail and thereby increases the driving force of the mainsail.

I believe that this simple experiment, which any one can try in a few minutes, will prove my theories as well as complicated wind tunnel tests have done, and may put aside all doubts.

If the reader is interested enough to continue these experiments he may try the following: Enlarge the slots which were cut at the luff of the mainsail, as in Drawing VII. This experiment shows the advantage and disadvantage of having a slot between the mast and the luff of the mainsail. Then repeat the former experiment and again blow along the upper side of A, as in Drawings III and IV. You will notice that the sail (with same curve) does not lift as high as it did with the thinner slots. (See Drawing VIII.)

This experiment proves the great disadvantage of any rig having a slot between the mast and the luff of the mainsail. I found this result in my wind tunnel tests of 1924-25.

These experiments illustrate an entirely new principle of the forces acting on sails. The most important discovery is the fact that the much-feared back-wind caused by the wind off the jib striking the leeward side of the mainsail is not harmful, but advantageous, and increases the driving force of the sail if an artificially arched surface — the batten system — is applied.

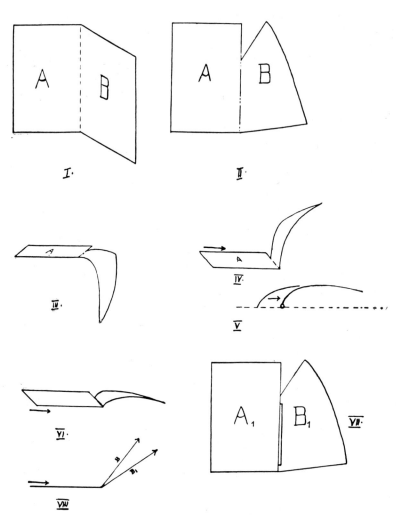

An interesting experiment with paper cut-outs illustrates the effect of the negative pressure on the leeward side of a sail

Permit me to insert here a short note published in *Yachting* May, 1932.

Testing the Rig in American Waters
By HERBERT L. STONE, Editor of "Yachting"

During the past winter several of the 20 square-meter class of racers designed by Dr. Curry were brought to this country, largely for experimental purposes, as there is no regular class here, and the first of these to be tried out was the *Barracuda,* owned by C. T. Ludington. This boat was sailed during March on Biscayne Bay, Florida, and the editor of YACHTING had the privilege of both watching and sailing her. The results were most interesting and the effectiveness of the batten sails seemed to be demonstrated.

This boat is 28 feet long over all, and has about 212 square feet of sail, measured, and about 280 actual, if the overlapping jib is measured instead of the fore triangle. In light breezes the boat was surprisingly fast. She seemed to move in the lightest zephyr. Undoubtedly, the shape of this hull, with its minimum of wetted surface, had much to do with this. In breezes of from 5 to 12 miles' strength the value of the batten mainsail and the so-called funnel effect was most apparent, and the *Barracuda* had no difficulty in passing her competitors on every point of sailing, but particularly on a reach. With the sails properly trimmed she sailed at times three feet to her competitors' two, and on reaches her advantage was even greater. In breezes of 15-mile strength, or over, she was overpowered with full sail (she has no ballast), but with a reef rolled on the boom she seemed to go just as fast, and her comparative superiority was just as marked. She proved easy to handle, once one got used to the type, but undoubtedly we were not getting the most out of her that was possible, due to our unfamiliarity with the rig. Also, the competition was not of the type to let one really get a line on the boat's potential capabilities. In the five races she sailed she met, among other boats, one Star, the best of the Suicide Class in those waters, and the Herreshoff centerboard sloop *Water Lily,* of about the same, or perhaps a trifle more sail area. These boats she beat by from one-half to three-quarters of a mile over a short 3-mile triangular course.

Experiments in the Aerodynamic Laboratory of Professor Junkers

Starting from the premise that the surface that produces no eddies develops about 60% more drive than one that promotes the formation of eddies, such as our present sails, which due alone to the disturbance caused by the mast, especially on the wind, must be regarded as most ineffective, my friend C. A. Bembé and I were engaged for several years in constructing a sail on which the wind might operate undisturbed. According to our view, this could be accomplished only by profiling the mast and sail *strictly according to the form of the bird's wing.* At the same time, aside from attempting to suppress the formation of the large eddies on both sides of the mainsail just abaft the mast, which had been confirmed by the experiments with the down, we sought to reduce the resistance of the sail to a minimum and to prevent the premature disturbance or so-called "breaking down" of the eddy-less current flowing in the lee of and parallel to the mainsail — The ideal sail should *bend* the lines of flow, *not break* them and thus promote the formation of eddies.

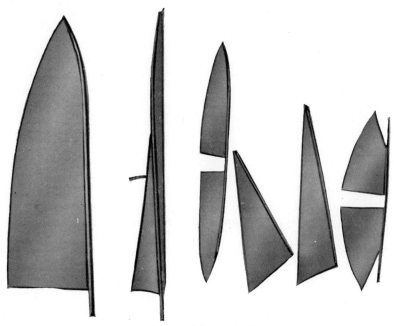

Tin Models of Sails

Professor Junkers,* who showed a keen interest in our investigations, kindly invited us to visit his laboratory at Dessau and placed the wind tunnel at our disposal for experiments. Tin model sails with masts and spars were made, which corresponded exactly in their form to our racing sails. We even went so far as to give the upper part of these tin models the sagging out so characteristic of our boat sails, especially those of the gaff rig.

Among others, the following experiments were undertaken on the *Marconi tin sail,* and exact measurements of the pressures developed recorded. The model was given eight different forms with respect to arching, profiling of mast, etc., by hammering and other means (see the given cross sections I to VIII appended to diagram of curves on page 71).

EXPERIMENT I. Here the tin model is given the form of the customary Marconi sail, being moderately arched, slightly twisted in its upper part and with a slit between the mast and luff through which the air flowing forward on the windward side of the sail can escape to leeward (cf. cross section I). The pressures developed by this model are represented in the diagram by curve I. The angles of opposition are inserted on the curve itself. The side pressure (drive) developed by the model is represented by the height or ordinate of the curve, the resistance by the distance of the curve from the vertical on the left of the diagram — by its abscissa.

* The leading authority on aeroplane construction in Europe.

70

Polar Curves of Models investigated
in Aerodynamic Laboratory of Professor Junkers at Dessau, October 1923.

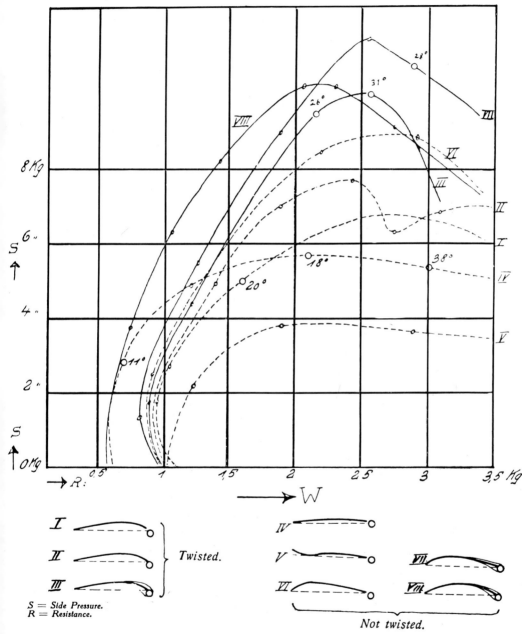

S = Side Pressure.
R = Resistance.

Twisted.

Not twisted.

EXPERIMENT II. The same tin sail is used, but the slit between the mast and the luff is sealed with plastilina (cf. cross section II). The pressures measured on this model are represented by curve II of the diagram; its path shows a *higher* development of pressure, at least of side pressure (drive), and hence a decided improvement over curve I. For the middle angles of opposition, corresponding to the wind abeam, a slight *momentary* inferiority is apparent. As we should expect, the slit between the mast and the sail appears here to have little influence on the development of pressure, whereas on all other courses a decided improvement is gained by *closing it*.

EXPERIMENT III. The corners or angles formed by the junction of the tin sail (I) with the mast, on both sides of the latter, are now filled out with plastilina, whereby smooth, uniformly profiled surfaces, similar to those of the bird's wing, are achieved (cf. cross section III). The measurements of pressure on this model, represented by curve III, confirmed, to our great satisfaction, the verification of our surmises on the efficiency of this model. A surprisingly large increase of pressure, amounting to a third more than for the ordinary sail (cf. cross section I and III) resulted from this change, the profiling or so-called "streamlining" of the mast and sail.

In the first three experiments the tin model was given the usual sagging out of the upper part of the sail or gaff to leeward; but in all the subsequent experiments it was hammered until the upper part of the sail stood at the same angle to the wind as its lower portion; that is, no outward twist was given to the upper portion of the tin models investigated in the following experiments (cf. cross sections IV to VIII).

EXPERIMENT IV. The tin sail, now without any outward twist, toward its head, was hammered relatively flat. The extremely unfavorable form of the corresponding curve IV of the diagram for the pressures indicates how small a pressure (drive) and how great a resistance this slightly arched surface — without the streamlined mast — developed. A comparison with curves I to III and the other curves IV to VIII of the diagram shows, indirectly, what an unfavorable influence the twisting or sagging out of the upper part of the sail in the first three experiments has. We may thus conclude that the flat sail used in this experiment, had it been twisted in its upper part — as is the case in practice, especially with the gaff rigged sails, would have given a still more unfavorable result than that indicated by the curve IV of the diagram.

EXPERIMENT V. The flat sail IV was hammered so that its leech hangs off a bit to leeward (see cross section V). This model was designed to represent those sails, whose leech is flat or even hangs off somewhat to leeward. As the corresponding curve V shows, the result is a considerable further loss of energy. We may, therefore, designate this form of sail as the most ineffective of all, developing hardly half the pressure (drive) of the sail, where the arching extends to the leech.* It is thus proved that it is an error to suppose that a flat leech, or one with the tendency to hang off to leeward, be advantageous, in that it facilitate the flow or escape of the wind off the sail.

EXPERIMENT VI. The tin sail was now given a decided arching, largest in its after third (see cross section VI); this cross section resembles cross section I except for the change in the position of its greatest arching and the

* Advantage of transverse battens.

72

twist or sagging out of the upper part of the latter. The corresponding curve is remarkably favorable. Its advantage over curve I seems to be due not only to the unfavorable twist of the latter, but, contrary to what one might expect, more to the greater bellying toward its leech, which is apparently most favorable for the development of pressure.

EXPERIMENT VII. The metal sail — cross section VII — retained the same form as in experiment VI, except that the *mast and sail were streamlined,* as in experiment III (cf. cross sections III and IV). Here the pressure attained a maximum, which was nearly double that developed by the ordinary form of sail, as shown by a comparison of the corresponding curve VII with that IV of the diagram (cf. also text to experiment IV).

EXPERIMENT VIII. The mast and sail of this model — cross section VIII — were given the same streamlining as that of model VII, but the greatest arching was shifted more toward the middle of the sail. The pressure developed is represented by curve VIII of the diagram.

These last two models furnished the most favorable curves. Curve VIII is of special interest; although the pressure developed by this model (VIII) is not quite as large as that of model VII, the small resistance to which it is subjected is most striking; in spite of its relatively greater arching the resistance of this model is the least of all the eight, in fact, less than that of the almost flat sail — cross section IV.

Briefly summarized, the experiments show the following:

1. The closing of the slit between the mast and sail increases the average pressure about 15%.
2. The sagging out of the sail means a loss of pressure of 20% to 30%.
3. The streamlining of the mast and sail is equivalent to an increment in pressure of 30% to 40% over that of our present sails, which corresponds to an increase in pressure of from 6 to 10 units per square meter; at the same time the resistance is reduced about one-half.

As we have just observed and as is confirmed by the curves of the above diagram, the streamlining of the mast and sail has the advantage not only of increasing the pressure but also of reducing the resistance. The former may be effected to a certain degree by giving the mast itself — its cross sections — the streamline or "drop" form, but the resistance can be reduced appreciably only by streamlining both mast and sail in such a manner, that the lining or envelope extends so far aft onto the sail, that its surface forms a continuous surface with it. On the other hand, the idea of a streamlined Marconi mast, which is *capable of turning* on its axis, adjusting itself always according to the direction of the wind, is surely justified. It has two advantages: First, the streamline form (of mast) always adjusts itself in the desired position to the wind; secondly, in the case of a bent mast the unfavorable distortion of the whole sail *before the wind* is avoided, as it will set as well on this course as on the wind. The mast must, of course, be pivoted so that it will turn.

In order not to tire the reader with further descriptions of less important experiments, I wish only to state that various other gaff rigged and Marconi models were investigated in a similar manner to those already mentioned and that the measurements recorded confirmed the general conclusions already drawn.

With regard to the measurements themselves, I may observe that the current of air generated in the wind tunnel could be given any velocity, ranging from three to thirty three meters (about 10 to 110 feet) per second, but that no appreciable difference in the relation of the forces acting due to any change in the velocity of the air current could be detected. Furthermore, it should be stated that the size of the models compared to that of our yacht sails played no noteworthy role.

Profile sails have been used with great success, especially on ice boats. One of the many possible constructions of a profile sail is shown in Figs. A, B, C. The cover must be made of veneer wood which will retain its form and hold the bows apart in their proper position. Attempts to use canvas instead of veneer wood have been unsuccessful. The wooden envelope must remain set on the mast and always ready for use. The sail is hoisted and lowered within it. If a pivoted streamlined mast is used, a profile sail is not essential.

Several months later two more experiments were performed at our request at the Aerodynamic Laboratory in Dessau. They were prompted by the following considerations:

If we compare the pressures developed by an arched sail and a flat sail (see diagrams on pp. 28 and 31), we observe that the latter develops little more than half as much pressure as the former. We must, therefore, conclude that the main boom exercises an unfavorable influence on the sail by flattening out its foot and lower seams and thus reducing the development of pressure in that area.

The bird's wing retains its arching up to the body of the bird. And the barks and fishermen's boats of the waters of Southern Europe — the Mediterranean — carry no booms, using sails with arched, i. e., loose-footed lower seams (see the photographs on page 77).

The following measurements were made:

EXPERIMENT IX. A Marconi tin sail with a relation of length to breadth of 3:1 and a straight foot corresponding to the straight boom was investigated with regard to the pressure developed. The maximum pressure was reached at an angle of opposition of 20° and amounted here to exactly 4 kilograms (about 9 pounds), as indicated by curve IX of the diagram on page 78.

EXPERIMENT X. The same model sail was given an arching of 1/13 throughout, that is, its foot or mainboom was arched or "bent" accordingly. The corresponding curve Xa of the diagram shows that the pressure developed due to this change increased from 4 to 4.5 kilograms (from about 8 pounds, 12 ounces to 10 pounds). As these measurements were

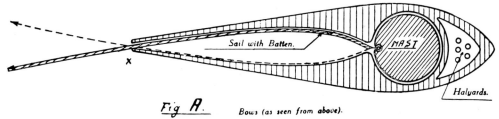

Fig. A.   Bows (as seen from above).

Sail with Batten.

MAST

Halyards.

X

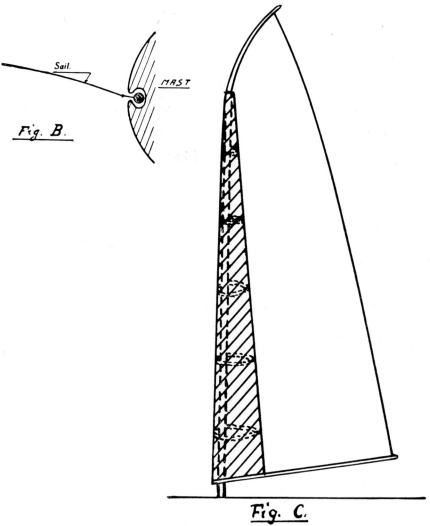

Sail.

MAST

Fig. B.

Fig. C.

The Profiled Sail.

75

Ice-boats Use Profiled and Turning Masts as Well as Transverse Battens.

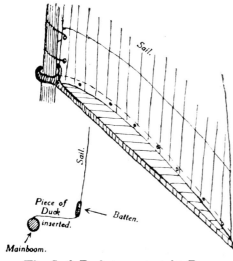

The Sail Pocket on straight Boom.

(best solution)

made with a relatively short boom — of relation of length to breadth of sail of 3:1 — we should, therefore be justified in assuming that the pressure developed by a sail of the same surface area but with a boom of twice the length, that is, by a sail of relation of length to breadth of 3:2, which corresponds to the gaff rig, would increase double that amount, from 4 to 5 kilograms (from about 8 pounds, 12 ounces to 11 pounds). This was confirmed by curve Xb of the diagram, which represents the pressure developed by this model.

From these experiments we see how important it is to extend the arching to the foot of the sail. This can be effected to a certain extent by using battens in its lower part, which should extend to its luff; but the

Barks on Lake Geneva—Switzerland.
(Observe Loose Foot of Sail — Without Boom)

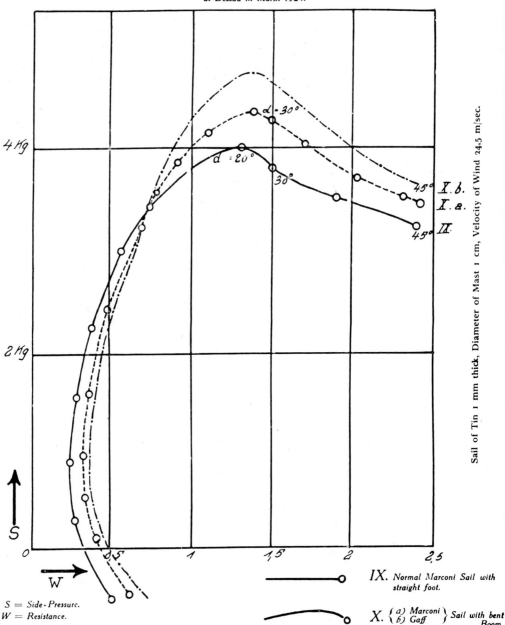

Experiments in Wind Tunnel
at Dessau in March 1924.

S = Side-Pressure.
W = Resistance.

IX. *Normal Marconi Sail with straight foot.*

X. $\left\{\begin{array}{l}a)\ Marconi\\b)\ Gaff\end{array}\right\}$ *Sail with bent Boom.*

Sail of Tin 1 mm thick, Diameter of Mast 1 cm, Velocity of Wind 24.5 m/sec.

primary problem of replacing the straight boom by a bent one, if we wish to take full advantage of this further means of increasing the development of pressure in the sail, still remained to be solved.

78

Before I had found satisfactory solutions or rather constructions for the various innovations referred to above, I set myself the task of constructing a bent boom; upon its completion I tested it thoroughly, and I am able to report the following on its construction and the results achieved:

My various tests with the bent boom showed that it improved the boat strikingly in light and moderate breezes. A boat inclined to a lee helm with a straight boom, had a tendency to luff with a bent boom, an absolute proof that more pressure is developed by the mainsail in the latter case. In a strong wind, however, the bent boom appears to be disadvantageous. This is obviously due to the fact that in the flaws the relatively large resistance of the arched surface cannot be reduced, while, by easing the sheets, the side pressure can naturally be diminished. By this change in the relation between resistance and side pressure the direction of the driving force is, however, influenced unfavorably.

The arching of the foot of the sail may be accomplished in various ways. One may use a straight boom, on which the sail is bent indirectly by inserting a piece of duck, the outer contour of which is given the desired arching, between the boom and the foot of the sail; the inner straight edge of this piece of duck is fastened to the boom and its arched edge sewed onto the foot of the sail; it thus forms a right angle with the sail proper, into the foot of which a batten is inserted under such tension that the piece of duck is stretched laterally, that is, held in a horizontal position at — right angles to the sail (cf. the drawing, on page 77).

The Bent Boom

This so-called "pocket" construction has proved the most practical of all. It has the advantage in a strong wind of permitting the removal of the batten and the lashing of the sail, by means of a leech line and grommets provided for that purpose, directly to the boom, whereby the smaller arching so desirable in heavy winds is achieved.

The bent boom used in the above tests was constructed as follows: The boom, seven meters (about 23½ ft.) long, is "built-up" of three lengths of wood limed together. It has its greatest arching in the first third, becoming straighter toward its after end. The boom terminates at the mast in a universal joint, so that it can be reversed on tacking half a turn upward, either by hand or automatically. Practice has proved it necessary to insert a stop device in the joint to prevent the boom from hanging through due to its arching or outward

The Bent Boom

bend. While the boom is making its turn of 180°, the foot of the sail slides around it on a wire leech rope that passes under about twenty little travellers on the boom. This mechanism however has proved impractical, although it insures a perfect set of the sail with a *uniform* arching from head to foot. It does not permit a reefing of the sail, but, with the boat in question, designed for heavy weather, reefing was not necessary. The accompanying photographs show the bent boom in use. Altogether I do not recommend this construction.

We now come to the last experiment, XI. For its better understanding, I will first state the considerations upon which it is based.

Let the reader recall the measurements of pressure in the chapter on "The Distribution of Pressure." We have seen that the suction on the leeward side of the sail amounts to from three to five times the positive pressure on its windward surface and that the maximum suction lies in the fore quarter of the sail. We also know from the chapter on the "Reciprocal Influence of the Sails" that the suction is generated by the *partial vacuum or region of low pressure* in the lee of the sail. Also, the experiments with the down have indicated the presence of this region of low pressure, and we were able to observe how pronounced the tendency of the air was to stream into and to fill it — according to the physical law that air flows from regions of higher toward those of lower pressure. The air, especially that of the eddies formed along the leeches of the sail, thus tends to stream into this region of low pressure from all directions. We have seen that the down held under the boom near the mast was sucked with accelerated velocity *around the boom* toward the lee (see the drawing on page 20). The reader already knows that the current of air that passes round the mast to the lee can be deflected from its path by the wind off a properly cut and trimmed jib and thus prevented to a considerable degree from flowing into and filling up the region of low pressure in the lee of the mainsail.

But we have not tried to deflect the air flowing in from below the boom (and upward) from its natural path. *Would it not be possible to intercept this current of air that flows in under the boom* onto the lee of the sail?

It was such considerations that suggested the idea of affixing a long, narrow, thin *plank horizontally* to the boom. This should prevent not only the

air on the wind- ward side of the sail from escap- ing downward, tending rather to compress it, but also the currents flowing in under the boom from streaming to lee and upward into the region of low pressure.

This "plank boom" (patented in 1924) was in- vestigated in the Junker Aerody- namic Labora- tory, and my hy- pothesis proved to be correct.*

The Travellers on Bent Boom

* This idea found and first applied by the author was many years later taken up in America and the boom called "Park Avenue boom." It was successfully applied on the cup defender "Enterprise." See pictures on pages 86 and 87.

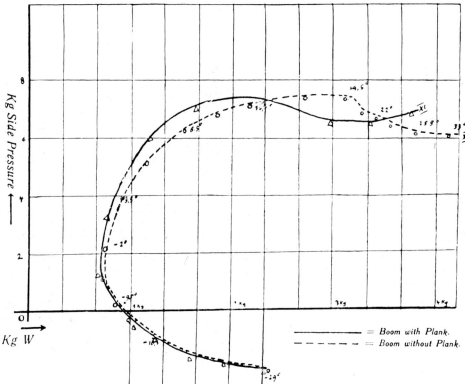

The Plank Boom
Experiments in Wind Tunnel at Dessau in February 1925.

Kg Side Pressure →

Kg W →

———————— = Boom with Plank.
— — — — — — = Boom without Plank.

EXPERIMENT XI. The tin Marconi model employed here is that with the "bent" boom, already investigated in experiment X, both with the plank affixed to it in *lee* (cf. the annexed drawing). The pressure developed by this model, measured in the wind tunnel, is represented by curve XI of the above diagram; compared with curve X it shows that for angles of opposition up to 15.5° not only a greater pressure but also a smaller resistance are attained with this model. The increase in pressure amounted to from 15 to 20 per cent.

Unfortunately, the experiment was performed with the plank on only one side of the boom, the leeward side; it may, therefore, be assumed that the increase in pressure developed by the use of a double plank, as represented in the photograph on the next page, would be appreciably greater. Also, the advantage gained, increment of pressure, by the use of a longer boom would have been greater, as the one in question was relatively short — corresponding to a sail of relation of length to breadth of 3:1 (see experiment X).

Whether the plank is affixed to a straight or to a bent boom, the improvement would, naturally, be the same.

Boom with Plank on Lee Side.

82

However a combination of the two devices, the bent boom and the plank, should give the combined effect of the two.

Nature also takes advantage of the "plank" device in the *body* of the bird, which prevents the air from streaming round the inner end of the wing onto its under surface. Flettner makes use of it on his rotor by affixing large circular plates or discs to the upper and lower ends of the rotor cylinder — of such diameter that they project considerably beyond the walls of the cylinder. At the Göttingen Laboratory the remarkable fact was revealed that the rotor develops only a little more than half the pressure without the plates.

The fastening of the plank to the straight boom ought not to present any serious difficulties; it should be effected in such a manner that it could be taken off readily. As regards its form, we should be guided by the pressure and suction curves in the neighborhood of the boom, making the plank broadest in its fore quarter, where the suction is greatest, and letting it taper from that point fore and aft. Constructed on this principle the plank assumes, strange to say, approximately the streamline form.

Boom Replaced by Plank

The boom itself might even be quite discarded and replaced by a thick (horizontal) plank, over which the foot of the sail is enabled to glide back and forth on small travellers inserted in the plank, as indicated in the photograph; these travellers run directly across the plank, from edge to edge, and thus being of different lengths allow the lower part of the sail to assume the given arching.*

* Later experiments revealed that the most successful solution was the use of batten sails with the batten pocket as shown on pages 77 and 85. The Plank-Boom is heavy and the travellers cause too much air resistance.

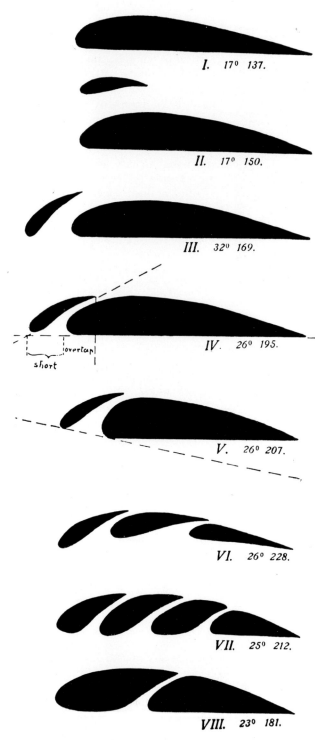

I. 17° 137.

II. 17° 150.

III. 32° 169.

IV. 26° 195.

overlap

short

V. 26° 207.

VI. 26° 228.

VII. 25° 212.

VIII. 23° 181.

Aeroplane Wings and Yacht Sails

The accompanying drawing represents eight different types of aeroplane wings, which were investigated with regard to their efficiency — lift, in the wind tunnel at Göttingen by Professor Prandtl. Although the surface area, projected on a horizontal plane, is the same for every wing, the lift developed varied according to the type of wing, as indicated by the numbers inserted directly below the wings in the drawing. The reason for this variation in lift is to be ascribed to the slit or slits in the wing, which due to the funnel effect thereby produced are known to increase the lift developed (cf. chapter on "Reciprocal Influence of the Sails," p. 49).

The by far most favorable types of wing are those numbered IV, V and VI in the drawing. The similarity in the cross-sections or profiles of wings IV and V and yacht sails is most striking: the narrow slit, the short distance of the fore edge of the air guiding auxiliary wing from that of the main wing and the overlapping of the latter by the former. We observe that the lift of wings IV and V for an angle of opposition of 26° amounts to 195 and 207 units respectively, whereas wing I, which has no air guiding auxiliary plane in

front of the main wing, develops a lift of only 137 units. The most favorable wing is that with the two slits, number VI, which develops a lift of 228 units or almost 100% more lift than wing I does. As the arching of the leeward side of a sail is the decisive factor in the drive developed by an arched surface and the arching of sails corresponds exactly to that of the upper surfaces of the wing profiles, a comparison of the yacht sail and the wing of an aeroplane is surely justified.

The author's 10 sq-m Racer with Sailpocket and Adjustable Centerboard.

10 Sq. M. Racer Design and Rig M. Curry 1927

The boat shown in the photographs on page is 6.5 meters or about 21 feet long over all and has a correspondingly small initial stability. The centerboard box is wedge form, being considerably broader at its rear end, as shown in the first photograph, so that the centerboard can be placed at an angle of about 5° to the keel of the boat on beating to windward. The board is adjusted by means of a crank with a spiral shaft, which acts on its rear edge and holds it in the desired position — at the given angle to the keel, on the wind. The broad slit formed at the bottom of the centerboard box is closed by a movable horizontal plate inserted in the keel. To the stern is attached a rectangular aluminum plate, the upper edge of which hangs on hinges parallel to and a few inches above the water line; it can be pulled down into the water from its normal horizontal position by means of a hand lever in the cockpit; in the vertical position it stands at right angles to the keel or course and acts as a brake. The boat can be stopped almost on the spot by pulling the hand lever entirely back. This brake can be used to great advantage in retarding the speed, at will and without change of course, as, for instance, at the start or upon running up to a landing or mooring. See a similar form of "brake" in pictures on page 297 where the break is attached to the stern of a 20 sq. m. Racer. It proved *most successful* in racing and most practical on small boats.

The boat has a "double mast" (cf. p. 90), which sits in two joints made fast to the deck on either side and can thus be clapped over aft onto the boat when not in use. The two spars of this mast are given a streamline form, that they may offer a minimum resistance to the wind. The mainsail — its fore leech, runs between the two spars of the mast and is hoisted by a halyard that passes over a block at the top of the mast, where its two spars

Cup Defenders

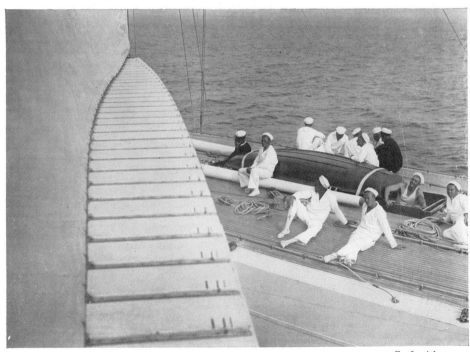

The "Park Avenue Boom" of the Cup Defender "Enterprise"

meet. The jib halyard passes through a block fastened to a cross tree joining the two spars somewhat lower down. Both halyards run within the mast, i.e. its two spars, which are sufficiently hollow for that purpose. The fore leech of the mainsail is hauled taut below by a wire rope that passes through the deck to a stretcher or pulley in the bottom of the boat; the other end of this rope is made fast to the main boom. The jib is made fast not on deck but to the main boom, which is prolonged forward to the distance required; it thus swings up to windward, when the mainsail is payed out. The advantage thereby gained is that the slit between the two sails becomes narrower and hence the desired funnel effect more pronounced. The mainsail is given the desired arching by means of long traverse battens that extend to its fore leech, and in its lower portion — next to the boom, is inserted the pocket as shown in the photographs on pages 77 and 85. The jib sheets run through outriggers affixed to the after part of the boom. This rig has proved successful only on small boats.*

E. Levick

Park Avenue Boom

Blanketing

This chapter belongs properly to the practical part of the book, Part II, but I insert it here, because it should be included among our preliminary observations, being of a purely theoretical, more general nature.

Practice has taught us that blanketing, one of the most important weapons of contest — and a race should be a real contest, not merely an agreeable cruise — is always most successful at a certain distance from one's competitor. This distance, which varies according to the strength of the wind and course sailed, is often difficult to determine.

* On larger boats the construction does not stand up.

Furthermore, the yachtsman will have noticed that, when the blanketing is most effective, the lee boat is not merely blanketed — with hardly a breath of air — but her sails and even battens are often pressed over to windward; this means that they are subjected to *pressure from the opposite direction.*

To confirm the correctness of these observations and explain their cause, we shall make use of an apparatus employed by Eiffel to determine the extent to which blanketing is effective and the actual amounts of positive and negative pressure on both the blanketed and the blanketing sails at various distances apart. A surface, which may be given the form of a sail, is fastened at its center of gravity to the end of a horizontal rod. A similar surface is placed, also at its (same) center of gravity, on this rod in such a manner that it is capable of being moved — with least possible friction — along it (see the first drawing on next page). When the wind is directed against the fixed surface in the direction of the movable one, the latter will recede from or, apparently against the wind, approach the former, or it will remain stationary at a distance of about twice the height of the blanketing surface from the latter. In a strong wind this critical distance is somewhat greater, in a light wind somewhat smaller.

Let us now apply the various results found by Eiffel to our sails, with due consideration for the few slight differences or corrections necessary. We may state at once that the distances in question hold for a wind of 10 m/sec. velocity and must, therefore, be somewhat shortened for lighter winds. The pressures in kilograms in their direction of action, to which both the blanketed and the blanketing sails are subjected, are inserted in the drawings on the next page for the two courses in question — on the beam and before the wind.

I. When the distance between the two sails is *less* than twice the mast length,* the blanketed sail is under the action of air currents of opposite direction to that of the wind, that is, it is subjected to a pressure opposite to that developed by the blanketing sail (see drawings B, C and D); this (negative) pressure is greatest at a distance of *one* mast length (see drawing D) ; it is, therefore, at this distance that the blanketing is most effective. Drawing A shows the extent of action of the blanketing — *four mast lengths.*

II. It is a highly interesting and hitherto entirely unknown fact that not only the blanketed boat is handicapped, but also the blanketing one gains an absolute advantage, that is, an increase in pressure of about 15% on her own sails by the act of blanketing. To be more exact, the positive pressure remains the same, but the suction and hence the total pressure or drive is intensified in consequence of the change in the formation and development of the eddies (cf. the pressure in drawing A with those developed by the blanketing boat in drawings B to G).

III. Drawing G is most significant. It shows that the wind cone, that is, the region of the blanketing, is not, as one might infer from drawing A, newly formed by every blanketed sail, but that it extends only to the blanketing zone of the first boat. It thus follows that a boat (I) may be able to sail *unimpeded through the lee of another boat (II), provided the latter is in her turn blanketed by a third (III).*

* The distances are reckoned for gaff sails in mast lengths, because this is the most convenient unit of measure. For Marconi sails the distances must be taken correspondingly shorter, that is, the unit is somewhat smaller than the mast length.

Blanketing.

Wind abeam and before the Wind — Velocity of Wind 10 m/sec.

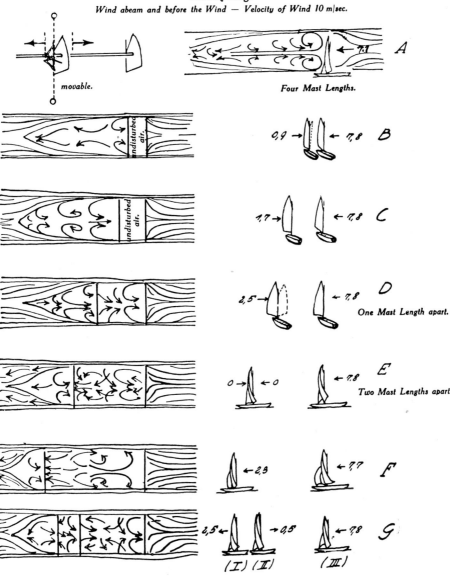

A — Four Mast Lengths.

movable.

B

C

D — One Mast Length apart.

E — Two Mast Lengths apart.

F

G

(I) (II)   (III)

Now we know why we often succeed in breaking through in the lee of another boat, and we can judge in the future, when this should succeed and when not. In a flawy wind the matter is naturally more complicated.

On the wind, blanketing is governed by entirely different laws — even for eased sheets the above statements must be somewhat modified. Here, on account of the more pointed form of the wind cone, the blanketing is most effective at about *half* a mast length.

10 sq-meter Racer with Double Mast

The Double Funnel Effect on Sails

On comparing the efficiency of aeroplane wings of different forms, we find that an aeroplane with a small plane in front of the main plane is more effective than the standard plane. (See page 84.) The wind tunnel tests referred to, confirm, that if a plane of one and the same area is divided into *three smaller ones* (compare cross-section of aeroplane wing VI on page 84), a still greater efficiency is obtained. As we see from these tests, the pressure developed by plane VI amounts to 228 units, whereas that obtained from a plane with only one funnel gives 195 units (see page 84).

The Lower Jib Being Backwinded Demonstrates That the Double Funnel Effect Is Not Achieved in This Rig

These experiments made with aeroplane wings suggest the question:

"Would it be advantageous to divide up our sail area for three rather than two sails?"

On comparing a three sail rig with a three plane aeroplane system we must not overlook a fundamental difference between the two; the surfaces of the aeroplane are arranged on an arch, whereby a significant disturbance can be avoided, whereas this is not the case with the ordinary three sail rig.

Manifold Subdivision of Sail Area

Which sails should overlap? Tests made with three jibs have proved that it is difficult to let several sails overlap to advantage. *Either the middle sail does not draw or, if the foremost jib is let out far enough not to disturb the former, the boat cannot point high enough on the wind,* because the essential graduation of the angles of opposition to the wind of the three sails necessitates too large an angle of opposition for the rearmost sail.

In the following we shall explain how it is possible to achieve a correct overlapping of two or more sails, i. e. to achieve the smallest possible angle of opposition to the wind for the rear sail and at the same time the largest possible overlaps without having the sails disturb one another.

On most American yachts (including those built by Abeking & Rasmussen) the fore-triangle is divided into two areas on the correct assumption that a divided surface produces more driving power than an undivided one (valve-effect, etc.). The two sails, however, overlap hardly at all. Upon the introduction of large overlapping jibs on German yachts and the success of the Scandinavian yachts with their large overlapping jib in the international races of the 6-m class, the American sails were changed. On the 10-m yachts the experiment was made of cutting *both* jibs with large overlaps, but the practical success of this innovation has *not* been proved.

During the last two years I have made a careful study of the subdivision of sails and sail areas. A series of experiments has led to the following conclusions:

On undertaking to divide the fore-triangle into two or three areas, we must discriminate between:

1. the arrangement of the sails and 2. the shape of the sails.

A *double* or manifold overlapping can be achieved to a certain degree *without mutual disturbance* and with a small maximum angle of opposition, provided due attention be paid to these two conditions.

With regard to the arrangement of the jibs, we have three possibilities:

1. The sails are fastened to the deck at different distances from the mast and to the mast at one and the same height above deck (cf. sketch D).

2. The sails are fastened to the deck at one and the same distance from mast and to the mast at different heights from the deck (cf. sketches A, C, E, F, G).

3. The sails are fastened to the deck as also to the mast at different distances from the mast and heights from deck respectively, their luffs thus running more or less parallel to one another (cf. sketch B).

In order to form a conception of the intrinsic difference between arrange-

E. Levick

Too Large Jibs Are Not Favorable, Espe-
cially with Wind Abeam When the Jib
Is Blanketed by the Mainsail

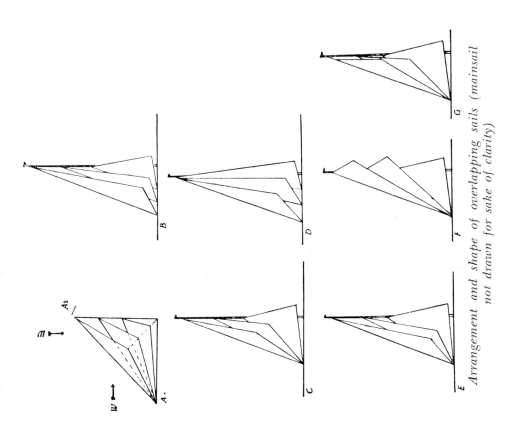

Arrangement and shape of overlapping sails (mainsail
not drawn for sake of clarity)

93

ments 1 and 2, the reader should first regard sketch A in an upright position (first possibility) and then turn it through an angle of 90° in the direction of the movement of the hands of a watch (sketch A_2), which represents the second arrangement or possibility.

An advantage of position A_1 over A_2 lies in the fact that the currents of air flowing off all three sails are not impeded in any way, whereas in position A_2 (also D) the air is caught as in a pocket at the common point of intersection of the three sails. It is a well-known phenomenon that the wind flows upward on a properly cut jib. In as much as the three jibs of A_2 or D meet above on the mast, it is to be expected that the air congested in that region will hamper the flow of the currents and direct them horizontally, to the detriment of their driving power. However, there is a disadvantage peculiar to position A_1: the luffs of the sails are more slanting (to the direction of the wind) than in A_2.

Sketch B shows a compromise between the first two arrangements, which is relatively advantageous, though the exploitation of the fore-triangle is incomplete.

Beside the arrangement of the jibs, their *shape* is also of immediate importance. "Why is the foot of the foremost jib (flying jib) usually steeper than that of the middle one, and the latter in turn steeper than that of the rear jib?" this question is often asked. Beside other advantages, there seem to be aerodynamical reasons for this peculiar cut of the foot of the jibs, which has proved successful in practice, though it may be difficult to explain it satisfactorily.

On the assumption that it be more advantageous to fasten all three sails to one and the same point on the deck — thus permitting a greater overlapping — let us investigate the rigs C, E, F and G of this type or arrangement.

The feet of the jibs approach the horizontal in E, ascend more aft in C, are still steeper in G and steepest in F. The rig seems to become more advantageous, the steeper the foot is cut. If it were not for the difficulty of leading the sheets to such heights above deck and for the necessity of taking the center of gravity of the sails into consideration, rig F would be the most favorable. On the above supposition that a common fastening point on deck for all three jibs be the more advantageous, rigs C and G would seem the most favorable and practical ones.

To return to rig F, which in my opinion has perhaps the most favorably shaped jibs, disregarding however the impossibility of tending same, attention must be called to the important fact that the mainsail is overlapped by the jibs in its total height. From the aerodynamical point of view, this is most desirable, especially for light-weather rigs, as also on account of the greater velocity of the wind at increased height.

A rather unusual suggestion, but one not to be rejected, would be to set the two upper jibs upside down in a heavy wind. By this means the center of gravity could be lowered. The considerations on which these rigs are based are the following:

1. It is essential that the air flow off the sails unhampered, without being congested, which is the case (congestion), when the jibs are fastened to the mast at one and the same point or close together.

94

2. The closer together the jibs are fastened to the deck, the more they may overlap and the more canvas can be carried without detriment.

3. The steeper the feet of the jibs, the more they can overlap without spilling back wind on the sail overlapped. As every jib develops maximum pressure and suction in its lower part (wind tunnel tests), a low overlap disturbs and a high one increases the suction; it is, therefore, better to have the jibs overlap as high as possible.

4. The greatest arch of the jib lies in the neighborhood of the clew where the air current is directed most inward. As this is the part of the sail that tends to produce back wind, it should, if possible, overlap so far that its leech extends aft beyond that of the jib directly behind it.

Dividing a System of Sails Into Various Systems

Should we not be able to achieve the desired overlap by the above method, there still remains an alternative, which should surely lead to success provided we keep in mind the conditions already mentioned.

This alternative — to attain manifold overlapping of the sails without mutual disturbance —, is especially advisable for yachts with several jibs. Let us suppose that a yacht with several sails is rigged so that every sail overlaps the one behind it. If no sail is to produce back wind on the one overlapped, i. e. to disturb it, the chord of its arch must oppose the wind at an angle that is at least 10° smaller than that of the sail behind it. In the case of 6 sails this would mean an angle of opposition of 5 × 10° or 50° for the rearmost sail. If the wind falls on the first sail at an angle of say 5°, the last sail would have to be set at an angle of 55°. In other words, the boat could not point high on the wind (cf. sketch I).

Knowing by experience that in the case of two sails *one* may overlap, we can divide a rig of six sails into three double rigs, having the first, third and fifth sails overlap and the second, fourth and sixth sails not overlap. A sail which does not overlap has no effect on the angle of opposition to the wind of the sail behind it, so the latter may be set at any desired angle. By this means we can let half the sails overlap and yet retain the same angle of opposition, as if the yacht had only two sails. In this case, even with six sails, the maximum angle is only 25° (cf. sketch II). In spite of having a large number of photographs at my disposal, I could find

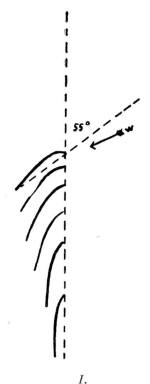

I.

An angle of 55° is essential that all 6 sails may draw. (Boat can not point high!)

95

II.
An angle of only 25°
is essential, if every
other *sail overlaps.*
(System I: boat points
high.)

very few yachts rigged according to this system. For this reason it is all the more surprising that an English yacht adopted this system of rig *more than forty years ago* (cf. photograph, p. 97). It is astonishing that in those days a rigging was conceived which can hardly be surpassed today. Note the large overlap of the foremost jib, which is possible only, when the two jibs are fastened to one and the same point on deck or bowsprit. The steep foot of the flying jib with its high clew also coincides with my theories. Furthermore, the third jib has an overlap hardly surpassed by our most modern racers. It is interesting that this yacht was considered by far the fastest boat of her class.

According to this, system I, the dividing resp. overlapping for 3, 4, 5 and 6 sails, one behind the other, would be that indicated in the diagram on page 98, first column.

The question remains to be answered, if one should have the first sail (from fore to aft) overlap, or if the first sail should be small — not overlapping, and the second large — with overlap. My personal opinion is that it is more advantageous to have the last, i. e. the mainsail, overlapped by the jib next to it. To achieve this in the case of two sails (mainsail always included) the jib would have to be large; in the case of three sails the first jib would be small, of four sails large, of five sails small, of six sails large, etc.

The reason for this division lies in the fact that an overlapped mainsail has shown to be an improvement and that the jib nearest to the mainsail has the shortest luff. This short luff has the advantage that it is stiffer. Furthermore, it lowers the center of gravity.

System II: Should one care to be more cautious, one may make two triple instead of three double subdivisions and let one overlapping sail be followed by two that do not overlap (see diagram on page 98).

In my opinion System I is the more favorable one and has proved successful in practice.

I may observe that many fast yachts have adopted this triple division more for practical than theoretical reasons ("Advance").

System III: Sailing with the wind abeam allows a change in the shape of the sails, in as much as we may let all the sails overlap or at least two of every three, in which latter case every third sail does not overlap.

Old English Yacht (System I)

	I. System	II. System	III. System

Wind abeam.

with 3 sails.

with 4 sails.

with 5 sails.

with 6 sails.

System of overlapping with 3, 4, 5 and 6 sails, one behind the other.

Quadrilateral Jib

M. Rosenfeld

*"Ranger," America's Cup
Class Off Newport*

Cinematographic Investigations of the
Effect of Wind on Spinnakers
With Holes

"Is it advisable to provide a sail with one or more holes at certain places?" This question arose many years ago but has not yet been answered.

In England, Germany and, especially, America, spinnakers with a hole in the center, or a row of holes down the center, have been used off and on. The opinions regarding the value of such holes have varied with the success of the respective yacht. But, as we know, success is not dependent on one, but on many factors, and cannot be set up as a standard for the value of a novelty.

However, these experiments were not without reason. It was believed that the pocketing of the air current, caused by the wind hitting the sail at right angles, could be prevented by a hole which permitted the wind to escape.

For two reasons I have always doubted the advantage of such discharge holes. In the first place, I was of the opinion that the wind would not pass through the smaller holes at all, because the air cushion in front of the sail would ward off the wind current, even diverting it sideways at a relatively great distance in front of the sail. As may be seen in the sketch on page 106, the air cushion divides the wind current in such a manner as to divert its course towards both sides of the sail at some distance from the sail, this distance depending on the area of the sail.

In the second place, although the air passing through larger holes would increase the pressure by continuing the current on the windward side, I feared that the suction effect of the sail would be greatly impaired by the filling up of the vacuum. For these two reasons, any advantage seemed improbable to me, on the whole, even though the accelerated wind current might avert the rebound of the main lateral eddies.

As this problem was only to be solved by examinations of the current with the help of smoke, and simultaneous measurements in the wind channel, I decided to experiment along these lines.

I used a spinnaker with a hole in the center. For the first experiment the hole was a little larger than a fist. At a velocity of 3 to 5 yards per second, the air current was made visible by smoke and photographed from the front, the rear and the side. The photographs on next pages have been cut out from my film *Wind and Water* (a film on yacht racing). Photographs 1, 2 and 3 of the smoke experiment clearly show that not only does the wind not go through the hole but that it does not even reach the proximity of the opening. The presence and effect of the aforementioned air cushion on the windward side of the sail are clearly shown in 1 and 2. The air current visibly resists approaching the sail and evades it in every direction (in this case downwards and sidewards). Photograph 3 shows the lee side of the same sail. Here also, it is apparent that the smoke does not touch the hole. The laterally diverted current and the eddies formed at the edges are clearly depicted. A comparison with the sketch proves the correctness of the currents on the spinnaker, as assumed in 1923.

Photograph 4 shows a sail from the side with a hole twice as large. Here the impeding effect of the air cushion is particularly evident. The wind is thrown directly backward, *i.e.,* it rebounds from the cushion and only then flows toward the lateral sail edge. These currents also agree with those of the sketch. The arrows on the windward side of the sail in the sketch show the smoke rebounding in the opposite direction of the wind. As in Photograph 3, the curved side eddies are beautifully clear. Naturally, the moving picture shows the flow of the current much better.

Photograph 5 demonstrates the surprising fact that the smoke does not even flow through a hole 7 inches in diameter. Here, too, we find the same obstructive effect of the air cushion, forcing the air sideways without touching the hole. Even with a hole of 10 inches, the smoke flows sideways.

On enlarging the hole to 11¼ inches, we see for the first time, in Photograph 6, a change in the flow. The effect of the air cushion is decreased, and part of the smoke passes through the hole. But even now, most of it flows past the edges. It was interesting to note that the smoke passed through the hole, especially when the wind struck the sail from the side.

The next experiment, made with a hole 12½ inches in diameter, brought about an entire change in the flow. The smoke now flowed through the opening. The evasion towards the edges ceased abruptly. Photographs 7, 8, 9 and 10 show the course of the current through a hole of this size, 7, 8 and 9 being taken from the windward side, 10 from the lee.

This sudden appearance of the funnel effect seems to depend on the relation of the size of the hole to the breadth of the sail. It may be assumed that in a small sail a small hole will suffice, whereas a broader sail needs a larger hole to produce this effect.

It is natural (and, furthermore, proved by the experiments) that the air current passing through the hole is accelerated. I reasoned that it might be advantageous to catch and use this current again. By fastening a sail to the spinnaker behind the hole, I constructed a sort of "funnel spinnaker." As the resistance of an area increases with the square of the velocity of the flow, a triple accelerated current passing through a hole should produce a nine-fold pressure on an area lying in back of it. In other words, a sail area of 1 square yard should have the effect of an area of 9 square yards.

As it seemed impossible to get exact results regarding the development of pressure *in natura,* I sent a spinnaker, reduced in size, with its auxiliary

Photo 1.

The small hole placed in the center of the spinnaker is insufficient to discharge the air cushion, and the air current passes around the edge of sail, as indicated by the smoke

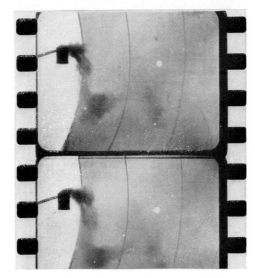

Photo 2.

The smoke, as soon as it reaches the air cushion, is deflected around the cushion, indicating that there is no air flow through the hole

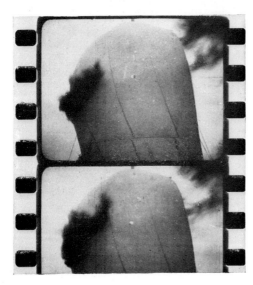

Photo 3.

All of the smoke flows around the sail

Photo 4.

The *impeding effect of the air cushion is distinctly indicated by the smoke being thrown back from the air cushion. After rebounding, it flows around the sail, following the usual course of the air flow as shown in the sketch*

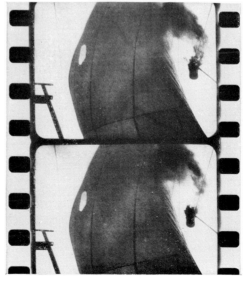

Photo 5.

Smoke will not flow through a seven-inch hole

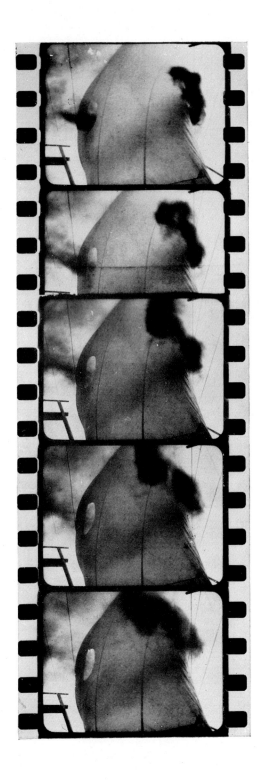

Photo 6.

Some smoke passes through the 11¼-inch hole

Photo 7.

Flow with a 12½-inch hole

Photo 8.

Smoke flows through hole

Photo 9.

Abrupt change with 12-inch hole

Photo 10.

All of the smoke flowed through the 12-inch hole

sail, to the experimental laboratories of Professor Junkers, who was kind enough to measure its pressure with various sized holes, with and without the auxiliary sail. The following results prove that a sail with holes is less effective than one without. The development of power diminishes as the hole increases in size.

The assumed increase of power by making use of the funnel with an extra sail area was also confirmed. A hole 4 inches in diameter (in the miniature sail) produced a pressure increased to $6\frac{1}{4}$ per cent above that of a normal sail wihout holes, even in the first experiment.

The two most important factors for obtaining greatest pressure seem to be to get:

1. The most advantageous relation in size of the hole to the auxiliary sail.

2. The most advantageous distance of the auxiliary sail from the hole.

Later on, measurements showed that the best effect is obtained when the two model sails were $2\frac{1}{2}$ to 3 inches apart.

In this early experimental stage it is naturally impossible to judge of the practical value of this funnel spinnaker. Therefore let us consider these investigations as entirely experimental.

RESULTS OF THE MEASUREMENTS MADE IN THE WIND TUNNEL OF PROFESSOR JUNKERS ON A SPINNAKER (JANUARY 1931)

Height of measured sail: 600 mm. length of sides
Diameter of sail at the height of the hole: 260 mm.

Spinnaker without funnel

Sail without hole. . . . . .10270 g. pressure
Sail with hole 20 mm. in diameter. . . . . .10050 g. pressure
Sail with hole 55 mm. in diameter. . . . . 9640 g. pressure

Funnel spinnaker

With auxiliary sail with hole 55 mm. in diameter. . . . . 9900 g. pressure
With auxiliary sail with hole 120 mm. in diameter. . . . .10220 g. pressure
With auxiliary sail with hole 160 mm. in diameter. . . . .10870 g. pressure

The diameter of the auxiliary sail was 160 mm.; the distance between the sails, 90 mm. However, the effect of the funnel spinnaker was more favorable at a distance of 100 to 120 mm. from the main area.

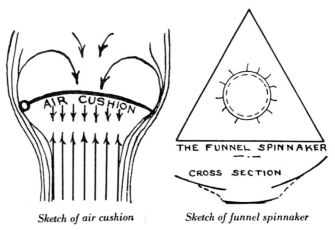

Sketch of air cushion   *Sketch of funnel spinnaker*

Resistance of Air and Water

When we speak of resistance, we understand the sum of two retarding forces, which we call *form (displacement) resistance* and *surface friction*.

Form resistance is called forth by the form or rather volume of the object and determined by the resistance it must overcome in displacing the permeated medium. Surface friction is the resistance encountered by the surface of the object in releasing itself from the particles of the medium, which tend to adhere to it. The surface friction of small bodies can be so great that, in spite of their weight, they do not fall through the medium, but remain suspended in it. This accounts, for example, for the small particles of dust, which one sees hovering in the air, when made visible by the rays of the sun.

As is well known, the condition of the outer surface of a boat's hull is of great importance in a race. The smoother we can get it, the less will be its surface friction. The scaly skin of a fish is as "slippery as an eel," in fact, so slippery that it is almost impossible to hold the live fish with one's hands. We should, therefore, follow Nature's example in treating the surfaces of our boats. One might ask, "How does the fish acquire this slippery surface or rather slimy coating; is it due to a chemical process?" Such an assumption would, however, be erroneous. Not the fish, but the water is the generator of this coating on the body of the fish. However, this does not mean that such a deposit will act to advantage on all surfaces. How does the yachtsman prepare the skin of his boat? One greases it below the water line; another soaps it shortly before the race; and a third rubs and polishes it with a preparation of graphite (black lead or stove polish). All these procedures require much time and trouble, and their value may be doubted. Putting fat or oil on the hull — below the water line — has the disadvantage that all the dirt, even the smallest particles, clings to it, forming in a short time a rough emulsic smear. Soaping is folly, because in a few minutes the soap is all washed off. With rowing shells, which are put in the water a few minutes before the start, it is, naturally, somewhat different. The third method is to give the hull below the water line a coat of graphite, a mixture of graphite and linseed oil, which is applied with a cloth, rubbed into the surface and then polished. This last method of treating the hull is without doubt the most advantageous of the above and has proved such — by experience; but it is not every yachtsman's taste to smear a beautiful white coat of paint with black lead or stove polish. Especially on this account, I wish to recommend another extremely simple method, which, however, can be applied only in fresh water.

We imitate the fish and allow the water to produce a slime over the boat's hull. To prepare for a race, haul the boat out, rub down her hull with sand paper and then give it, also the keel, centerboard (fin) and rudder, a thin coat of paint. Black varnish is especially suited to the quick formation of slime. About the third day after the boat has been launched the slimy coat has formed and the surface is as smooth as glass. If we wish to be especially painstaking, we can treat the hull above the water line with oil. Whereas on varnish, with every heeling of the boat, drops adhere to the surface, giving it the appearance of a grater, water does not remain on an oiled surface but flows off it with practically no friction.

Now let us return to our general observations. The *relation* of the form resistance to the surface friction is of great importance for the attainment of the least total resistance. This relation is not the same for air and water. In air, the surface friction has a *relatively* larger value compared with the form resistance than in water.

If the most favorable relation, that corresponding to the least total resistance, occurs, when the surface friction equals the form resistance, we should find the forms of the animals that fly in the air different from the forms of those that swim in the water. And we do. Swiftly swimming fish have slenderer bodies than fast flying birds, and this is to be attributed to the relatively greater surface friction of the air compared to its form

Wild Geese in Flight
Not in Wake of one another but in Arrow Head Formation

resistance. For example, if we should give the body of a bird an unproportionately great length compared to its thickness, then the surface friction would exceed the form resistance to such a degree that the total resistance would be greatly increased. With a relation of length to breadth of four to one the surface friction of the air begins to become a prominent factor.

The following phenomenon, confirmed by experiment, is of special interest here. Upon moving bodies first through undisturbed air and then at the same speed through air that is full of eddies, it was found that the resistance in the latter case was 60% greater than in the former. In the water as well as in the air, this fact plays a role that can not be underestimated. I need only refer to the extremely unpleasant experience one undergoes, when one falls into the wake of a yacht or into the region of her disturbed wind. Observe also the flight of geese; they never fly directly behind one another, but always either in arrow head formation or so grouped as not to fall into the air disturbed by those flying ahead. In other words, the yachtsman should observe the rule: *Never sail in the wake of another boat!*

We now come to the principle of the "drop form." The expression "drop form" is misleading, because a drop of falling water does not have the so-called "drop form" originally attributed to it; on the contrary, in consequence of its surface tension, it is almost round — this is confirmed indirectly by the circular arch of the rainbow. In order to be strictly correct we should, therefore, speak of a "streamline form." The form resistance, to which the forward blunt end of the ideal so-called "streamline" body is subjected, is counteracted in part by the forces or pressures exerted by the surrounding medium on its after portions; it is the forward components of these laterally directed forces that tend to drive the body ahead and thus to counteract to a great degree the form resistance of its fore portion; and there remains only the surface friction as a retarding factor. Thus we have in the streamline form the most favorable form for cutting through wind or water with the least possible form resistance or expenditure of energy.

The mode of action of the "streamline form" has been determined experimentally. The positive and negative pressures acting on the surface of the streamline body are measured by means of a specially designed apparatus, the so-called "pitot tube," which is supplied with a registering gauge, that is applied to the different points or sections of the surface (see first drawing on next page). In the regions of positive pressure the air particles are thrown against the surface and thus exert pressure, in those of negative pressure they are detached or drawn from it and thus create suction. These pressures, which are indicated in the drawing by arrows, alternate in their direction of action, as we pass along the surface, in such a manner that their resultant action creates, theoretically, a state of approximate equilibrium. This action of the air on the surface of a pliable, non-rigid body may be beautifully observed on the envelope of an air ship, which shows sections that are pressed inward or outward according to the direction of the pressure.

Cakes or sheets of ice held fast in a flowing stream are worn into streamline forms by the water, continuously and violently gnawing at their sides, until they finally assume shapes of least resistance or hindrance to the flow of the stream. To verify this, sheets of ice were towed through the

The Streamline Body.

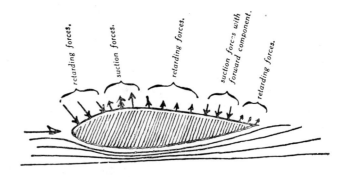

Disc.

The Resistances called forth by above streamline Body and Disc on left are the same.

Resistances called forth by Bodies of same Cross section but different Profile.

water, but, in consequence of the water in the wake of the boat being disturbed, no accurate results were obtainable from these experiments.

We have already observed that the length of the streamline form is dependent on its velocity of propagation or that of the streaming medium in which it is held, as the case may be, and that the greater the velocity, the longer and narrower the form finally developed.

I was fortunate enough to be able to avail myself of the opportunity of photographing a sheet of ice held fast in the bed of a stream; the speed of the current was about double that of a good walker. As it was a rare opportunity of observing Nature in the process of forming pure lines of flow on an object subjected to the action of that element, I am reproducing two of these photographs on the next page; the one was taken from the side the other from behind — down stream.

Many will recall the so-called "tears" formed by pouring melted lead into water. They present naught else than the forms of least resistance assumed by lead, as it falls through the water and, being cooled by the surrounding medium, solidifies.

To what extent the resistance of the air on various forms or bodies of the same cross section may be reduced by profiling the cross section in the direction of flow is indicated in the above drawing. We see that, by giving it the most favorable profile we may attain a reduction of about 92% in the resistance.

110

Sheet of Ice Subjected to Action of Flowing Water

Same Sheet of Ice as Seen From Behind — Down Stream

Eddy Formation on Ordinary Closed Car
(Eddy Formation, Visible from Dust, Causes Suction Behind Car That Retards
Speed More Than Frontal Resistance)

Most interesting is the effect produced by streamlining automobile bodies. Compare the two accompanying sketches. In the latter the air flows off the body and top of the car smoothly and without any formation of eddies; in the former the dust stirred up by the passage of the car, as also the leaves or bits of paper sucked along after it, show how intense the action of the suction of these eddies is. It has, in fact, been determined experimentally by Jarry, who found the following remarkable results for the resistance to be overcome by the ordinary closed and by the streamlined car:

Speed (miles per hour)	38	44	50
The ordinary closed car	7.0	11.0	16.5 horse power
The streamline body	2.4	3.8	5.7 " "

We thus see that approximately three times as much horsepower is necessary to run at a given speed with the ordinary closed car as with the same car with the streamline body and top. In other words, if we built our automobiles with streamlined bodies, we could attain the same results

Streamlined Car
(Air Flows Off Smoothly Without Harmful Eddy Formation)

Graphic Representation of Air Resistance with and without Envelope at Speeds of 10 and 30 Kilometers an Hour.

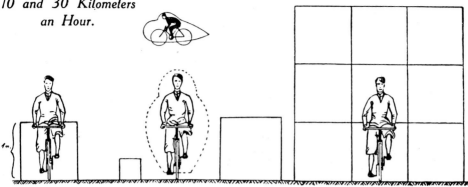

At 10 km. Speed without Envelope Resistance represented by Surface of 1 sq. m.

With Envelope Resistance represented by Surface of
¹/₅ sq. m. at 10 km Speed.
⁹/₅ sq. m. at 30 km Speed.

At 30 km. Speed without Envelope Resistance represented by Surface of 9 sq. m.

or speed with a much less powerful motor, that is, with a much smaller consumption of gasolene. Similar experiments may be made with the bicycle. If we recall how hard it is to drive a bicycle against the wind, we shall not be likely to underrate the great resistance to be overcome. The above sketches illustrate graphically the resistance to the air that must be overcome at two different speeds, 10 and 30 kilometers an hour, by the cyclist with and without the streamline envelope.

It is an error to suppose that the resistance of the air plays a considerable role only at *high* speeds. It is true that the resistance increases as the square of the velocity, but it becomes a most important factor at a speed of only six or eight miles an hour. This has also been confirmed in a most surprising manner by experiments with the "Landskiff," a machine for "rowing on land," which was invented by the author (cf. the two photographs on next page). This machine, which is propelled alone by the arms and legs, with the body on a sliding seat, attains a maximum speed of 30 miles an hour. In comparative trials of two "Landskiffs" — the one enveloped in a streamline cover, the other uncovered, and both propelled against a moderate wind with the same power — the former attained a maximum speed of 30 miles an hour and the latter one of only 18. A great expenditure of energy was required to row the uncovered machine against a strong wind at moderate speed, while the same machine could be propelled at a fair speed with little effort, when no wind was blowing. On the other hand, it was a pleasure to row against the wind in the machine with the streamline envelope, there being scarcely any appreciable difference in effort, whether running against the wind or with it.

For these machines, propelled alone by the muscles of the human body, which is capable of developing about half a horse power, the different resistances can be determined with remarkable accuracy. The least unnecessary expenditure of energy is felt at once and most decidedly by the working body — in spite of the comparatively light weight of the machine.

Curry, Aerodynamics of Sails and Racing Tactics.

All the above phenomena are of importance to the yachtsman, but he seldom pays sufficient attention to them. For example, a centerboard cut out of sheet iron, no matter how thin it may be or how sharp its fore edge, is by no means as favorable as a centerboard of greater thickness with a blunt fore edge that tapers aft to a point or rather line — not even to mention the streamline centerboard. This is due to the greater resistance of the former to the water. This subject will be treated more in detail in the following section on "New Forms for Centerboard and Rudder."

With regard to the mast, should the streamlining of the mast and sail in the manner described in the section on "The Construction of a Profiled Sail" prove to be too impractical, the mast itself should at all events be given

The Curry "Landskiff" — Double Scull (Uncovered. Driven by Curry and Bembe)

the streamline form as proposed. It is likewise most important that the *fin* (keel) should have the streamline form — as also the spreaders. The turn buckles of the stays, that drag in the water when the boat heels, should be covered with a streamline envelope, not only to reduce their greater resistance in the water but also to prevent unnecessary spray. And the halyards should run down the mast not side by side, but one behind the other. Their resistance, which one may readily detect even in a moderate breeze by their familiar humming or whistling, is greatly underestimated. We should realize that in a storm small boats may

The Curry "Landskiff" — Single Scull (Streamlined)
in Race on Avus Racing Track, Berlin

be overturned by the resistance of the mast and rigging alone. One should also consider the possibility of a hollow mast, provided such be permitted by the racing regulations, without stays and with the halyards running within it. As the hollow planes of the aeroplane withstand the enormous pressure to which they are subjected without bending, it ought to be possible to build a hollow mast with a system of inner trusses — of duralumin — that would require no stays.

Finally, the water line of the boat ought to conform to the streamline form. And, should this be impossible, as in the case of the *modern* Sonder boat on account of her extreme form, due to the rule of measurement, the skipper — and this is one of the secrets peculiar to this type of boat — should trim his boat to a streamline form under water. In the case of most boats this can be achieved by heeling the boat of shifting the ballast — the live ballast — forward. We can thus understand why the Sonder boat is always heeled artificially in light air or thrown on her nose. The former manipulation was necessary with the German 22 sq. m. centerboard racers of previous years, but it is not essential to heel the present boats of this class, as they have the correct tapering streamline form aft, when sailed erect.

It is easy to imagine that also the *sail* may give rise to a certain resistance or *surface friction* on account of its comparatively rough surface. It is of interest to know just how great this retarding action is and whether it is worth taking into account. To this end ordinary duck has been investigated, and it was found that 100 square meters of duck hung lengthwise and allowed to flap in the wind produced a surface friction or resistance equal approximately to the pressure or resistance on more than one square meter of the same material held at right angles to it. For a sail of 25 square yards, corresponding to that of the German 22 sq. m. racer, the surface friction would, therefore, in terms of the total resistance, to which the human body is subjected from the wind, correspond to the resistance of two men sitting on deck; for the Sonder boat this surface friction would equal that of four to five men. We thus see that the retarding action resulting from the surface friction of the sail is greater than is usually assumed.

Nature also lays great stress on the smoothness of the bird's wing. The quality or structure of the duck used for racing sails is, therefore, a matter to which we yachtsmen should not be indifferent. I had four different kinds of duck photographed under the microscope, in order to investigate the action of the wind on its surface (see the photographs on next page). Number 1 shows a smooth duck of better quality, number 2 a rough material and numbers 3 and 4 are of moderately rough duck, the latter dipped in kerosene. The photographs show marked differences in the structure of the three materials, scarcely visible to the naked eye, but undoubtedly perceptible to the air. We also observe that the duck dipped in kerosene undergoes thereby no material change with respect to its smoothness and that the fibres hanging from its surface have been little influenced by the treatment — in producing a smoother surface.

Measurements of surface friction on duck, which were made in the Laboratory at Göttingen, reveal the following results:

Surface friction of ordinary, smooth duck . . . . 83 units
The same duck with the fibres singed by a flame . . . . 50 "
The same duck with a triple coat of Zellon varnish . . . . 47 "

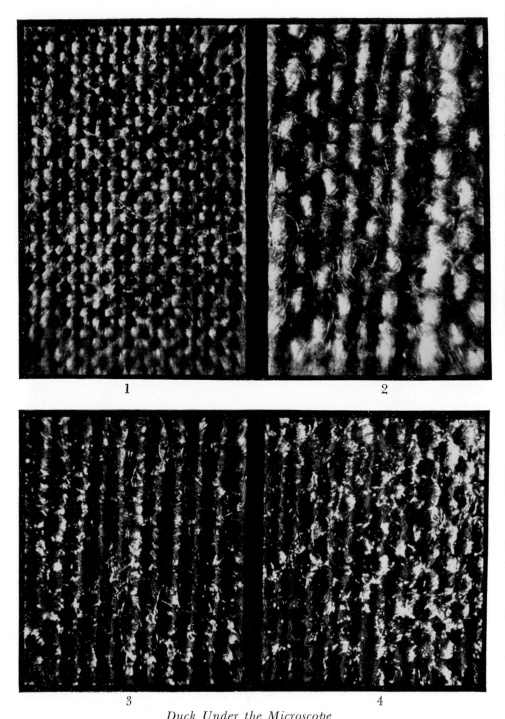

1   2

3   4

Duck Under the Microscope

(*The readers attention is called to the following optical phenomenon: Upon turning duck No. 1 so that the light strikes it from the other side the slight elevations in the duck appear as indentations and vice versa.*)

116

We thus see that it is possible to reduce this surface friction or resistance about 40%; this would correspond approximately to the resistance of at least one man sitting on deck for every 25 square yards of sail area. This is certainly a proof that the choice of the duck for a racing sail is a matter that should receive the attention of every yachtsman. Some advise, before a race, rubbing the sail in the direction of the seams toward the leech with a wet cloth, or, in case of large sails, sprinkling them with water. The chief thing accomplished by this treatment is that the fibres hanging from the surface of the duck tend to adhere to it and thus produce a smoother surface; but the wetting of the sail may do more harm than good by causing wrinkles and otherwise a badly setting sail. On the other hand, I am convinced that *if the sail could be given a coat of varnish* — light Duco varnish that would not impair its natural flexibility, it would prove *much superior* with regard to surface friction to the untreated sail of the best quality of duck.

Finally, in order to form a better conception of the total retarding effect due to the resistances called into action by the mast, stays, halyards, etc., I am appending a scale, in which these different resistances are represented quantitatively (cf. drawing A below); they have been calculated most exactly by an expert for a 15 sq. m. German racer. The driving force of the sail was found to be 8 kilograms for a wind of 6 m/sec. velocity. The rigging alone, not including the sail, offers a resistance of 1 kilogram to the wind; so that the driving force that comes into consideration for the propulsion of the boat amounts to only 7 kilograms.

In order to demonstrate the importance of a correct mast form and the eventual reduction of the other resistances called into action by the rigging, these also have been calculated and represented on a scale (cf. drawing B below). On simply streamlining the mast and arranging the ropes (halyards) one behind the other, we observe that we can reduce the total resistance in question by 56%, which means an increment in the driving force of from 7 to 7.56 kilograms (about 15 to 16.2 pounds). What a difference an increase of 1.2 pounds in power signifies need hardly be mentioned. I think I am justified in maintaining that we yachtsmen have taken far too little account of these retarding forces and that we ough to direct our attention, in the future, more to an elimination of the various harmful effects arising from the resistance of the air that still predominate on our yachts.

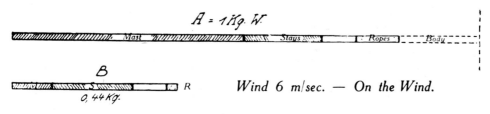

$A = 1 Kg. W.$

Mast   Stays   Ropes   Body

B

R

0,44 Kg.

Wind 6 m/sec. — On the Wind.

A { Pressure on Sail in Direction of Course: 8 kg. } = *7 kg. for Rigging A = 14 lbs. driving Force.*
{ Resistance of Rigging . . . . 1 kg. }

B Resistance with streamlined Mast and Halyards one behind the other — Driving Force 15.12 lbs.

New Form for Centerboard and Rudder

In the following I am reporting on preliminary hydrodynamic investigations, the practical realization and verification of which have so far been frustrated from lack of requisite funds for building a larger racing boat — for the purpose of testing and utilizing the results already found.

The first really exact experiments with models were undertaken in 1922 by C. A. Bembé and myself, though the various problems concerned had engaged our most careful attention for several years previous to that date. As is well known, an arched surface, which is opposed to a current of air or water, develops almost double the force or pressure that a flat surface does. But the surprising thing with the arched surface is the fact that even when it is held in the direction of flow of the current, that is, when its angle of opposition is zero, it reveals a component force in the direction of its arching (cf. the drawings on p. 9 and also the accompanying text.

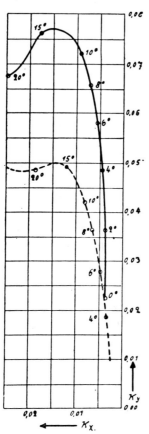

On the other hand, the detrimental resistance to which the surface is subjected is very small, and, in the case of a bird, which sails against the wind with motionless wings, it is practically counterbalanced by the horizontal component of the force directed upward (apparently due to the wind blowing slightly — about 4° — upward), which acts in the direction of flight. As a proof of the presence of this upward directed force we may cite again the fact that an umbrella, which is held horizontally, that is, with the handle vertical, tends to be lifted. Or let us recall the characteristic but instructive picture of the wash flapping in the wind, which, in consequence of its arching, is blown above the horizontal (cf. p. 8). An absolute verification of this display of force is given by the polar curves for the arched surfaces measured in the wind tunnel (cf. the section on "The Arching"). It was the knowledge of these facts which convinced us of the advantages of the strongly bellied sail.

Such reflections suggested the question: *Why not an arched centerboard?* With this possibility in view, let us recall the conditions in the water. We know that the drift of our boats to leeward amounts to about 5°; we may confirm this, when, heading for a mark close-hauled, we observe all at once that we can no longer fetch it; not that the wind has shifted, but the boat has drifted somewhat to leeward. Provided the skipper has made no allowance for the drift, the mistake must be corrected by taking another tack — or two — with the accompanying unpleasant consequences, especially in a race. Or the novice may be surprised on seeing the mark which he thought he could fetch, apparently travelling against the wind. To realize the drift of a boat it is only necessary to observe her wake, which, especially in a light wind

Polar Curves for flat and arched Plate.

————— = Arched Plate.
— — — — = Flat Plate.
(Eiffel.)

118

is visible to a considerable distance astern. It is quite immaterial, whether we speak of a drift of 5° or say that the water flows against the centerboard at an angle of 5° from the leeward side of the boat. The angle at which the water strikes that side of the centerboard is determined by the propagation (speed) of the boat and her lateral movement, termed "drift."

Now let us compare the polar curves for a flat and for an arched surface at an angle of opposition of flow of 5° (cf. the diagram on page 118). We observe that the detrimental resistance K_x, determined by the distance of the curve from the vertical on the right of the diagram (abscissa) is only a trifle greater for the arched than for the flat plate, but that the side pressure K_y, the distance of the curve from the lowest horizontal (ordinate), i. e. the height of the curve, is more than twice as great for the arched plate as for the flat one.

To what is this great difference in the action of the two plates due? The answer is indicated in the lines of flow for these two plates (cf. sketches C and D of the *annexed* drawing). These two sketches, which have already been referred to on page 19, are reproduced here in order to demonstrate more readily the relative action of two similarly constructed centerboards. We observe, even for these small angles of opposition of flow, how the flat plate tears the water; small eddies are formed along both sides of the plate from its fore to after end. As every eddy contains energy, and that energy is taken from the cur-

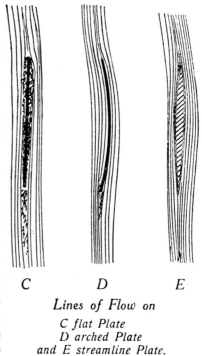

C   D   E

Lines of Flow on

C flat Plate
D arched Plate
and E streamline Plate.

rent, the action of the latter on the plate is thus diminished accordingly. The lines of flow on the arched plate present an entirely different aspect. The flow is continuous; it is only bent. It is this bending of the lines of flow that accounts for the great pressure developed by the arched plate; and this pressure would thus be imparted to a boat with a similarly arched centerboard. As the strong suction action on the leeward side of an arched surface is an established fact, as determined by experiment, to be three to five times as great as the pressure on its windward side, we easily understand why aeroplane designers give the upper surface of the profiled plane a large convex arching and the lower surface almost none. The form of the under surface is of so little importance with regard to the development of pressure compared to that of the upper surface that, for constructive purposes — the thicker the profile the fewer the trusses necessary — and also to reduce the resistance somewhat, the under one is made almost flat.

To return to our subject; if the arched surface develops a pressure or pull in the direction of its arching, then a boat with an arched centerboard could be driven almost against the wind, provided we were able to eliminate the resistance to which the body of the boat and her rigging are subjected. If we compare the normal relations of a boat with a flat centerboard and

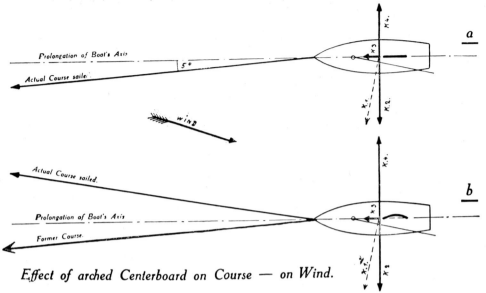

Effect of arched Centerboard on Course — on Wind.

one with a centerboard arched to windward, the above considerations would give us approximately the courses indicated in the above drawings for the two boats high on the wind. The boat *a* with the flat centerboard drifts about the afore-mentioned 5° to leeward — a proof that the force K_1 developed by her sail, which can be resolved into two components K_2, acting at right angles to the centerboard, and K_3, the force acting in the direction of the keel that drives the boat forward, is greater than the supporting force called into action by the pressure of the water on the centerboard. In other words, since the force developed by the sail is greater than that exercised by the centerboard, the driving force K_3 is not in a position to drive the boat forward exactly in the direction of the keel, and consequently she will drift somewhat to leeward (cf. drawing *a*). On the other hand, the boat with the centerboard arched to windward does not drift to leeward but tends rather to work up to windward, since the component force K_2 developed by her sail is smaller than that K_4 exercised by the water on her centerboard (cf. drawing *b*).

The reader is begged to bear in mind that these, as also the following drawings, are merely sketches intended more to facilitate the conveyance of ideas than to serve constructive purposes.

But before we proceed further, let us consider whether the arched surface cannot also be applied to the rudder. The blade of the rudder is of pliable steel and can be arched on either side by means of a wire rope that passes over the ends of a cross-bar, inserted in the blade, to its rear edge, to which it is made fast (cf. the drawings).

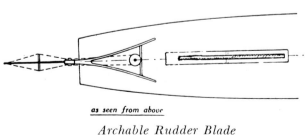

as seen from above

Archable Rudder Blade

According to the tension brought to bear on the wire rope on the one or the other side of the rudder, this pliant blade is bent or arched in the direction desired. The remarkable effect of the arching is manifested in the tendency of the stern of the boat to be pushed toward the side; this action of the arched blade should, therefore, enable one to steer the boat without calling into action the retarding forces of the rudder. A comparison of this new type of rudder with the ordinary form, as represented in the two drawings on this page, shows that one need not move the tiller — from its normal midship position — to produce the steering effect necessary. The arched surface develops a force acting in the direction of its arching without calling forth those retarding forces that otherwise impede the progress of the boat; and this force is called into action even when the current strikes the rudder directly from ahead, i. e., at an angle of opposition of 0° (cf. the drawings below and those on pp. 9 and 10). On the other hand, the pressure that must be brought to bear on the flat rudder for steering has a retarding component, which is transferred to the boat; it is represented by the force K_2 in the first drawing. With the new rudder the boat can be steered by adjusting the arching of its blade alone, which may be effected by a small lever or steering wheel made fast to the tiller, as indicated in the drawing on page 120. Of course we could not discard the tiller entirely. For example, on a free course, where the boat often has, as we know, a strong weather helm — with great pressure on the rudder — we could adjust the arching of the blade by means of the wire rope in such a manner that the boat would just hold her course with the tiller midships, using the latter only as an auxiliary means for correcting slight deviations in course.

There is an advantage gained in efficiency by the use of an arched surface for the centerboard over the rudder in that the former operates in quiet water and the latter in water that has been disturbed by the passage of the hull of the boat through it, to the effect that the efficiency of the rudder is greatly diminished. But it must be conceded that our modern centerboard boats set little water in motion and that only on the surface on account of their small draft.

But we can also treat the present problem from another point of view and conclude that, if an arched surface produces double the effect, it would suffice to have the centerboard half as large; the friction resistance of the centerboard would then be reduced one half and hence the total friction resistance of hull, centerboard and rudder, or the so-called "wetted" surface appreciably. What an important factor the wetted surface plays is evident from the various means

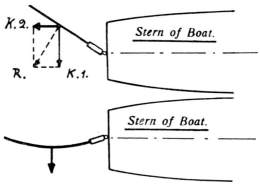

Flat and arched Rudder Blade in Action.

employed by yacht designers to reduce the wetted surface of the hull to a minimum. We may observe that the centerboard comprises about *half the total wetted surface* of a craft, a fact that is often overlooked.

The practical experiments with model boats gave surprising results. The difficulty in carrying out such experiments lies in the fact that the boats become very sensitive due to the arched centerboard, showing a marked tendency to turn, and are consequently hard to hold on any course. This made it difficult to obtain accurate angular measurements on the wind. But it was interesting to observe, nevertheless, how these little boats worked up to windward by a series of jerks.

Let us now go a step further and investigate the streamline or symmetrically formed narrow, profile centerboard (cf. the drawing). Such a finboard is a certain retrogression with respect to effectiveness, but it has the advantage of being more practical and easy to construct. Let the ordinary flat board serve again as comparison. The streamline centerboard shows, similarly to, the arched surface, that for the small angle of opposition of 5°, which concerns us here, the flow is not disturbed, that is, it has, in fact, not begun to form eddies (cf. sketch *E* on page 119), whereas we know that the flat plate shows marked signs of eddy formation at that angle. As the streamline centerboard in question — with its

Streamline Centerboard — most effective Profile.

(Goettingen No. 444.)

two arched surfaces — presents on both tacks an arched surface to the flow, on which the so important suction action can be developed, a greater efficiency must be attained by this form of centerboard. A comparison of the polar curves for a flat surface with those for a symmetrically profiled form shows that, although the side pressure on the latter is not so much greater, at least not as great as the excess of pressure on the arched centerboard over that developed by this profiled form, the harmfull resistance is only about ⅓ that of the normal, flat centerboard.

The same advantage is gained by the use of a profiled rudder blade, but to a greater degree, in that the flow "breaks down" much later — for larger angles of opposition; in the case of the rudder we have to deal, as we know, with such angles — up to 30°. The moment the flow breaks down and the large eddies appear, the efficiency diminishes rapidly. For this reason the rudder should never be held at a greater angle than 30° to the flow. The thicker the profiling, the later begins the eddy formation as the angle of opposition is increased. For this reason we may make the profile of the rudder somewhat thicker than that of the centerboard. The greater efficiency of the profiled rudder allows us also to make it smaller, whereby its harmful resistance is reduced.

The advantage gained by giving the fin of a yacht a thick profile is that the lead ballast may be not only increased in amount but also concentrated at a greater depth, without increasing appreciably the resistance of the fin; the distance of its center of gravity below the water line may be still further increased by making the lowest horizontal sections of the fin broader than its upper ones. On the assumption that the fin is given the streamline form — with greatest breadth in its foreportion or third and tapering aft — its resistance is seldom greater, in fact, often smaller, than that of a narrow fin. Towing experiments which I made with various yachts confirmed this. But we must realize that an actual advantage is gained by the broadly profiled fin only when it is inclined at *an angle to the flow,* as on the wind, and not, where the *angle of opposition is zero.*

A third possibility of improving the boat by a change in the lateral plane is the following: We know that the lateral plane of a boat is the projection of that part of her hull that is below the water line on the vertical plane passing through her keel. The pressure of the sail is transferred to this lateral plane or rather to the body of the boat — to her hull and centerboard, which jointly constitute her support in the water. As is well known, with fast racing boats the centerboard offers the principal support, and it is not mere chance that the aim of modern yacht designers is directed toward making the *centerboard carry the greatest possible amount of this support, and the hull proper as little as possible;* or, in other words, the latter *is given the least possible draught.* This tendency may have been carried to an extreme in the flat lines of the latest Sonder boats; but for this very reason, they presented an unsurpassable type, that as an all-round boat was superior, especially in speed, to any of our present types in smooth water. We realize how small the lateral plane of the hull proper of our modern racing boats is, upon hoisting the centerboard, when the boat is on the wind; she drifts at once almost directly sideways, especially when she is sailed upright. We may ask, why does the yacht designer try to reduce the support of the hull and transfer it as much as possible to the centerboard? For the obvious reason that the centerboard develops the greatest support with the least retarding resistance to the direction of propagation. If we support the boat by the hull, *this resistance is not only large, but it increases disproportionately with the speed of the boat.* She can not plane.

A centerboard boat sailed high on the wind is known to drift about 5° to leeward. The centerboard of normal size does not suffice to hinder this drift, and the unfavorable result is that the boat does not advance exactly in the direction of her axis, but, by reason of the drift, is shoved slightly to the side; in other words, the actual course sailed and the axis of the boat do not coincide. We can easily imagine that this pushing aside of the water, which is in fact manifested by the larger wave on the lee bow of the boat, exerts an extraordinarily unfavorable influence on her speed, that is, that it gives rise to an excessively great resistance in the direction of propagation. We are thus confronted with the important question: Is it absolutely essential that the boat's hull act as a support in the water? Could we not leave the entire support to the *centerboard alone and regard the hull only as the buoyant body?* In other words, how would it be possible to prevent this drift that is so detrimental not only to the direction of the course but also to the speed of the boat?

This problem can be solved by adjusting the centerboard in such a manner that it makes an angle to the weather of about 3° with the keel of the boat, whereby the latter and the direction of propagation are brought to coincide. The centerboard, as indicated in the *annexed* sketch below, would have to be inclined about 3° to the weather or nearer to the wind, that is, at a sharper angle to it, than the hull of the boat. The result of this change would be that the boat's hull would move straight ahead without being retarded in the least in her speed by the resistance otherwise caused by the lateral pressure on her lee side (bow) due to the aforesaid drift, while the whole support in the water would be carried by the centerboard under the most favorable relation of resistance to support.

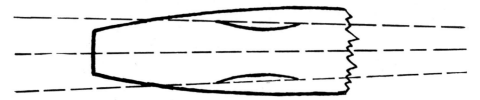

Adjustable Centerboard
making Angle 3-5° with Keel on either Side of same

Arched centerboards set at an angle of about 3° toward the windward side are being used with success by scows on the middle western lakes. These boats use so-called bilgeboards, that is, one slightly curved centerboard on each side (see Fig. above, in which the arching is exaggerated to demonstrate it more clearly). When the boat is sailed, the centerboard on the windward side is pulled out of the water.

THE PENETRABILITY OF THE SAIL

Discussion about the penetrability or, rather, permeability of the sail has been extensive and exhaustive; although I have sought to consider every possible factor that might tend to promote efficiency, I am convinced that the non-porosity of sail duck does not play the important part generally attributed to it. With this in view I performed a special experiment with an expert on this subject, and the results obtained confirmed not only the various observations I had made myself on sails but also the conclusion I had drawn.

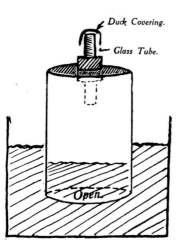

Apparatus for measuring Penetrability of Duck.

The experiment was the following: In an ordinary tin can with an open bottom but closed top a hole is made in the latter, into which a glass tube is inserted. A piece of very loosely woven duck (cf. the adjacent sketch) is stretched over the top of this tube. When the can is placed in water, the latter cannot flow in from below into the former, although the can is entirely open, any faster than the air escapes above through the glass tube with the duck covering. The can sinks slowly deeper and deeper from its own weight, as the air is thereby displaced. The permeability of the duck can be calculated from the time the can takes to become submerged, i. e., from the time that elapses for the air to escape through the opening covered by the duck under the pressure of its weight, this pressure corresponding to a certain strength of wind.

Under an initial upward pressure of a column of water of 9.55 millimeters, the duck shows a permeability of 0.0387 cubic meters of air per square meter. This initial pressure, which is equivalent to a wind pressure of 9.55 kilograms per square meter, corresponds to a wind of a velocity of about 12 meters per second along the sail. But the penetration of the air through the sail to leeward in the same time amounts to only 0.0387 meters, that is, to only about 1/300 the velocity of the wind that passes over the sail. If we take into account the decrease in the pressure toward the leech (cf. pp. 26-27), there results an average air penetration of only about 1 centimeter.

It thus follows that the permeable sail — and it was easy to blow through this sample of duck with the mouth — guides the wind approximately along the dotted line in the annexed drawing.

Since the wind is deflected from its normal path by the pressure developed by the sail, the conclusion may be drawn that the efficiency of this permeable sail would be the same as that of an impermeable one that is payed off at its leech about 2 centimeters more than the former. In other words, to attain the same wind pressure, we must trim the permeable sail about two centimeters closer than the impermeable one. However, the forward drive

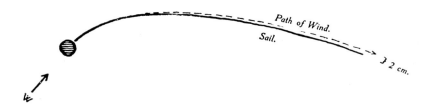

in the direction of the keel will be only a trifle smaller, about 1/167. These values are so infinitesimally small that, practically speaking, they may be neglected. Even when the sail is not trimmed close, its drive — at an angle of 10° — is reduced by only 2%. Closely woven ducks may, therefore, be regarded as practically impermeable. A comparison with the bird's wing confirms that, although *one can easily blow through it in any direction*, it is the most effective surface that exists.

Many of our yachtsmen discard their sails after only a year's use, "because they are no longer dense!" I hope they may now be convinced how erroneous this assumption is, as also that even the lightest duck may be regarded as impermeable in a light breeze and that in a strong wind it tends only to increase the boat's stability.

We shall now offer a comparative summary of the various properties peculiar to the high (Marconi) and the gaff rig, whereby the advantages of the former should be established:

High Rig	Gaff Rig
Develops more pressure on the wind due to the favorable relation of length to breadth. (ratio)	Shows inferior qualities to windward on account of the shorter fore edge opposed to the wind.
The sail sags off less.	The sail sags out more, especially along the gaff, and thus develops less pressure or drive.

The lever arm is smaller on account of the shorter boom; and hence the tendency to luff not so great when running free.

Develops less pressure or drive off the wind on account of the greater relation of length to breadth of sail.

The shorter the boom the less the weight.

No gaff, hence weight and resistance greatly reduced.

Except near the boom the sail is properly bellied *up to its head* and hence more effective.

Only the mast disturbs the flow of the wind onto the luff of the sail.

As the center of gravity of the sail often lies only apparently higher, the stability of the boat is only slightly affected.

One may carry a permanent rear stay.

The boat is rendered more manageable from the sail being concentrated nearer the center of effort.

The tendency to luff in a strong wind is slight.

The sail catches the upper wind under the lee of the land.

Advantage can be taken of the increase in the velocity of the wind with its height above the water.

Is harder for another boat to blanket.

The sail sets somewhat worse dead before the wind. — Remedy: mast straight or capable of turning!

The sail is easily reefed.

The sail is more quickly set, lowered and furled. The pressure is more evenly distributed along the mast.

The pressure on the rudder is greater off the wind.

Develops more drive with wind abeam, but more difficult to hold under maximum pressure.

The longer the boom the greater the weight and hence the greater the tendency to roll before the wind.

Weight of gaff plus its resistance to the wind.

Since there are *two* spars, the sail is flattened *both above and below,* especially when not properly peaked.

Both the mast and the gaff disturb the flow of the wind in the upper part of the sail, opposite the gaff.

The sagging off of the gaff promotes the stability of the boat in a strong wind.

One has to tend *two* back stays.

The tiller is less sensitive and hence the feeling for the boat rendered more difficult.

The tendency to luff in the flaws is greater.

The sail does not reach so high up into these upper currents.

Less advantage can be gained from this property of the wind.

Is more easily blanketed.

The sail sets well before the wind, except for the sagging off of the gaff.

Two halyards to tend instead of one in reefing.

The gaff presses the mast forward at their mutual point of contact, thus rendering a jumper stay necessary.

Practically speaking, upon every re-rigging from gaff to high rig, I have noticed a remarkable improvement in the boat's sailing qualities, that was indirectly confirmed by the various successes achieved with the new rig.*

C u r r y , Aerodynamics of Sails and Racing Tactics.

* On courses with long wind-abeam stretches the Gaff Rig has proved faster on small boats.

126

Wind and Water

Lashed by the wind, the clouds and waves
Inspired us with awe,
Yet each dark cloud and storm tossed wave
Was subject to beauty's law.

Many people think that the wind is arbitrary and indeterminable in its fluctuations of strength and direction. But even if the fickle nature of this mobile element often leads to deception, it is the privilege of the wise to read its signs and to recognize certain fixed laws that it obeys. Before the storm breaks loose we are warned by its harbingers whose cries resound from countless natural phenomena: Clouds race by and we may read their warning from their forms and colors. From the distance the murmur of forests and the sounds of bells and voices, borne by invisible vibrations, strike our ear with unusual clarity. Yonder, on the land, a flag flutters: on the distant horizon the smoke of a steamship lashed by the wind is visible, the long, dark banner from its funnel indicating the trend of the atmosphere. On shore a cloud of dust eddies and whirls along the road; leaves dance in the air; fields of grain wave and bend restlessly. The storm spreads over the water; we hear the flapping of a sail, seized by the wind; the water becomes that typical steely blue to blackish gray; the roar of the waves grows nearer; the sweet fragrance of hay, forest or meadow is often wafted our way; it grows cooler; masses of clouds are driven in wild flight past and beyond us.

All the signs of the threatening storm may be noticed betimes by him who knows them and, seeking for them, turns his glass in all directions; his senses of hearing, smell and feeling are awakened to the slightest suspicious premonition. Forewarned, he can prepare for the worst; danger finds him armed. All these storm signals sound quite natural, still to many they are unfamiliar, if they appear singly or in such apparent guise. Many a sailor is awakened from pleasant dreams by being thrown into violent reality unawares, his sail flapping madly in the wind.

However at night there are storm signals that are most deceptive. To these belongs, above all others, the muffled roar of water. If this roar, which may arise from the high seas as well as from the surf and, especially in the dark, throws him who cannot discriminate into strained expectancy, lasts more than a few minutes, nothing baneful may be anticipated. In this case the storm has swept by at considerable distance, on the one side or the other — or else a brief gust of wind has spent its force before it could reach the boat, while the waves and surf on the distant shore still echo the raging of the storm on its path of destruction.

Often it is not easy to discriminate between sun rays and sheets of rain which glitter through the clouds. The difference is that sun rays are propagated radially or diverge, whereas rain falls in parallel sheets. The direction of the ensuing wind may be discerned from the sheets of rain driven by the wind, provided their direction does not coincide with the vertical plane of observation.

Let us now examine the nature of the wind more particularly.

The wind as such is caused by the flow of air from regions of higher to those of lower pressure. It is thus dependent on the fluctuations of pressure, which are in most cases caused by differences in temperature. In order that the term *"speed of wind"* may be clearly understood, the following table is appended, which may serve to obviate the constant confusion, current even in yachting circles, between *"strength of wind"* (ten different grades according to Beaufort) and *"speed of wind"* in meters per second.

Strength of wind	Meters per second	Designation	Characteristics
0	0	Calm	Water not rippled.
1	1.7	Light	Leaves rustle; pennant is wafted out; water begins to ruffle.
2	3.1	Moderate	Boughs sway and bend; waves begin to form.
3	4.8	Fresh	Boat heels perceptibly.
4	6.7	Strong	Wind whistles softly in the rigging; small boats consider the advisability of reefing.
5	8.8	Stronger	Trees sway; most small boats should reef.
6	10.7	Very Strong	Walking is noticeably impeded; yachts reef.
7	12.9	Stormy	Trees are bent and boughs are broken off; small boats seek shelter.
8	15.4	Storm	The mainsail is lowered and furled, and the trysail is set.
9	18.0	Gale	Trees are uprooted.
10	21	Hurricane	

A practical means for the transformation of speed of wind in meters per second into kilometers per hour is approximately the following: Multiply the former by four and subtract 10% therefrom. For the reverse, the transformation of kilometers per hour into meters per second, divide the former by four and add 10% thereto. For example:

$$8 \text{ m'sec.} = 8 \times 4 - \frac{8 \times 4}{10} = 32 - 3.2 = 28.8 \text{ km. per hour.}$$

M. Rosenfeld

Local Thunderstorm

For the transformation of the Beaufort scale into that of meters per second the following relation holds approximately:

2 x Beaufort $- 1 =$ m/sec. scale, where x denotes Beaufort grade in question. For example: Strength of wind 5 (Beaufort) gives $2\times5 - 1 = 9$ m/sec.

In consequence of the friction on the surface of the earth, the speed of the wind decreases the nearer we approach the ground or water. In the higher layers of the atmosphere the speed of the wind, in general, increases at the rate of about 1.5 m/sec. per kilometer. But the rate of change close to the ground or water is much greater, and that is what interests us here — in sailing.

On an open field the following wind speeds were measured:

Distance above ground	Speed of wind
0.2 meters	1.5 meters per second
1 "	2.5 " " "
2 "	3 " " "
3 "	3.5 " " "
4 "	3.9 " " "

On account of the less surface friction of water, the speed of the wind over the water is almost twice as great as that on the land. These values undergo the following change at the heights given over the water:

Distance above water	Speed of wind
0.2 meters	2.5 meters per second
1 "	4 " " "
2 "	5 " " "
3 "	5.5 " " "
4 "	6 " " "
6 "	6.4 " " "
8 "	6.7 " " "
10 "	7 " " "
15 "	7.2 " " "

Although the wind conditions may not always be expressed exactly by these values, the latter, nevertheless, represent the average speeds from a number of measurements. The advantage of the high Marconi rig will again be obvious here, especially when we realize that under the lee of the land, where the wind reaches down only to the head of the sail, the difference in the two rigs must be much greater. "The rapid increase in the speed of the wind with height" is beautifully illustrated in Nature in the case of birds flying off the ground. When a bird first leaves the ground, it has to work hard to attain height, but once three meters or more above the surface it begins to mount quickly and at a steeper angle — a result of the increase in the speed of the wind with the distance above the ground.

The *veering of the wind* with increasing height is also of significance to the yachtsman. As we ascend into the upper layers of the atmosphere, the wind veers more and more to the *"right;"* it can amount to 15° at an altitude of several kilometers. This phenomenon, which appears especially in summer, is significant for the yachtsman, inasmuch as he can determine from the direction, in which the clouds are moving in the upper layers of the atmosphere, the direction of the subsequent wind, that has not yet reached the lower regions, by assuming a wind direction 15° to the *left* of that above.

130

Deflection in Direction of Wind from Horizontal

Average Deflection about 4° upward.

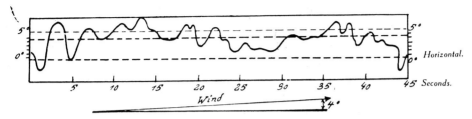

The *direction of the wind* is not, as is commonly supposed, horizontal. As we have observed on page 9 and later, the wind is directed on an average of about 4° *upward.* We are indebted to Lilienthal for this discovery. The curve represented here is a short piece of one of the many determined from measurements made by Lilienthal with an extremely simple apparatus (cf. the above sketch), which registers the given fluctuations or deflections of the wind on a self-revolving cylinder; it represents the deflections during a period of only 45 seconds. The maxima shown in the various curves lie between + 16° and − 9°. The upward direction of the wind is, in general, independent of the speed, direction, season of year and time of day.*

We obtain a confirmation of the upward directed movement of the wind, which appears to have its cause in the greater velocity of the higher layers of the air exercising a certain suction effect on the lower ones, when we observe the smoke from a chimney. Even though one might contend that gases rise on account of their heat, we may assume that they are cooled in a few minutes; for the column of smoke from a chimney ascends first rapidly and then gradually. On the other hand, it may also happen that with a low barometer, especially before a thunderstorm, the smoke is blown over the water horizontally without showing the least tendency to ascend, in spite of the strong wind that may prevail. If the reason for the upward directed tendency of the wind is to be sought in the suction effect of the higher, more rapidly moving layers of the air, then this horizontal flow of the lower layers before a thunderstorm would be the best proof for the validity of this theory

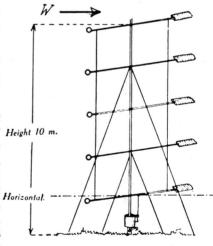

Upward Direction of Wind.

---

* The socalled "turbulence" of the wind is often offered as an explanation for this phenomenon, in that the energy, which, arising from the resistance of the air on the earth, is continually being transformed into turbulence and stored up in the air, rises perpendicular to the frictional surface, wanders upward and, in greater height, is partly transformed into heat.

131

— for the obvious reason that the familiar *reactionary* wind that blows in the lowest layers is opposite in direction to that of the storm wind; in which case the speed of the lower wind does not increase but decreases with the height, in consequence of the mutual friction of the two oppositely directed air currents on the dividing surface between them. Here the air of the lower layers will, therefore, be sucked not upward but downward by and into the more rapidly moving lower layers, that is, the wind will in this case be directed not upward but either horizontally or even downward. So it happens that smoke often travels as if pressed *"down"* on the water. As already mentioned in the first chapter, this upward directory tendency of the wind is the principal secret in the flight of birds. I may recall in this connection the familiar experiment with the umbrella, to which I have referred so often. This peculiar property of the wind should interest the yachtsman for the following reason: If we wish the *wind to strike the luff of the sail at right angles* — with the boat on the wind, we must incline the mast about 4° forward. At all events, we should advise giving the seams of the sail and the pockets for the battens an *upward slope aft*. To be exact, the upward slope of the seams and pockets should be made to coincide with the *direction of flow* of the wind on the sail. The upper battens should, therefore, slope 5° to 10° more upward than the lower, and the boom should also be given a corresponding tend upward.

As to the *variation in the direction of the wind* it is generally known that the wind remains comparatively steady in direction up to about wind strength 3 (cf. table on p. 128). With further increase in velocity the socalled "turbulent" wind flow appears, bringing with it a constant veering in the direction of the wind. From this moment the helmsman should not take his eye off the pennant, unless he wants to risk having a favorable flaw escape his notice.

Now the question: How does the wind veer — from ahead and from the quarter? A good helmsman will try to perceive a strong flaw the moment it strikes the water — *before* it reaches the boat, and determine its exact direction by the ruffling of the water. It has already been explained, why the wind during the flaw veers apparently more from the beam than one might expect (cf. pp. 46-47) ; this we may designate as its first peculiarity. Our explanation for this was the following: the pennant indicates the direction of the apparent wind, which is the resultant of the (real) wind and that created by the speed of the boat; as the velocity of the wind increases, when the flaw sets in, proportionately more than the speed of the boat, the resultant direction of the apparent wind in the flaw will be more on the beam, as indicated by the pennant, which will tend more in the direction of the (real) wind than in that of the wind created by the boat.

The second peculiarity, which is intrinsic to the puff and has not yet been mentioned, is that it blows in different directions in its different parts or sectors: it can, in fact, as is often the case, strike in from directly ahead. The reason for this variation in the direction of the flaw is the following:

The flaw rebounds, as it were, from the surface of the water and thereupon diverges radially. According to the sector, in which the boat is struck by the flaw, the wind is found to come more from ahead or from the beam. Let us examine the three cases represented by the sketches on the next page.

Radial Propagation of Flow.

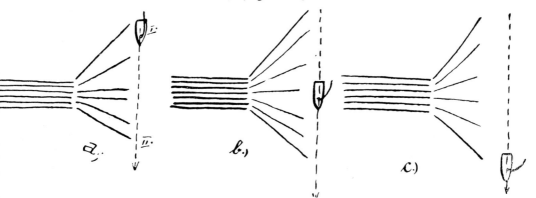

Case a. The boat runs into the outer sector of the flaw; this thus strikes the boat more or less *from ahead,* and she must bear off or trim closer. As she continues on her course, the wind veers more and more quarterly.

Case b. The boat is hit by the flaw in its central sector; there is, therefore, no appreciable change in the direction of the wind. As the boat proceeds on her course, the wind comes *more and more from the quarter.*

Case c. The boat is struck by the flaw, as she is passing out of it; here the wind is blowing so quarterly that the boat can point much higher or ease her sheets accordingly.

Cases b and c confirm the yachtsman's view that a flaw veers more and more from the quarter, as one sails through it. Case a is by no means an exception, but the veering of the wind from ahead is not so noticeable, since its increased velocity in the flaw, which causes a veering of the "apparent" wind in the opposite direction (first peculiarity of the flaw), tends to offset this effect. The sectors of a flaw may extend *laterally* to a much *greater distance* than its depth; in this case the boat would get the benefit of only a small portion of the flaw or, in other words, the flaw may be of such short duration that it passes by before the boat has been able to sail through it. For this reason "bear off in a flaw." If the lateral extension of the flaw is small, the force developed by it will be less intense, and, in case it should strike the water just ahead of the boat, she would be able to sail entirely through it — first higher on the wind, then more off the wind and finally with the wind on her quarter.

As an observant critic, Herr Belitz, so beloved in European yachting circles, found that the radial divergence of a flaw upon striking the water could be distinguished best, when a broad flaw falls upon a *field of boats* that are all on the same tack. The boats are hit quite differently by the same flaw; some profit by it greatly, others not at all. A flaw approaching from ahead is anticipated by an observant helmsman by bearing off somewhat — he falls off *before* the flaw sets in. What happens then? As the boat has still little headway, she is heeled over at first; this should be parried by paying off the main sheet. This may not answer, whereupon the boat will bury her lee bow in the water, and the wave thereby formed will act like a cushion, against which the boat presses with her whole shoulder; she is thereby pressed to windward, suddenly running much higher on the wind and faster than

133

before — "Aha! The flaw is more from the quarter" observes the inexperienced helmsman. But if it should occur to him to glance at the pennant, he may find that it is streaming out directly over the gaff or even to the other side of it — *to windward*. How is this possible? Are we confronted with another problem, for which there is apparently no solution? How can the *sail* still be full and drawing in its upper part? One would suppose the *wind* could exert no pressure whatever on this portion of the sail that is sagging out more than ever, rather that it should strike in from lee and cause the sail to flap!

The explanation follows: The force that now keeps the head of the sail full and drawing is not acting from without directly on it. The more the boat heels, the more does the wind tend to flow from below upward over the sail, the boom becoming, in this heeled position, more the wind cutting edge than the mast, which runs more parallel to the direction of the wind. The wind, upon falling on the lower part of the sail, which makes a greater angle with the wind than its upper one does, is directed upward over the sail, becoming the predominant factor there. The head of the sail, in spite of its negative angle of opposition, is, therefore, still kept full and drawing. With birds also the outer end of the wing has generally a negative angle of opposition; it is twisted toward the end in a similar manner — here it is the so-called "ram" eddy, formed near the body (under the wing), that flows out toward the end of the wing.

Thus we see that there are a number of influences, some having their origin in the form and course of the flaw, others in the sail itself, which jointly determine the direction of the wind on the sail.

The ensuing investigations deal with the nature or structure of the wind proper in its various details.

The aeronautic observatory near Lindenburg has been carrying on most instructive research work on this subject, and I am presenting here from their records on flaws the final results — averages of measurements, extended over a period of several years.

The wind measurements, the socalled "fast" and "slow" registrations, are made with an anemograph, which records the given speeds of the wind on a cylinder that revolves fast or slow according to the registrations to be recorded (see the registration curves on the next page). *The* most striking peculiarity of these curves is that, especially with moderate winds, the strength of the wind increases "suddenly," but decreases "slowly" — in a series of stages (of gradually diminishing strength). To detect this rhythm, to steer in conformity to it and to take advantage of it, is *the* art, which enables the lightest craft to withstand many a heavy flaw or series of such. The first impact — the maximum strength of the wind, must be parried by letting off the sheets or luffing, and not a fraction of a second is to be lost in this manoeuvre. Then the sheets should immediately be trimmed closer and speed acquired, in order to be able to luff up the moment the next wind maximum sets in. It is hardly possible for a boat running at high speed to capsize, if she retains her ability to parry the various gusts. No flaw is so strong that there are not intervals between the gusts that can be utilized for this purpose. Provided one man tends the helm, another the sheets, and their cooperation is correct and quick as lightning, it is almost impossible to capsize a boat with the normal rig, unless something unforeseen happens.

Registration Curves of Flaws.

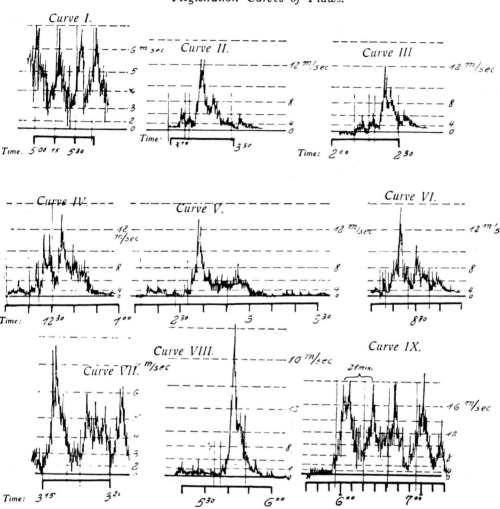

Curve I: Periodic Nature of Flaw.
Curves IV and VI: Exceptionelly pronounced Development
of "Fore" and "After" Runner.

Curves II, III and V: "Long Flaws".
Curve VII: "Fast" Registration of Flaw.
Curve IX: Flaw of long Duration.

Besides the sudden increase and gradual decrease in the strength of the flaws, the socalled *wind periods* are distinctly visible in the above curves. These periodic maxima or oscillations, that re-occur at given *equal* intervals, are evidently subject to some law of Nature; they seem to be caused by certain regular eddy-like formations of *extraordinary size*, the durations of action of which are measured by minutes, not seconds. The dimensions of these elements of turbulence stand in a certain relation to the average strength of the prevailing wind. The horizontal dimensions or extension of the eddy can be calculated from the periodic interval and the average speed of the wind. This periodic behavior of the wind is visible in the registration curves I to IX. For curve I the horizontal extension of the eddy, determined from the speed

135

of the wind and the period of duration of its action, amounts to 4500 meters; for curve IX to 12,600 meters. These measurements do not correspond exactly to the increase in the speed of the wind, or more, correctly, the horizontal extension of the eddy is not always a linear function of this speed but it increases more rapidly than it — the average speed of the wind.

Let me call attention here to the remarkable fact that in a heavy sea the *"big waves"* always roll by in groups of three or five and that also the interval between the groups appears to be always the same, being dependent upon the strength of the wind. May not the formation of these waves, which are distinguished by their size from the average waves, stand perhaps in the closest relation to the afore-mentioned turbulence of the wind? Is it not conceivable that these "big waves," which as all other waves acquire their energy from the air, are related in some way in respect to their periodicity as well as to their size to the wind periods?

With slightly ruffled water very characteristic bright streaks may be noticed, especially on the ocean, which are at approximately equal distances apart. These bright streaks appear to be windless zones, which are caused by the upward movement of the turbulent eddy; whereas its downward movement on striking the water produces the "big waves." As the wind increases in strength the distances between these bright streaks become greater. Are not all these phenomena to be traced to some such periodic system? It would divert our attention too much from the subject to follow up this matter further, but they may afford interesting inquiries for others.

Aside from these periods we recognize the secondary fluctuations, which take place during, that is *"within,"* the former. These phenomena are most pronounced in a strong and apparently steady wind, as indicated by the registration curves. There thus remain only the *flaws,* with the nature and structure of which we should become more familiar.

Meteorologists discriminate between two kinds of flaws, the socalled *"long flaws"* and the *"wind flaws."*

I. The *"long flaws,"* or, for brevity "flaws," are gusts of wind that appear on a calm day or in a light breeze; they spring up suddenly and pass by quickly, being of short duration. The best example of such flaws is offered by light airs on a quiet day, when the fickle wind springs around from all four points of the compass, or, to a more pronounced degree, by the atmospheric disturbances accompanying a thunderstorm, after the passage of which tranquillity is again restored.

II. The *"wind flaws,"* are characterized by a series of wind maxima with the intermediate temporary minima peculiar to the steady wind. These, including their periodicity, have already been discussed.

The *"long flaw"* is constituted as follows:

I. A first fore-runner, which blows in the *opposite* direction to the main flaw.

II. A second fore-runner, which is a weak puff that sets in just before the main flaw and in the same direction as the latter.

III. The main flaw, in which the wind has the direction of the path of the flaw.

IV. An after-runner that follows in the path of the main flaw, but is weaker.

Beauty in Clouds and Water

M. Rosenfeld

The curves II, III, V and VIII of the registrations on page 135 represent such flaws. In the development of a long flaw there is, generally, an interval of comparative tranquillity between the first and second fore-runners and also between the latter and the main flaw. Then the main flaw sets in "suddenly" with its maximum strength, whereupon it subsides gradually. Several minutes later follows the after-runner, a flow conditioned by the principle of continuity, to the effect that the masses of air carried off by the passage of the main flaw must be replaced. This is the general structure of the long flaw, but exceptions occur, where the fore-runner is stronger than the main flaw (cf. curve IV) or the after-runner develops remarkable strength (cf. curve VI).

How much the knowledge of the characteristic peculiarities of the wind may benefit the yachtsman, the experienced skipper surely realizes. In the first place, before every thunderstorm the first fore-runner, the socalled *"reactionary wind,"* may be expected. This can often be quite strong and of considerable duration — a quarter of an hour for example. Therefore, when a thunderstorm is collecting on the western horizon, one should not hasten immediately to the west shore, but first await the east wind that is certain to set in from that direction. After one has had the full benefit of this reactionary fore-runner, one should not be tempted to linger longer in that quarter, for this wind is sure to let up just as *suddenly* as it set in, and, before this occurs, one should have already worked over toward the west, in order to get the benefit of the storm wind before it reaches one's competitors.

After the main flaw has struck the boat with its full strength, it is naturally too late to think of reefing. Generally, this first blast has such an effect on the skipper that he decides on precautionary measures, which are likely to prove fatal at such a critical moment or, in case, they are successfully carried out, are of little avail, as the wind, in the meantime, has subsided and become harmless. The following should be noted: If one has not decided to reef during the wind pauses, which occur between the first and second fore-runners or between the latter and the setting in of the main flaw or storm, one may reckon safely on the gradual subsidence of the wind shortly after the storm has broken loose.

After the main flaw, which may last for five to fifteen minutes, has passed by, the brunt of the storm is broken, but the after-runner should not be overlooked. One must keep in mind that, in spite of the present let up, the after-runner is to be expected under all circumstances, and, before that has passed by, one cannot count on the wind setting in from another quarter. Later, however, one must reckon with an eventual return of the storm and its accompanying disturbances — change of wind, etc.

Now we come to the *wind flaws,* with regard to which there is nothing special to be observed. They are characterized by the highest development of wind strength measured. As mentioned at the beginning of our discussion, they show the same gradual decrease in the strength of the wind, only during much shorter intervals than is the case with the long flaws. Especially in moderate, flawy winds the periodic oscillations, already mentioned above, are more or less pronounced here, the length of the periods increasing with the strength of the wind. For a wind of 5 m/sec. their period is about 15 minutes (cf. curve I, page 135); for a wind of 10 m/sec. it is about 21 minutes (cf. curve IX).

A reference to the lateral extension of the flaw — whether a "long" flaw or a "wind" flaw, should not be omitted. Judging from the intensity of the wind in the different parts of a flaw, as well as from the image that many flaws cast on the water, it is not to be denied that there is often a great similarity between the general form or contour of the flaw and the streamline form. The flaws often appear to have a relatively well rounded off fore edge and to taper gradually more and more as they pass off. This is also to be inferred from the strength of the wind in the different parts of the flaw.

In the following section the wind is treated from the point of view of its local peculiarities from a purely practical standpoint. The first question which every yachtsman puts to himself, when he goes on board his boat on the morning of a race, is: "Will there be wind today?"

This question is best answered from the following points of view:

1. How does the barometer stand? *Every sudden change in the barometer is a sign of wind.* Even during a race the detection of any such change may be of service.

2. In what direction is the air moving in the higher strata of the atmosphere? Is such a movement only local or is the wind observed to have the same direction over the whole firmament? A local movement in the upper strata seldom reaches down to the lower ones, whereas, if the wind has one and the same direction throughout the upper strata and is not at too great an altitude, it will surely work down to the surface of the water sooner or later. In the case, where the clouds are travelling by at great height, the wind will, generally, spring up from the opposite direction on the surface.

3. Of what nature are the clouds? A *uniformly overcast* sky indicates a calm. A *cloudless sky* or single, torn clouds mean wind, which is contrary to current opinion. The appearance, of clouds or mist, later in the day, may indicate wind. We know that the degree of cloudiness has a significant influence on the strength of the wind.

A *clear sky*, as it admits of unhindered radiation, acts in two ways: in the day time it favors the ascensional movement of the air and hence convectional circulation, thereby tending to increase the strength of the wind in the lowest stratum, which concerns us here. At night, due to the cooling of the lower strata, it creates a state of stable equilibrium (in the vertical direction), thereby retarding the convectional circulation and thus withdrawing the air on the surface of the land or water *from the influence of the upper, more rapidly moving strata.* Therefore, the same barometric gradients would indicate a stronger wind on a clear day than on a cloudy one; at night, on the other hand, less wind; and furthermore, the same gradients with a clear sky would give rise at night to much lighter winds than by day, whereas in the day time the relation between the strength of the wind and the gradients remains nearly the same at all times of the day, being subject only to nonperiodic variations.

On the other hand, an *overcast sky* retards radiation, which latter, as observed, promotes convection between the lower and the upper strata; and so it may happen that on a cloudy day there is *wind in the upper strata* and *none below* — a calm on the water.

4. From what quarter may the wind be expected? On the lakes of Upper Bavaria, aside from the peculiar and familiar local shifting of the wind from south through the east to north in the course of the day in fair weather, we may observe that the longer the southerly wind holds in the morning, so much the weaker will be the north-easter, when it sets in later. An east wind with no northerly trend means unsettled weather; it is usually strong but does not last long. And, in general, it holds that any wind which springs up *suddenly* also dies out *suddenly*.

Characteristic of the Bavarian lakes are the following atmospheric conditions: Over the water blue sky, but on the distant horizon clouds — in the east in the north and in the west. The boats becalmed for hours! The question is: "From what quarter may the wind be expected?" This is not difficult to predict. If wind comes at all, it will set in from the direction where the clouds are thickest. The clouds, which have collected on the lake in other quarters, gradually rise and disappear, while from the direction, where the clouds are still assembling, the longed-for "blue streaks" begin to appear on the water. This mutual war of the clouds is a wonderful sight for the spectator and, when in the direction, from which the offensive in the mass of clouds approaches, the air becomes thicker and thicker and finally the characteristic haze appears over the water, then the diagnosis is no longer doubtful.

Let us now consider the influence *of the land* on the wind, and put the question: What influence has the land on the atmosphere? There are two ways in which it may act:

I. *It creates wind by the process either of emission of air from or of suction of air toward it.*

II. *It retards the prevailing wind by the process either of blanketing or of banking up air.*

The property of the land to create wind is to be observed only on fine days and to be attributed to the adjustment of the different temperatures — of the land and water. As every yachtsman knows, if by chance he has been drifting about, becalmed for many hours in the afternoon, he may safely reckon on the well-known "evening breeze," which blows off shore and springs up at the latest the moment the sun disappears below the horizon; similarly, he ought to realize also that the same process takes place in the day time, but in the reverse order or direction.

The property of the land to produce a suction effect or, in other words, the singular circumstance that on calm sunny days, immediately under the land, a light on-shore wind is encountered — the fact that on such days the boats that are directly under the land draw ahead, while only one or two hundred yards off shore there is not a breath of wind — is also to be ascribed to the adjustment of the prevailing temperatures; and this effect is most pronounced, when the difference of temperature between the land and water is greatest, which is the case in the afternoon between one and three o'clock. *On this account the course or start close under the shore is the one to be chosen at midday in sunny, calm weather.*

Briefly, the natural process of the adjustment of the temperatures is as follows:

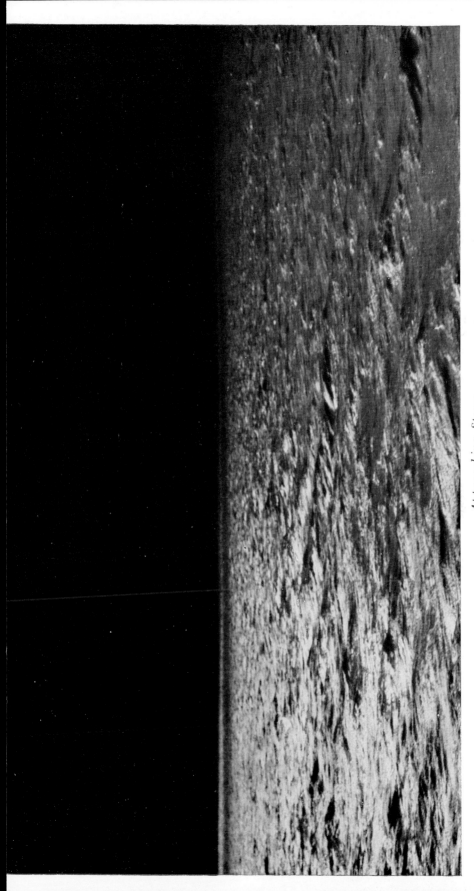

Approaching Storm

In the day time the land warms up more than the water; the warmer air lying over the land ascends and the colder air collected on the water is sucked into its place; thus arises a steady circulation caused by the adjustment of the air, which lasts until the difference in temperature disappears (cf. first of sketches below).

In the evening and at night the reverse process occurs; the land cools off more than the water, and it is over the water that the relatively warmer air rises and the colder air of the adjacent shore streams into the place of the air that has ascended from the water. This process is represented in the second sketch.

The same relation of warmth that exists between water and land also holds between earth and rock and between forest and field. Therefore, on a wooded shore we should expect the *evening breeze* later and then not so strong, whereas the land wind should set in earlier in the evening and stronger under a shore, where fields and rocks (quays) abound. These facts would justify us in not keeping in too close to the land at night, if there are forests on its banks.

On the other hand, *during the day*, stone walls and open fields exercise a strong suction effect; and on calm days, in contradistinction to wooded banks, they give rise to stationary on-shore winds, that extend to definite or sharply defined distances from the shore.

The suction wind can be observed best in the *spring* and *autumn*, because at these seasons the differences in temperature between the land and water are exceptionally great. This wind, which is to be attributed to the action of the sun alone is, therefore, always the more pronounced on that bank which is the more exposed to the direct action of the sun's rays, that is, which is the more inclined or at right angles to their direction of propagation. Inasmuch as this wind may extend to a great distance from the shore, for example, to the middle of a small lake or often even over its whole surface, especially when the bank in question is exposed in a marked degree to the rays of the sun, it is frequently difficult to judge whether one has to do with a suction or with an ordinary wind. The difference between the two winds is that the suction wind *is propagated over the water in the direction opposite to that in which it is blowing.*

This very interesting characteristic may be explained as follows: If one sucks in cigar smoke, the layers of air next to the mouth are the first that are drawn toward it; and as one sucks harder the layers of air farther off begin to move toward the mouth. The propagation of this movement in the air is,

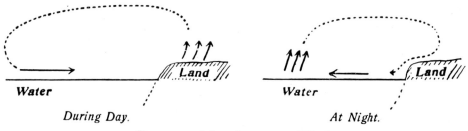

During Day.   At Night.

Property of Land to create Wind.

Curry, Aerodynamics of Sails.

142

therefore, opposite in direction to that of the current of air itself — from the moment the latter arises and continues to increase in intensity.

The reader may now rightly ask the question: "Of what interest is it to the practical yachtsman to know whether the wind in question is diagnosed as a suction or an ordinary wind?" We had already laid stress on the fact that one can predict early in the morning that there will be wind on the one bank in the forenoon, and on the other bank in the afternoon; this knowledge is of importance to the racing man that, on the one hand, the suction wind is generally stationary, or, in other words, may be confined to a given zone for hours, so that one must strive to reach it, but, on the other hand, the outer limits to which this wind extends may be continually shifting somewhat. It often recedes, and one may have to run after it for a while, which is a painful task on its outskirts, where calm prevails. Therefore, if one succeeds in reaching the outer boundary of a suction wind, one should not be satisfied, but then should sail a good distance into it, so that, in case of a retrogression of its front, one may not become suddenly becalmed. Late in the afternoon nothing is gained in running after this suction wind because then it generally ceases all at once. This sudden cessation is a special characteristic of the suction wind.

Another peculiarity of the suction wind is that *it never changes its direction;* it always blows at right angles to the shore. It also shows a marked tendency to spread out over the whole surface of smaller bays. In summer the evening or nocturnal suction wind is stronger than the diurnal suction or solar wind; on the other hand, in spring the former cannot generally be expected, because the temperature of the land seldom sinks below that of the colder water at that season.

Let us consider the few practical cases represented in the sketches on the next page. Sketch A demonstrates that with a regatta course, which is laid out diagonally across a lake, to benefit from the on-shore wind that prevails on its opposite bank, one should not as a rule sail a direct course — from mark to mark — but steer straight across the lake to the wind zone, in which one can travel faster. In spite of the greater distance, one generally reaches the mark sooner. In the reverse case (sketch B), where the on-shore suction wind lies on the bank where we start, we should sail in this streak of wind along the shore to a point opposite the mark on the other bank and then hold straight across the lake.

Sketch C shows a regatta course that runs into a small bay. As the suction wind, represented by the dash lines, is stronger near the shore, we should choose course II, indicated in the sketch, close under the shore. But as we know that the suction wind always blows at right angles to the bank, the shift of the wind caused by the bend in the shore line should not be overlooked, and it would be a great mistake after rounding the mark under the shore to go about onto the other tack, off into the lake, as indicated by course I of sketch. As the suction wind behaves in all smaller bays as indicated in this sketch, the secret of success in many a hard contested race may often be ascribed to advantages gained from a thorough knowledge of its origin and various peculiarities.

We have been speaking of the land with regard to its wind creating properties; let us now turn to its second peculiarity, that of retarding the wind.

Change of Course in Case of Suction Wind.

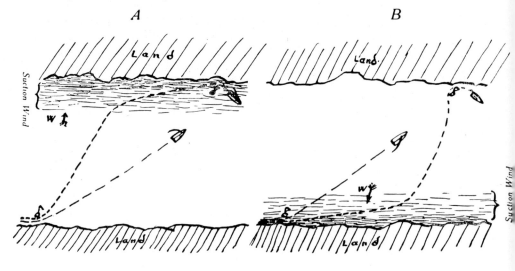

A   B

Change of Direction of Suction Wind in Bay.

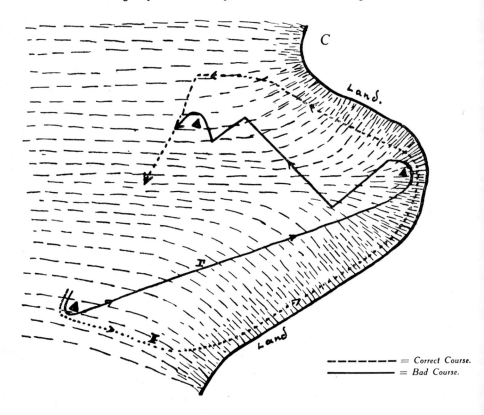

C

- - - - - = Correct Course.
———— = Bad Course.

The blanketing effect of the land is well known to all, and perhaps it need only be added that, generally speaking, this blanketing effect extends to about four times the height of the shore bank and that it increases as we approach the shore. A comparison with the laws of blanketing from boat to boat, already investigated in the section on "Blanketing," will explain also, how it happens that boats that are entirely blanketed by the land are sometimes seen to work ahead with a light contrary wind, that is with an air current, which is opposite to the general direction of the prevailing wind. Experience has also taught us that the extent of the blanketing zone is dependent not only on the height of the obstacle, but also on its nature. For example, a forest standing on a low shore and thus not offering any particularly high obstacle to the passage of the wind, may nevertheless be observed to cast a remarkably long blanketing shadow. Measurements have shown that this shadow extends on an average to 200 yards from the shore. This is to be attributed to the *retardation of the wind* due to the *greater friction* developed in its passage over the crowns of the trees. We have been discussing the off-shore wind.

The second retarding effect occurs with *an on-shore breeze*, that is when the wind blows off the water onto the land. The phenomenon of a reactionary or rebounding wind will probably be familiar to most yachtsmen, that is, they will, at least, have had the experience of being at the mercy of not only the waves but also the wind that rebounds from a wall or stone quay. This retarding effect, which every shore presents to a more or less degree, I had an opportunity to study in the formation of snowdrifts, two photographs, which are reproduced here and on the next page. Every reader, on examining the pictures, will be able to recall such formations, but few will have stopped to consider their cause or origin. The photographs show haystacks, as seen from the side, exposed to the wind, on which snowdrifts have been formed by the storm. We observe that the snow is drifted not close up to the stack but at a distance of about two yards from it, thus forming a deep furrow between it and the stack.

But how is this to be explained? The same process or phenomenon may be observed, when snow, sand or dust is blown up against a wall. The dust or sand settles at a certain distance from the wall and forms heaps, that is, it is precipitated to the ground at that spot, and after a short interval a small heap forms in front of the

Snowdrifts

145

wall, which grows steadily larger. Further, one may recognize from the little particles of dust, which are eddying in the air, that in front of the wall a large eddy is in action, which on the ground is revolving in the direction opposite to the prevailing wind. At the point, where the two currents of air meet, the resultant state of the air is one of comparative rest, and it is at the common or "dead" point that this sand, which has been carried hither by the wind, falls to the ground and collects. It is, moreover, interesting to note that the little heap of sand is just as far away from the wall as the latter is high (cf. the drawings on next page). Furthermore, it may be observed that this small sand heap in front of the wall, which, in turn, presents a new obstacle to the wind, gives rise to the formation of another, but smaller heap at a given distance from the former (cf. drawing B). The angle of inclination the first sand heap forms with the top of the wall amounts to 45°, which is exactly half that the wall itself makes with the ground; the corresponding angle for the second heap is found to be 22.5°, which is again half the angle the first sand heap forms with the top of the wall. We thus see that the extent of action of the eddy is equal to the height of the obstacle, but that the action itself

Snowdrift Due to Action of Eddy

becomes weaker as one recedes from the wall. The upward draft of the eddy in front of a wall is manifested in a most drastic manner, when women find themselves by chance within its confines. Relentlessly the air current catches the skirts of the surprised victims and lifts them, umbrella-like, over their heads. A painful experience for those not familiar with aerodynamics!

The above experiments confirmed the following: With an on-shore wind that

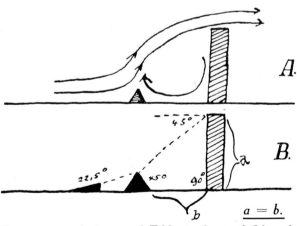

Formation and Action of Eddy in front of Obstacle.

extends over large areas, as those subjected to the influence of a cyclonic low, or, in other words, with a wind that is not of local character, such as that caused by the adjustment of temperatures over land and water, one should never run too near under the shore, because there the reactionary or rebounding wind extends to a distance from the shore of at least that of the height of the bank.

These observations led to the following experiment, which I will not withhold from the reader, as it is of interest from the point of view of the impenetrability of sail duck and of the resistance of the air in general: On the same day that I photographed the snowdrifts I placed a wire grating with its meshed surface at right angles to the wind on an open field and, upon observing it the next day, I found that the snow had drifted up in front of the grating, whose meshes were of the size of one's fist, exactly as it had done in the case of the haystack or, in fact, any compact obstacle, the main drift being at a distance of the height of the grating from it. I may recall here the peculiar action of the grating often used in a stove or fireplace for safety's sake; it lets hardly any heat into the room. Just as a thin hedge offers complete shelter to the wind, so is the manner, in which the snow, blown up against the wire grating, drifts, a further proof:

I. Of the absolute impenetrability to air of any duck or cloth, however thin it may be; for if a coarse grating lets the wind through scarcely at all, and if, for example, a sail made of surgical gauze permits the passage of air through it only under relatively high pressure, then the penetration of wind through ordinary sail duck must be entirely out of the question.

II. Of the fact that the total resistance to the wind of the grating is not that offered by the sum alone of the actual surface areas of the various wires of which the grating is composed but that it is much greater than that sum. In other words, translated into sailing language: Several halyards, arranged side by side along the mast, offer a total resistance to the air that is not merely that of the surfaces of these wires or ropes, but each rope produces by the peculiarity of its reciprocal influence perhaps more than double the resistance of its actual surface area.

But to return to our observations on the influence on the wind, the change in its direction, caused by the land. In the preceding we have been considering the influence of the land *on the strength of the wind;* we shall now investigate its influence *on the direction of the wind.*

The property of the land of influencing the direction of the wind in its neighborhood, causing it to veer, is indeed a phenomenon frequently observed. With a wind

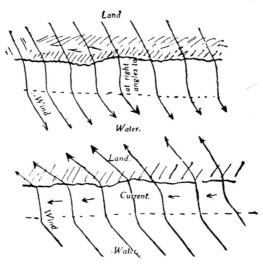

Influence of Land on Direction of Wind.

147

that blows obliquely off the shore, the wind near the land veers in such a manner that it is directed more at right angles to the shore line. In other words, the nearer one approaches the land, the more does the wind tend to blow directly off it (cf. the first of the drawings on page 147). One can make use of this veering of the wind under the shore to advantage on beating to windward by hugging the shore, i. e. by taking short tacks toward and close under the land and then longer ones directly under and along it, while farther out one is doomed to beat dead to windward.

An on-shore wind veers in the same manner as it approaches the land, if it is blowing obliquely to the shore; it is directed more at right angles to the shore line, though, after it has reached the land, it gradually assumes its original direction. Here the veering of the wind more at right angles to the shore, as we approach the land, has the effect that close under the land the water forms a current parallel to the bank in the direction of the component of the prevailing wind along the shore — a certain amount of the energy of the wind has, as it were, been conveyed to the water (cf. the second drawing). Under certain circumstances it is therefore advisable here to avoid the immediate vicinity of the land.

To summarize briefly:

With winds blowing diagonally on or off shore.

In beating to windward:

With the wind *blowing* off the shore, hug the land.

With the wind blowing on the shore be guided by the direction and strength of the current of water along the bank.

On other courses;

With an off-shore wind, avoid the proximity of the land on account of its blanketing effect.

With an on-shore breeze, also avoid running too close under the land, on account of the retarding or rebounding effect of the wind near the shore, which tends to form an air cushion.

On hot, calm days:

Run close up under the land, especially at midday; there a suction wind may be expected, caused by the adjustment of temperatures; and

Toward evening:

Also hug the land (unless it be a wooded shore), that you may take advantage of the off-shore evening breeze.

The Water

Although this subject does not, strictly speaking, belong in the treatise it should nevertheless not be omitted from the realm of observation of the thoughtful yachtsman, as it certainly will be useful to him to become better

M. Rosenfeld

Start of International Class Groups, Larchmont, N. Y.

acquainted with the element to which he stands indirectly in such intimate relations.

Waves are phenomena of friction at the surface of contact of two fluid media. The wind which blows over the water is retarded by friction, while the energy withdrawn from it is transformed into eddies. These eddies, as they hasten over the water, burrow into its surface and form wave troughs. The greater the strength and the extent of the wind over the water, the larger and stronger will be the eddies developed and the higher and longer the waves thereby formed. All waves are thus to be regarded as generated by eddies, which are, in turn, caused by the friction of the air on the surface of the water. In the case of large waves or ocean billows, our leading authorities differ on one point; some are of the opinion that calm reigns in their troughs, the wind or eddies acting only on their crests, while others maintain that the eddies reach down into the troughs. I am inclined to the belief that the eddies are also active in the troughs of the large waves — from the rippling of the surface of the water that may be observed even at the bottom of the trough (cf. also the photographs of the desert on next page). It is quite remarkable also, how easily gulls glide over the waves and sweep down into their troughs, and how relatively poorly they soar over the land; one gains the impression that they are able to take advantage of the ascending currents of the eddies. The formation of eddies and the creation of waves caused by the action (friction) of the former, appear, as already stated, on the surface of contact between all fluid and similar media; their action can, for example, be beautifully observed on a sandy beach, after the waves have rolled back into the sea. Similarly, as between water and sand, the *tiny* sand waves on the dunes are formed by the action of the wind. The desert presents a remarkably beautiful picture, with large, far stretching billows and neat, curling wavelets on the billows themselves. A picture, as it were, of a sea grown stiff and rigid! And here also wavelets may be observed in the troughs of the sand waves.

Similarly, the process of eddy formation also occurs between two strata of air of different temperature or density; the socalled "cirrus or lambs' fleece" clouds are nought but phenomena that are to be ascribed to this process. Professor Ahlborn, who has investigated the nature of water and its eddying action by means of under-water photography has made the following interesting observations: He confirms the fact, already established (also photographically) by Professor Morey of Paris, that the particles of a wave swing in elliptical paths; the vertical or minor axes of these ellipses become shorter with the depth, until, at a depth of about one hundred times the height of the wave, the particles oscillate in approximately horizontal planes (cf. the photograph on page 152).

Let us now investigate the waves produced by the passage of the hull of a boat. When a craft is forced through the water, it produces, according to the speed developed, smaller or larger waves. The more favorable the boat's form the less the driving force required for her propulsion, and hence the less the amount of energy imparted to the water and expended in the formation of waves. *We are able, therefore, to judge of the merits of the hull of any particular boat by the size of the waves generated.*

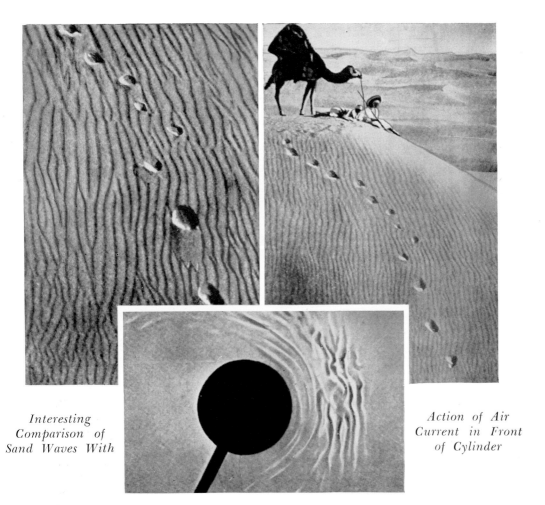

Interesting Comparison of Sand Waves With

Action of Air Current in Front of Cylinder

On observing any craft in motion, we can distinguish between the following forms of waves: First, the familiar *bow waves,* which, according to the lines of the boat's hull, assume a more or less parabolic form; they are formed by the impact of two masses of water — of opposite direction of flow. Secondly, the *stern waves,* which *run obliquely to the direction of the course* and intersect the bow waves at given distances from the boat; according to the speed of the boat the crest of such a wave assumes either a straight front or one that is inclined somewhat forward at its outer end — the more the greater the speed of the boat. These waves are formed by the eddies on the bottom of the boat that are directed upward. Finally, there appear at *right angles to the course* especially clearly defined stern waves, which follow the boat at given constant distances; these intersect or interfere with the obliquely directed stern waves at a considerable distance from the boat. Their height decreases with their distance astern. They are to be attributed to the striving tendency of the water to fill up the void space — the water displaced, caused by the passage of the boat.

151

Elliptic Paths Described by Particles of Water in Interior of Wave During Half Period of Oscillation

The familiar mounting of a craft at high speed, which motor boats show to an especially marked degree, is due to the fact that the bow wave is formed farther aft under the bow and thus lifts the forward part of the boat, while the first stern wave that follows the boat at right angles to her keel is also shifted farther aft; as the water does not succeed in filling in the void space under the stern of the boat — in replacing the water displaced by her passage — in time, the first stern wave will lie no longer under the stern of the boat, but behind it, and consequently she will settle or sink somewhat deeper aft.

Observations of the stern waves that follow the boat at right angles to her course have disclosed the interesting fact that, with respect to their *length*, they are entirely independent of the form and size of the boat, *but that they stand in a certain relation to her speed*, whereas their *height* is determined by the form and especially the draught of the boat; in other words, the distance between the crests of these waves — their wave length — increases for *all boats in the same ratio as the speed*. These waves thus offer a most practical method for the determination of the speed of a boat, in that one has only to estimate the distance from crest to crest in order to be able to calculate, according to the following table, which is based on the formula:

Photo 2. Lines of Force at Speed v = 66.4 cm./sec.

Waves Formed by Model Boat of 460 mm. Length

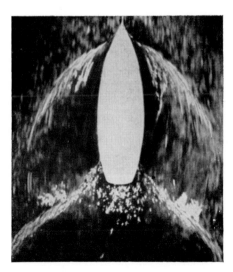 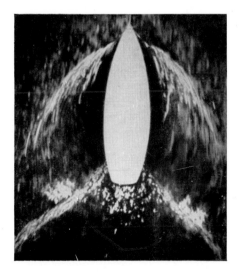

Photo 3. Stereoscip Pictures of Waves and Lines of Flow on Surface of Water at Speed v = 92 cm. /sec.

153

$$v = 1.25 \ \sqrt{\text{wave length}}$$

for her speed:

Wave length in meters	Speed in kilometers per hour
0.20	1.8
0.65	3.6
1.43	5.4
2.55	7.2
4.00	9.0
5.75	10.8
7.80	12.6
10.20	14.4
12.90	16.2
16.00	18.0
18.40	19.8

Practically one need only note the following three pairs of numbers which are easy to remember and between which one may easily interpolate:

1½ meters wave length	5½ kilometers per hour
2½ " " "	7 " " "
4 " " "	9 " " "

Further, in regard to the waves, the following results of *towing experiments* may be of interest to the yachtsman. Such experiments are of great value in diagnosing a boat, but are seldom undertaken, unfortunately. With a motor boat one can tow yachts of similar size and type at about one and the same speed and, by comparison, determine the most favorable form of hull (in upright position) by means of a spring balance or scales. For example, if one yacht can be towed a few kilograms easier than another, but, if at the same time she is always easily beaten by the latter, even in a light wind, that is, in approximately upright position, the conclusion is to be drawn that the difference in the merits of the two boats is to be sought in the rig; on the other hand, the diagnosis allows of a determination as to whether for a yacht, which is, for example, inclined to a lee helm on the one tack, the mistake in symmetry lies in her sails or rigging (for instance mast hanging to one side) or in her hull. Only by this method is it possible to confirm whether the hull is warped or the fin bent or twisted, as such asymmetries are not always perceptible to the naked eye. The greater the speed at which the yacht is towed, the more pronounced will be also any abnormal pressure on her tiller, which would localize the defect in the fin and not in the sails or rigging. For example, if the fin is twisted or warped in the one direction or the other, this would be manifested in the tendency of the yacht to deviate from the straight course, provided she is being towed in an upright position; but if she shows an inclination to luff or to fall off more on the one tack than on the other, when slightly heeled, this generally indicates a warped hull. If the whole fin is bent toward one side, the boat will lie awry in the water, and the trained eye will detect the defect in spite of the fact that the mast may be straight.

A further question:

At what distance astern should a tender be towed that the speed of one's yacht may be retarded as little as possible? Naturally, this does not directly concern the racing man, but even he may be placed in a situation, with a tender in tow, where he cannot well avoid having a little scrap

154

with another boat. The answer to this question is simple. The tender is towed with least resistance or tension on painter, when it is descending from the crest of the second stern wave that follows the yacht (cf. the annexed drawings). It is obvious that for a boat with a long overhang the first stern wave may lie under the overhang, in which case the tender must be given just so much painter that it rests on the *first visible* stern wave, as indicated in the second drawing. As to whether the reason for the easier towing of the tender is to be attributed to the fact that it is, as it were, always

Sonder Boat. Tender

At what Distance astern should Tender be towed.

descending from the crest of the wave, or because the stern wave formed by the tender itself coincides with the second stern wave of the yacht, we shall not attempt to decide here. At all events the exact amount of tension on the painter of the tender and the variation of this tension according to the length given it are probably unknown to most yachtsmen, and on this account some results on towing experiments performed by me and others may be of interest and instructive. From the diagram on the next page it is evident that the pull of the tender is proportional not alone to the length given the painter but that it varies according to the relative position of the tender on the wave; it is, for example, less, when the tender is descending from the crest of the third wave than from that of the fourth in the same relative position to crest. *The oscillatory variation of the tension or pull is a direct proof that the pull exerted by a boat in tow depends upon her position on the (stern) wave in question and that it is not, as one might suppose, to be attributed to the suction action of the towing yacht.* How great the difference in the pull of a tender that is correctly towed and one that is made fast to the yacht with a painter of arbitrary length is demonstrated by the curves of the diagram. When the motor boat was running at a speed of 10 kilometers an hour, the pull varied from 9 to 22 kilograms.

Finally, a few words on the *temperature of the water.*

In summer the water of lakes is warmer with an on-shore breeze than with an off-shore wind. Especially in fair weather this difference is considerable, amounting often to 6° C.; and the reason for this is that the upper layers of the water, which are warmed more by the sun, are blown by the wind toward the lee-ward shore and accumulate there. This gives rise to a convectional circulation of the water, in that the colder water of the deeper layers flows toward the windward shore and rises there to the surface, replacing the upper warmer layers that have been carried over to the opposite shore.

In *judging the temperature of water* one should keep in mind that mere estimates are most unreliable and always only relative, inasmuch as one compares the warmth of the water with the surface temperature of one's body. For example, if one gets wet to the skin or the air is cool or the wind fresh, water, which felt cold when the sun was shining, will seem luke warm; the uninitiated are, therefore, very apt to be deceived by such comparisons.

PART II

Racing Tactics

RACING TACTICS

In the ensuing chapters the handling of the large and the small boat is treated simultaneously, without further reference as to which is meant, it being taken for granted that this may be clear to the reader. It would also take too much space to enumerate here the fundamental principles of yacht racing, and we shall, therefore, confine our treatment of the present subject chiefly to matters less familiar to the yachtsman. It may, however, often be necessary to elucidate certain subjects that may be more or less familiar to the reader, that he may understand better the ensuing subject matter treated.

For those, to whom the resultant effect produced by the various forces acting on the sails and the hull of a boat may not be familiar — for example, how it is possible for a boat to beat to windward, — let the following brief explanation of this remarkable phenomenon be offered:

The *annexed* diagram represents a boat on the wind on the starboard tack. The direction and strength of the wind are represented graphically by the line A B. According to the parallelogram of forces this (resultant) force may be resolved into two component forces, the larger one A C, which acts parallel, to and along the sail, without producing any other effect than a certain amount of surface friction, and may thus be neglected, — and the smaller one A D acting at right angles to it. Although this latter component acts at right angles to the sail, due to the relative position of the sail to the keel of the boat, it is directed somewhat forward: it can, therefore, be resolved into two components the larger one A E acting at right angles to the keel and the smaller one A F that is directed forward in the direction of the keel or path of the boat. The lateral plane of the boat, that is, its hull and fin or centerboard, offers so

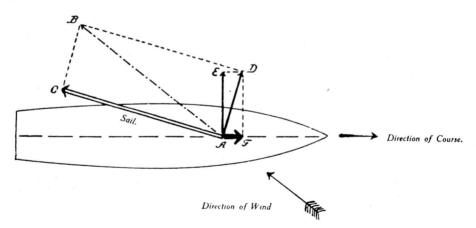

Graphical Explanation for "Beating to Windward".

great a resistance to this lateral component *A E,* that it is almost neutralized. There remains, therefore, only the other component *A F* acting in the direction of the keel, and this is the force that drives and is, in fact, sufficient to drive the boat forward. The socalled "drift" or sliding off of the boat is due to the fact that the resistance, the lateral plane offers the lateral component force *A E* is always somewhat smaller than the latter. The drift or amount of drift of a boat depends upon:

1. The general form of the hull (lateral plane).

2. The direction of the path or course with respect to that of the wind. The higher the boat is sailed on the wind, the greater the drift.

3. The speed. The greater the speed, the greater the number of particles of water that come in contact with the hull and fin or centerboard of the boat and thus the greater their resistance to the lateral component *A E* and hence the less the drift. On the wind the drift varies from 3° to 10° according to the form and size of the lateral plane of the boat.

The Author's 20 sq. m. Racer "Aero"
Winner of Over 200 First Prizes

Before the Start

Let us imagine ourselves in the position of a skipper, to whom a strange boat is entrusted to sail in a race the next day, and consider how he can become quickly acquainted with the boat and get her into trim.

We are already familiar with the manner in which the sail — mainsail — is to be tended, and it is necessary only from a practical point of view to call attention to the following: The trimming of a sail is generally understood by most would-be yachtsmen to be identical with a constant hauling out of the sail on the spars, with the fatal result that after a short time the graceful convex curve of its leech gradually disappears and finally becomes concave; the sail is supposed to be trimmed, but it is, in fact, so mistrimmed, that it can never be made to set properly again.

The worst mistake that can result from such "trimming" of a sail is that its fore, lower third, especially along the boom, becomes so stretched that it sets like a board, losing its entire arching, as indicated in the accompanying sketch. If we examine the average sail from the stern of the boat, looking up close to the boom obliquely over its surface toward the mast and gaff, we shall be able to observe that its fore, lower surface is as "flat as a board" — without the least arching; this is caused by the constant stretching out of the foot of the sail along the main boom, whereby the diagonal from the yaws of the gaff to the clew of the after foot of the sail is likewise stretched to the utmost. As a result, the other — after, upper — portion of the sail tends to sag off to leeward, especially the leech, and the battens describe the characteristic S curves (cf. annexed sketch). This is particularly pronounced, when the sail is not suffi-

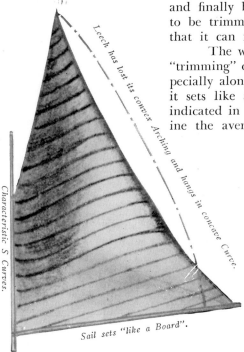

Leech has lost its convex Arching and hangs in concave Curve.

Characteristic S Curves.

Sail sets "like a Board".

Sail Mistrimmed by Overstretching Sail on Spars

ciently *peaked*. It is on this account that the rope in the luff of the sail is, generally, replaced by a wire rope, and we could recommend, for similar reasons, inserting a wire rope in the foot of the sail.

As a general rule we may advise every yachtsman to haul out his sail on the spars only before or during a race and on all other occasions to keep the foot of the sail loose or at most only "hand taut." *No harm is ever done* by stretching a sail apparently *too little* on the boom and gaff; should it become wet, it is then not necessary to loosen the sail on the spars, as it will shrink just enough to insure a good set.

The Marconi or Bermudian mainsail can be trimmed by proper *adjustment* of the stays that run fore and aft from the top and lower part of the mast; it must, of course, be possible to adjust these stays accordingly, to lengthen or to shorten them to a considerable extent; this can be accomplished most readily by running each stay through a block on or, better, below the deck and attaching its free end to a pulley that can be manipulated from the cockpit; in this manner the stay can be tautened or loosened at will, readily and to any extent. Upon setting the jib, which will cause the mast to incline somewhat forward, the head stay from the top of the mast will, for example, have to be drawn taut, as otherwise the top of the mast and also the upper part of the mainsail will rake or hang too much aft.

With regard to the deviation of the mast from the vertical, we have already observed that the mast should be either vertical or inclined only somewhat aft. It should never be trimmed much aft or, more correctly, be given a pronounced rake; * it is to be regretted that this bad habit has evidently become a fashion in certain European yachting centers and is often to be found in the designs of yacht constructors, who evidently from lack of original ideas for the lines of the hull hope to win the approval of the layman for their designs by the use of strange curves for the mast.

I wish to call brief attention here to the various advantages and disadvantages of the mast that is stepped vertically or with a slight inclination aft and that with a pronounced rake, as also to state at the outset that I have trimmed the masts of yachts of most various types of craft with the result that in every case, where the mast originally had a pronounced rake the sailing qualities of the boat were improved materially by inclining it more forward.

Certain slight advantages of the raking mast are the following:

1. The boats are "said" to stamp less in a heavy sea, due to the fact that the Marconi mast, which in its upper part acts more or less like a whip, does not swing forward of the vertical, so that the pressure (weight) of the mast upon the hull of the boat is brought to rest more on the broader stern than on the narrower and thus more sensitive bow.

2. The mainsail, provided it has no battens, will set or hang better on the raking mast. In the case of certain types of smaller boats, where the sail is held in form by long traverse battens that extend from luff to leech, this advantage of the raking mast does not come into consideration.

3. With boats that have a pronounced lee helm this fault can be rectified *somewhat* by giving the mast a rake, should it prove impossible to correct it otherwise — by stepping the mast farther aft.

* "Rake" is used here in the sense "inclination aft."

The main advantages of a vertical mast or one inclined only somewhat aft are the following:

1. The center of effort of the sail plan is somewhat higher; this is of advantage in light airs, whereas the weather helm that results from an increase in the velocity of the wind is favorably affected, that is, diminished.

2. The support of the mast by the shrouds and especially by the head stays, which run here at larger angles to the mast, is more effective.

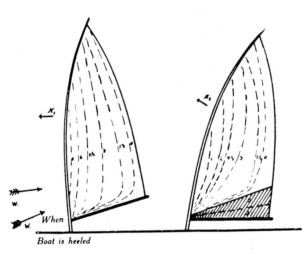

Drive developed with vertical and raking Mast.

Boat is heeled

3. The chief secret of the vertical mast or one inclined somewhat forward is the following: On the assumption that the maximum driving force is attained in the mainsail, when the wind strikes the luff of the sail, that is, the mast itself, at right angles, the latter should be inclined about 4° forward (when the boat is not heeled), since the wind is directed that amount upward in the lower layers of the air (cf. Part I). In this position the wind strikes the luff of the mainsail at right angles, and a maximum drive is thus developed by its arched surface. On the other hand, in the case of a raking mast, the resultant force K_2 acting in the belly of the sail is directed somewhat *upward* and not directly forward (cf. accompanying sketches).

These unfavorable conditions become even more pronounced, when the boat is heeled. Here the wind strikes and passes over the sail more from below — more parallel to the mast and at right angles to the boom. By inclining the mast somewhat forward, we are able to rectify this error to a certain degree at least, thereby causing the wind to pass over the mast rather than over the boom into the sail (cf. first sketch). It is for this reason that most sail makers give the seams of a sail a *marked upward* slope toward the leech, recognizing that, the farther the boat is heeled, the more upward is the wind directed as it passes over the sail. Aside from the fact that in the case of a raking mast the boom hangs lower and lower, as the mainsail is payed off, and that not only the boom but the lower part of the sail along this spar, as indicated by the shaded triangle in the second sketch, is thus blanketed by the hull of the boat, we observe that the farther the boat is heeled, the more pronounced is the blanketing of the sail by the hull. We have already called attention to the fact that a great advantage is gained, when the mainsail is cut in such a manner, that the boom is higher at its outer end than next to the mast and not, as is so often the case with raking masts, horizontally or even lower. The curves of equal pressure or the socalled "isobars" for the mainsail show that even in the erect position of the boat there is almost no driving force in the lower part of the sail, especially toward its leech (cf. chapter on "The Distribution of Pressure" in Part I). It is evident that this area of minimum drive increases, the more the boat is heeled.

Moreover, the eddies on the lee side of the sail undergo, as we have seen in Part I, a change that affects the driving force unfavorably, when the mast is given a rake.

4. Dead before the wind it is not the actual area of the mainsail but its projection on the plane at right angles to the direction of the wind that determines the drive of the sail, this area and hence the resulting drive decreasing, as the rake of the mast increases. The mainsail on the raking mast also tends to fall back midships and must be held out in its proper position by some device applied to the boom; this is absolutely necessary in light airs.

Measurements of the up-drive developed by an aeroplane model with wing I at right angles to the body and wing II inclined 23° backward on either side of it (cf. *annexed* drawings) were made by Professor Prantdl in the wind tunnel at Göttingen; they gave the following significant results:

Wing I		Wing II	
Angle of opposition	Up-drive	Angle of opposition	Up-drive
11.6°	133 units	11.6°	122.1 units
14.5°	142.7 "	14.5°	128.8 "

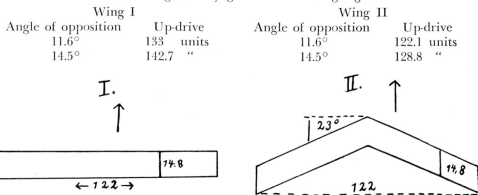

Wing of Aeroplane Model
at right angles to Body and inclined 23° backward

The aeroplane with the wing at right angles to the body may be compared to the boat with vertical mast — of no rake; that with wing inclined backward to the boat with raking mast. Although the resistance of the former is somewhat greater, the up-drive developed by the wing at right angles to the body is, as we see, about 11% greater than that of the inclined or raking wing.

Let us now return to the investigation of the boat we are to sail in the race; we proceed as follows:

The mainsail should be given a certain arching or belly, varying at the point of greatest depth (measured from the straight line from the mast to the leech of the sail) from 1/20 to 1/12 of the length of that line inversely as the strength of the wind; this can be effected by a proper adjustment of the various battens in the sail.

We first ascertain, whether the boat has a lee or a weather helm and to what degree; this serious fault can be corrected more or less in the following manner:

A weather helm is *diminished*   A weather helm is *increased*

I. Through an alteration of the *sails*
by

(a) Increasing the size or surface area of the jib.

(a) Decreasing the size of the jib.

(b) Decreasing the size of the mainsail.

(b) Increasing the size of the mainsail.

(c) Setting the jib farther forward (on deck).

(c) Setting the jib farther aft.

(d) Replacing a gaff by a Marconi or Bermudian rig.

(d) Replacing a Marconi or Bermudian by a gaff rig.

(e) Giving the mainsail less belly.

(e) Giving the mainsail more belly.

II. Through an alteration of the *mast*
by

(a) Stepping the mast farther forward.

(a) Stepping the mast farther aft.

(b) Inclining the mast more forward.

(b) Increasing the rake of the mast.

III. Through an alteration of the *lateral plane*
by

(a) Hanging the centerboard farther aft.

(a) Hanging the centerboard farther forward.

(b) Pulling up the centerboard somewhat — on the wind.

(b) Letting the centerboard down as far as it will go.

(c) Shifting the crew farther aft.*

(c) Shifting the crew farther forward.*

(d) Sailing the boat in an upright position.

(d) Sailing the boat more or less heeled.

Should the boat be properly balanced, having a lee helm in light airs and a more pronounced weather helm as the wind increases, we should then see, whether she sails equally well on both tacks. This can be ascertained most readily by racing the boat with another of the same type or size. It is sometimes the case that the sails have to be trimmed differently on the two tacks. If we observe that, in racing the boat, she beats to windward especially well under a certain trim of the sails, then we should note their position exactly, by taking bearings, for example, of the boom on deck or by some other simple device, that we may be able to trim the sails in that most favorable position, when racing under similar wind and weather conditions. We should also observe, whether the boat has the *same* lee or weather helm on both tacks; any variation should be investigated at once, the cause sought and, if possible, the

* Small boats can often be steered or properly balanced alone by shifting the live ballast fore or aft; in some cases they may actually be sailed to windward shifting from tack to tack, without the tiller being touched.

fault rectified; such tests can be made best by towing the boat behind a motor launch, to conform whether the cause lie in the hull or the rigging.

We should then determine under what conditions — strength of wind, etc., the largest jib we have at our disposal can be used to *advantage in windward work,* confirming at the same time whether the jib sheet reeving eye is at the proper place on deck — it is generally too far in. In the latter test we should be guided by the following principles: The position of the eye fore and aft should be such, that the foot of the jib can be trimmed so taut, that the wind flows upward off the sail. It should be placed well out toward the railing — so far that the jib begins to shiver, when the mainsail is full and drawing. To determine this point on deck, we luff the boat up more and more and watch both sails. Backwind should be avoided in the mainsail, if possible; this can be effected in the case of large jibs by hauling in the main sheet somewhat more than the jib sheet, which is seldom detrimental to larger yachts. We have already called attention to the importance of a correct cooperation of the jib and mainsail in Part I, where it was shown that the total driving force may be increased by 30 to 50%. For that reason I recommend an adjustable reeving eye for the jib sheet, that could be set more forward or aft and farther in or out on deck according to the prevailing wind and weather conditions; such a device offers no serious technical difficulties.

We next determine how high the boat can be sailed on the wind, whether she may be pressed and how close the main sheet may be trimmed in. Generally speaking, the main sheet may be hauled in so close on larger yachts, that the boom hangs just over the corner of the stern; this, of course, depends on the beam of the boat.

The modern yacht or smaller racing craft can be sailed extremely high on the wind; the main boom may be taken in almost midship without impeding her speed. The extraordinarily close trimming in of the mainsail on the smaller boat, for example, the German 22 qm. racer, may seem unnatural especially to the beginner, and it is universally supposed to be detrimental to her speed; this is not, however, the case.

The common error committed by most, even experienced skippers — especially those who claim a certain feeling for their boats — is that they ease the main sheet somewhat, in order not to "press her;" the result is that the mainsail is never given a good full. Upon analyzing this case theoretically, we shall be surprised at the result. According to the principle of the parallelogram of forces, the force that drives the boat forward may be increased perhaps 10% upon easing the main sheet somewhat and bearing off accordingly; on the other hand, the driving force can be increased 30% or more, if we trim in the main sheet as close as possible and fall off on that *same* course, as we thereby increase the angle at which the wind strikes the sail by about $5°$; this is confirmed by the system of polar curves for the different angles of opposition in Part I. We may also observe that on the wind the main sheet should always be made fast in lee, in order to avoid an unnecessary twisting of the mainsail, which is most harmful, and that its free end should rather not run through a block on deck but pass directly from the main boom to the man on the sheet, as it is possible only to feel the various forces acting on the sail, when these are conveyed directly — in the direction of their action.

On the other hand, a light jib sheet can be highly recommended for light winds, as it can be replaced readily and quickly by a heavier one, even when the boat is not on the wind. It is indispensable in racing, as the tendency of the jib to fall in is greatly diminished, the sail retaining its proper set — the belly that is so essential in light airs.

Another important matter is, how high should the mainsail be set? We know from experience that under no conditions should it be hoisted too high. I have investigated this matter empirically and confirmed beyond doubt that, when the main boom is set too high, the boat invariably sails worse, even in light airs, and especially on the wind. The reason for this is that, on the one hand, the eddies on the lee side of the mainsail are disturbed by the presence of the jib, when the latter is lower than the mainsail, and on the other hand, the favorable influence exerted by the jib on the upper part of the mainsail is diminished — the more, the higher the latter is hoisted. High set sails tend also to make a boat very unsteady. This can be illustrated by the following experiment: We shove a model boat forward by placing the hand on her mast; she will glide smoothly through the water when the shove is imparted to the lower part of the mast, but she will move unsteadily — in zigzags and off her course — when it is brought to act higher up — toward the top of the mast. We also know from experience that the higher the mainsail is set, the more the boat will slide off.

We may observe the following on the *tending of the centerboard and the rudder*. Should a boat have an extreme weather helm, pull up the center-board somewhat, even on the wind, and note how it will affect her. This causes the center of the lateral plane to wander farther aft and thus tends to reduce her weather helm. This test should be made with the greatest care, as only the experienced yachtsman is able to judge, whether the reduced surface of the centerboard still suffices to keep the boat from sliding off too much.

We can start a boat in light airs quicker on all courses by pulling up her centerboard for a few seconds; the wetted surface of the boat is thereby reduced to at least *one half* its normal surface. The boat will then begin to move at once with the slightest puff of wind; whereas she would otherwise just begin to get started by the time the puff had passed by. I have often sailed races in light airs, where the temporary pulling up of the centerboard upon every puff or breath of air was so universal, that the noise caused by the whole fleet making this manoeuvre and the ensuing one of letting down the board could be heard to a great distance.

The rudder with an *adjustable* or sinkable blade, which we should highly recommend to be made of hard aluminum, is quite universal on all smaller types of boat and has, naturally, advantages over the ordinary rudder or that with a stationary blade. The blade should, however, never be let down deeper than is essential for steering the boat. The more it can be pulled up, the faster the boat will sail, as not only the surface friction is diminished, but also a greater steering effect, with less impediment to speed, can be attained by the more horizontally extended surface of the blade with its correspondingly longer lever arm. A further advantage of this type of rudder over that with the stationary blade, that is of no small moment, is that the latter, due to its long fore edge, offers a much greater resistance to the water. During the start, however, the blade should be immersed somewhat deeper, as sharp turns and sudden changes of course may be required at any moment.

The distribution of the live ballast or crew. The first question is, on what lines should the boat sail? We recommend as the first test for this purpose to watch the boat from the shore with her full equipment and crew or live ballast on board, letting her sail by several times. Then go aboard the boat and steer her on the wind, as it is on this course that it is easiest to determine her proper trim, and shift the live ballast fore or aft, until you feel that the boat is correctly trimmed or balanced. It is often instructive for the skipper to go aft and observe the flow of water under the stern of the boat; of course, one of the crew should be sent forward, that the longitudinal trim of the boat may not be disturbed. It should be noted first, whether the boat, when on an even keel, is sailing on the lines on which she was designed, and secondly, whether the flow of water corresponds to those lines, that is, whether the water line itself is sharp, tapering to a point aft. If it is blunt or round or not under but at the stern of the boat, where it can assume a rectangular form, then we should note, whether by heeling the boat or shifting one of the crew farther forward the flow can be improved; if this is possible, then the proper trim can be maintained, in the latter case, by recalling the man sent forward and assigning him a position just as much farther aft as the helmsman will have to move forward to reach his seat at the tiller. When the proper trim has finally been determined, then it is of great importance to ascertain, how the boat will behave, when one or two men are sent forward to work on deck. Many boats are little affected either by a temporary shifting of the crew or by the commotion caused thereby, whereas others, especially smaller boats,* are most sensitive and lose their whole headway, even when the man on the jib goes on the fore deck. In the latter case the best way of avoiding the evil is to send the man who is to hoist the sail well aft, while the man on the jib is busy on deck.

Our next problem is to investigate the *"momentum"* of the boat which, upon sudden turns depends chiefly on the sharpness of her keel — its fore edge. We can then judge, whether the boat should be steered steadily or not; similarly we should note, to what degree the boat loses her headway on a sudden change of course, so that we may sail her accordingly on shifting tacks or on rounding marks. We can test this by steering the boat first rather freely and then more and more steadily and observing whether there is any change in speed. The "momentum" or headway a yacht is capable of retaining depends, aside from the general form of her under body, upon her *weight*. It may be of interest to consider how weight, in general, influences the speed of a boat. Should she be built as light as possible or not? This is a question that is never answered with any degree of assurance and probably will not be definitely settled for years to come. In general, it is assumed that "the lighter the boat the faster," but it is often the case, strange to say, that the heavier boat is faster than the lighter one of the same design; we might, therefore, conclude that a boat may be both *"too light"* and *"too heavy"* or, in

* Especially the scows.

167

other words, that there should be a certain definite weight for every class or type of boat. This is more or less confirmed by the fact that the same boat can be faster in light airs on one day with a crew of three and the next with only two. The explanation for this is, I think, to be sought not in the strength of the wind but in the *wind itself*. On comparing the behavior or course of a light boat with that of a heavy one in a *flawy wind*, we may call attention to the following characteristics of the two boats: the *light boat* starts somewhat quicker but loses her headway sooner and then lies dead on the water. On the other hand, the *heavy boat* possesses the ability of storing up more momentum, due to her greater weight, during the passage of a flaw and then of spending that surplus energy after the flaw has passed by; she thus retains her headway longer and is thereby enabled to glide through the ensuing calm or soft spot and perhaps into the next streak of wind beyond it, whereas the light boat cannot reckon on such good luck. The courses of the two boats are represented graphically in the diagrams below. We may call attention here to the analogous case of a sled or toboggan on a run; the sled with a heavy man will take longer to get started than the one with a boy, but, once in motion, it will retain its energy or momentum and finally, at the end of the run, will slide along for a considerable distance after the lighter laden sled has stopped. It is only in the rather exceptional case, where the flaw is of shortest duration — only a breath of air — that the light boat may attain its maximum speed before the puff has passed by, whereas the flaw is of too short duration for a heavy boat to acquire any *such* speed; in this case the light boat has the advantage over the heavy one.

In a *steady wind and no waves* the lighter boat always has the advantage, as she displaces less water and the surface friction is thus diminished correspondingly (cf. diagrams). On the other hand, the heavier boat is faster in a sea — due to her greater weight — as is also confirmed by experience.

The above can be summarized as follows: A boat should be as light as possible, but in cases, where additional weight in the form of live ballast may not be taken on board, her weight should never be less than the normal minimum that is recognized and empirically established. It is a false point of view that a boat must invariably be lightly built for light weather, as light

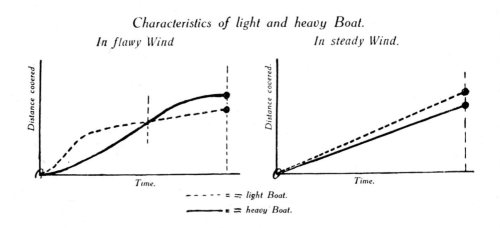

Characteristics of light and heavy Boat.

In flawy Wind   *In steady Wind.*

Distance covered   Distance covered.

Time.   Time.

- - - - = = light Boat.

———•ε = heavy Boat.

airs are generally very flawy. A heavy boat may, for example, be a good light weather boat, provided her wetted surface is small, and, therefore, a typical heavy weather boat may often be fast in light, flawy weather.

The small racer should be built as light as possible, at least as light as prescribed by the weight restrictions for her class, provided these are not further restricted as to live ballast. The German 15 qm. racer, for example, should be built as light as possible as the crew of two allowed in that class is sufficiently heavy. On the other hand, the German 10 qm. racer should not be too light, as her crew is usually restricted to one man only.

I came to a similar conclusion from comparative trials with the "Land-skiff," which is described in Part I (cf. page 114). As this machine is propelled by a series of jerks, which may be compared with the flaws of an unsteady wind, the heavier machine proved to be faster than the lighter one.

We conclude herewith our observations on this subject and proceed to our preparations for the race.

A few hours before the race we should test the whole rigging, both running and standing, most carefully, not overlooking the various shackles and turnbuckles, seeing that they are sufficiently taut and cannot loosen. After the sails have been set, the halyards, especially if not new, should be doubly secured by binding every such free end to the thimble in the end of the wire rope of the halyard in question and making it fast to a cleat or other-wise. Nothing is more aggravating than to lose a race that has been hotly contested through an accident that might have been avoided, had more care been taken. Nothing *should* break and nothing *will* break, if proper care has been taken, and it is the duty of the critical eye to discard all ropes, halyards or sheets that are in the least defective and to examine both rigging and boat with the proper understanding beforehand. We may observe here that so-called "hard luck" is not always the correct expression for defeat.

Many articles are most essential on a racing boat and should not be forgotten; we mention them here, classifying them according to the following *ten commandments:*

I. The fore leech or luff of the jib should always be well stretched by the halyard. It should, in fact, be stretched so taut, that no pressure whatever is brought to bear on the head stay. This is of great importance. If not sufficiently taut, the boat can show none of her good qualities on the wind. As the halyard may stretch somewhat during the race, this give must be allowed for on setting the sail. The upper head and the rear stays of the Marconi rig should be so arranged, that they can be adjusted readily.

II. A circular of the race should be on board. Not only the skipper but every member of the crew should be acquainted with its contents. How often it happens, especially in cases, where the racing course is changed at the last moment, that just before some mark is reached the circular is demanded and, if it is to be found, studied in the greatest excitement and, generally, with the fatal result that the mark is rounded in the wrong direction. Indif-ference to this commandment may be the cause of losing a race that has other-wise been sailed with the greatest care and success.

III. See that all necessary articles, including those prescribed by the circular, are on board.

Besides the pump, which is usually prescribed by the circular, a small bucket is most essential; it can be fastened to the end of a pole or the boat hook and used as a baler from the windward deck; this is to be highly recommended on smaller boats, as it does not necessitate any shift of live ballast — to leeward. The man on the fore deck should always have a few shackles and some tarred twine on his person — in his pocket should he be so unfortunate as to lose a shackle over board, when working forward; upon which the skipper otherwise may be obliged to crawl about under deck and search for an article that after all may not be on board.

A certain amount of reserve rope should be taken along, in case some halyard or rope has to be replaced or repaired.

IV. Never forget your yachting knife — with splicing iron. It is also advisable to have on board a chest of tools, including hammer, monkey wrench, pinchers, etc.; to which may be added a screw driver, tarred twine of various sizes, needles and thread and a broad strip of adhesive tape, that is most useful in patching tears in a sail. All these articles can be stowed away in a small drawer, that can readily be built into the boat under deck. It may sound peculiar to speak of "drawers" on a boat, but they are most practical for stowing away small articles and are to be recommended in preference to nets and other devices that are seldom accessible and generally hang so low — into the bottom of the boat — that everything they contain gets wet, when the boat is heeled.

V. A stop watch is indispensable in all races.

To attempt to make a good start with an ordinary watch or with none at all, counting the seconds by guess or feeling, is a crime for a skipper; the chances are that he will be surprised by the starting gun half a minute too early or too late. When a skipper boasts of sailing a race without a watch, he is more likely to be a fool than a sportsman. Your stop watch should be carefully tested before the race, as it is often the case that it will stop after a minute or so, strange to say, generally just before the starting gun is fired — due, perhaps, to a bath on the previous day or for some other unaccountable reason. Your watch should not be held in the hand nor attached to a chain that is always catching in everything — in preference in the tiller — but it should be worn in a leather strap or bracelet on the wrist, so that both hands are always free at critical moments to take in the main sheet or to assist in any necessary manoeuvre; otherwise you generally let your watch fall in the moment of excitement and have to search for it later in the bottom of the boat — in the water or at best in the pocket of some cast off garment. I have found it practical to set my stop watch two seconds ahead — of the official chronometer. You then have one second for starting the hand and need not hold your finger impatiently on the starting button for minutes awaiting the signal; the other second is for the propagation of the signal (gun) from the sailing committee's stand to the boats in the starting zone, which is generally a distance of about 330 yards, the velocity of propagation of sound per second. You need not then be anxious about starting your watch on the second, as it will point at the minute, when the starting gun is heard. This manipulation with the watch is to be recommended, especially when you belong to the first start. To effect it you have only to open the watch, lift up the hand and replace it two seconds ahead. In races of importance it is advisable to have two stop watches on board.

VI. See that the reefing apparatus works (also the main sheet rings). Is the man for the reefing apparatus strong enough for the purpose and does he understand how to manipulate it? First loosen the stretcher on the main boom, then rool up the sail on it by means of the reefing apparatus, thereupon lower the sail till the boom is in its normal position, etc., and finally tauten the stretcher.

VII. See that the racing pennant is in order. It is the soul of the boat and the skipper must be able to depend on it; it should be sensitive to the slightest breath of air. No skipper should be so conceited as to suppose he can sail a race properly without a pennant; he cannot steer his boat well on the wind and much less so on a free course, as he cannot possibly determine the correct relative position of his sails to the prevailing wind. The most practical device for flying a pennant is a system of light rods or a frame that turns on a central axle and is counter balanced on that axle by a weight attached to the upper rod of the frame, to which the pennant is sewed, that it may always fly out properly (cf. sketch below). The axle on which this frame turns is made fast to the mast.

VIII. A field glass should always be on board. It can be used to great advantage not only at sea but on inland waters and along the coast. By means of it the man on the fore deck can readily locate the turning marks well beforehand, recognize faint streaks or spots of wind at a distance not visible to the naked eye and search the neighboring shores for signs of wind, determining at the same time its prevailing direction. As we have observed, these are the functions of the crew and not of the skipper, who should be spared all such subordinate work during a race.

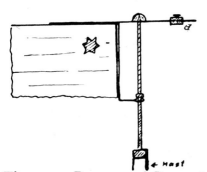

The racing Pennant and Device for flying it.

IX. See that you have a flag on board that can be set as a protest signal. We know that protesting is generally, confined to the inefficient; it is more or less characteristic of the beginner who, lacking efficiency, hopes to win prizes by other means. This is so often the case that we should not be convinced to the contrary by any false sense of honor. Nevertheless, there are cases, where it is a matter of duty to protest and for such an eventuality we should always have the necessary weapon — the protest flag — on board. If an unfair or fresh competitor attempts something mean and unsportsmanlike, the only means of retort is similar action on our part.

X. See that you have a candle or cigarettes and also matches on board. Although we have designated the racing pennant as the soul of the boat, we should not forget the qualities peculiar to a soul, namely, that it can easily fall asleep. The wind or rather the prevailing breath of air may be so lifeless that the pennant loses all interest in it and, although we may be able to waken it from occasional dreams for short intervals by giving it a good shake, it will often remain most indifferent and refuse to be wakened for longer periods. What is to be done in this case? The smoker will suggest *that he smoke,* giving the others to understand that he is only too willing to perform his duty and make any sacrifice — as if he had never had the least desire or intention of smoking; on the other hand, the man who does not smoke, hoping to lengthen his life by abstaining from the vice, will demand a candle. The candle will then, generally, be held in just the wrong place — where the air currents are of a most complicated nature, or placed indifferently somewhere on deck, that it may be watched most conveniently, but, generally where some one is sure to sit down unconsciously, when requested to do so, and, failing to jump up in due time, soon realizes that even a candle produces considerable heat. At all events the burning or smoking article in question — I do not mean the singed trousers — should be held or made fast on deck, where it is not exposed to the various air currents produced by the sails. Such regions can be determined most readily by tests with the light feather or down (cf. Part I). There is one region, however, that should be *avoided most carefully;* it is that *below* the main boom.

A small aeroid barometer will also be found to be most useful, as it registers all changes in the weather, as the approach of a thunderstorm or squall.

At sea a compass is, of course, indispensable.

The skipper must know the racing regulations, especially the rules of the right of way, by heart. In case the races are held in waters with which he is not familiar, he should, of course, try to acquire as much knowledge as possible of the winds peculiar to them and also locate the marks of the racing course from different points, taking bearings on the neighboring shore, before the races begin.

I should like to make a few suggestions on the apparel most appropriate for the racing man.

1. A *woollen* sweater is indispensable in cold and rainy weather.

2. Experience has taught that shoes with chrome leather soles cannot be worn in wet weather, as they have no hold whatever on a wet deck. For rainy weather rubbers or short rubber boots worn over the shoes can be highly recommended and, I am sure, will meet with the approval of everyone who has once tried them. He who has raced for years and knows what it means to have cold, wet feet for hours will surely appreciate the significance of a warm, dry body.

3. I have found gloves also most practical in heavy weather. The ropes do not slip through, nor chafe nor burn your hands, when you have to let them run. You also do not get tired so soon holding a rope or sheet, which is often essential on smaller boats, where you cannot let it out of your hands for hours. You need *only lay* the sheet of a small boat in your hand and you will be able to hold it easily due to the friction of the sheet on your glove or, if necessary, to ease it quite a piece without danger of burning your hand; whereas, if you wear no gloves, you generally have to wind the sheet at least once around your hand, in order to be able to hold it — without having it slip; the hand gets badly squeezed and becomes numb,

172

when the sheet is wound round it for hours, and it is, on the other hand, often quite impossible to loosen the sheet quickly, perhaps only by letting it run entirely. On small boats it is advisable, should you have only one hand free, to hold the sheet for the moment between your teeth, while you use your other hand to take it in.

All the preliminary preparations have now been made for the race and it is only in heavy weather that it is advisable to try your boat and give the rigging a final test; this should be done, however, a few hours before the race, so that, in case anything should break, it could be repaired in due time. On small boats one should not forget to observe, whether the waves splash up through the centerboard box into the boat; this can be remedied by stopping up the slit in the box with a rag. Under no conditions should you fail to pull up the centerboard, as also the sinkable blade of a rudder, just before the start, to clear it of any sea weed or other obstacles that may be hanging on it, as these greatly impede the speed of the boat, especially in light airs. To clear a yacht of such obstacles, put her in stays and let her drift astern a considerable distance.

Reefing. The skipper should decide, whether he should reef and, if necessary, how many reefs he should take in according to the following two principles:

I. *According to the strength of the wind.*

A certain advantage is gained, when the mainsail is somewhat reefed, as an extreme weather helm is thereby diminished and the boat will sail better, being more evenly balanced. The boat should be tried before in order to confirm definitely, whether she can carry the amount of canvas set, as it is quite impossible to judge this from the mere appearance of the water — wind and waves.

II. *According to the competition.*

(a) If you feel you can hold your most dangerous competitor under similar conditions, do not let the amount of canvas he is carrying influence you too much in regard to what you should set.

(b) Should your most dangerous competitor — and he alone comes into consideration, be faster than you are under normal conditions, you will be obliged to have recourse to extreme measures. You may gain a certain advantage either by taking along — on a small boat, a heavy, tall, "third man" or by carrying more canvas, if possible whole sail in despair. It can, of course, happen that you capsize before the end of the race, but the wind may let up somewhat, and then you will be able to carry your sail to advantage.

Should you intend to carry whole sail, do not disclose the fact to your competitors till necessary. Either set your sail at the last moment or, what is still better, reef down your mainsail at first even more than is necessary and shake out the reefs just before the start.

M. Rosenfeld

Note the Difference in Heeling.

(The leading boat sails in undisturbed wind—all the others do not.)

The Start

The time signal is given — the first gun, and at once the stop watch is started.

During the preparations for the race, scepticism was thoroughly justified on the part of the skipper, but from the moment the time signal is given it is his duty to have confidence in himself and implicit faith in his boat. He only who has self-confidence and confidence in his boat belongs at the helm. An old sailor's proverb, that is confirmed by experience, puts it: "The speed of your boat increases with your own confidence." The crew can contribute much to this purpose. A marvellous effect is produced, when, for example, the man on the jib sheet calls to the skipper in an assuring tone: "We shall overhaul her without doubt," "she can never catch us" or the like. I once had a crew that kept assuring me, when the whole fleet were close on our heels, how fast we were dropping them; I was quieted by this soothing assurance, until, taking advantage of an opportunity to look astern, I found to my dismay that they had all closed up on us; but the false information was well-meant, and both I and indirectly the boat surely profited by it. I am, therefore, thoroughly convinced that a critical situation will always prove fatal, unless the skipper has confidence that he will succeed in extricating himself from it or should the crew indulge in such exclamations as "there is nothing more to be done," "we are beaten" or, the Lord knows, what other even more despairing effeminate ejaculations of the sort.

It should hardly be necessary to observe that the skipper should remain as "cool" as possible and accustom himself not to yell at his crew but to convey his commands in a low voice or even whisper, should he find it advisable not to disclose his manoeuvres to his competitors. A good crew have a right to expect such treatment and, in return, should carry out all commands most strictly. To expect absolute "coolness" to reign on board during the start would, of course, be absurd, for then every fraction of a second counts and under such circumstances "coolness" would be equivalent to indifference, a quality that should never be tolerated in a race.

The chief points to be observed for the interval before the start are the following:

I. The man on the jib sheet should be made responsible for any collision; it is his duty to call the attention of the skipper to any obstacle in the course or to the approach of another boat; it is most important that this should be understood and agreed upon beforehand. It would be quite wrong to expect this trying function of being continually on the watch of the skipper, who has more than enough to attend to and to calculate. For similar reasons the crew and in this case the man on the main sheet should be made responsible for the *various signals* — their interpretation and immediate communication to the skipper; it should, for instance, be his function to inform the latter of any change in the racing course. Every member of the crew should also be familiar with the course — from the circular at least — and be able to inform the skipper of the location of any turning mark at any moment.

II. Do not make any unnecessary manoeuvres just before the start, as these tend only to cause a certain excitement or commotion on board. In light or moderate winds keep your boat in the immediate neighborhood of the starting line. In a stiff breeze your boat should always be well under way, especially in case you do not have the right of way and must keep clear of your competitors. In light airs let your boat have a *good full*, that you may always *have sufficient headway to manoeuvre.*

III. *Watch your competitors from the moment the preparatory signal is given as the majority, especially those on yachts, will then be practising the starts they intend to make;* you should watch them most carefully, as you must take this into account upon deciding on your own start.

IV. If considered essential, practise your own start a few times with your stop watch, that you may acquire a feeling for the speed of your boat and the distance she is travelling in a given time under the prevailing conditions — of wind, etc. Put the question: What distance can she travel in a minute? Inform the crew of the start you intend to make, that they may be prepared for it.

V. Observe whether the starting marks lie exactly in the starting line; if not, determine approximately — in yards or boat lengths, how much they have swung out of it.

The preparatory signal is given — the second gun.

See whether your stop watch is right — to the second. Be on the lookout for course signals.

VI. Remember that the race begins not with your starting but with your preparatory signal. From this moment you must watch your competitors and sail your boat accordingly; you may be obliged to work out a new plan of starting at the last moment. If, for example, you have the impression that the majority of the boats intend to start in a bunch close to the weather mark, you may bear off to leeward at the last moment and, running at full speed, attempt to reach the line on the gun, undisturbed by the others.

VII. Remember, it is not the boat that crosses the starting line first but the *one that is ahead a few minutes after the start* that has made the *best start.*

VIII. *Never* set an auxiliary sail before or during the start. The spinnaker may be on deck and everything prepared for setting it or breaking it out, but it should under no conditions be in action or drawing before you have crossed

176

the line and are clear. Starting "under spinnaker" may be compared with an air castle that vanishes the moment obstacles are encountered — in the case of a boat helpless drifting, imminence of a collision or a luffing match.

Then arises the question: "How shall I start?" *The talent for sailing is innate, but the ability to start a matter of practice.* This golden rule should be interpreted in the sense that one should lay out a definite plan of the kind of start intended, in which all possible situations that may arise are already included and *thoroughly considered beforehand.* It is hardly to be expected that your plan will always be successful; the reason for this is to be ascribed, however, not to your competitors, that fall upon you suddenly from every direction of the compass, nor to the gradual development of quite a new situation, but rather to an incorrect carrying out of your own correct plan of start — at the last moment.

The manner in which you should approach the starting line depends, of course, upon the *type of boat* you are sailing. Generally speaking, we may say: The smaller centerboard craft should approach the line with flapping sails, being *headed for it* at least two minutes after the preparatory gun has been fired. In other words, you approach the line with little headway — with flapping sails — and just a few yards before you reach it give the order to take in the sheets, and your boat, picking up headway quickly, shoots over the line at full speed. Although this manner of starting may be recommended for small boats that speed up quickly, it should not be attempted with a larger yacht. Generally speaking, a keel boat should approach the line in the following manner: Lie on or near the line for the first minute, then sail off at full speed in a direction more or less opposite to that of the racing course for $1\frac{1}{2}$ minutes and come about, allowing $\frac{1}{2}$ minute for the manoeuvre; you then have 2 minutes left to cover the distance to the starting line, for which you will need under similar conditions only $1\frac{1}{2}$ minutes. If the wind holds, you can let the sails flap somewhat and thus decrease your speed; if it lets up, you will have $\frac{1}{2}$ minute to spare, to reach the starting line in time.

However individual to the different types of boat the various stages of the start may be, they differ also according to the *strength of the prevailing wind.* In light airs you cannot run your boat close enough to the starting line, but this does not imply that you should not keep her constantly moving and at as high speed as possible. In this way a *certain reserve speed or momentum* remains stored in the boat — her mass — that can be spent, should the wind suddenly let up. While a boat not sailed on this principle will have to attempt in vain to get started at the last moment or, upon running into a soft spot, however narrow it may be, to work through it, the socalled "wild skipper" will shoot his boat over the starting line like a "cannon ball."

As the wind increases, you will have to increase the distance from which you approach the starting line. At all events your boat *should be headed for it and you should not risk putting her about during the last two minutes before the starting gun is fired,* as the time required for this manoeuvre can easily be underestimated.

The proper handling of the sheets is just as important as that of the helm of a boat. Here the following principle should be strictly adhered to:

Start your boat, especially the yacht, first with the mainsail, then with the jib.
In other words, let the jib flap and manoeuvre with the less readily adjustable
mainsail in the neighborhood of the starting line. The jib should not be used
till the last moment, when it can be brought into action by a single pull on
the sheet, to overcome the few remaining yards to the starting line. In light
airs the helmsman may hold the jib sheet in his hand during the start, in
order to procure the final trim desired more quickly. The commands for the
start would, therefore, be the following: "Let the jib flap, mainsail flap; in
with main sheet slowly — jib flapping; mainsail full — jib flapping; both sails
full." It is advisable to instruct the crew beforehand that the command
"full" is not necessarily to be interpreted as identical to the command "close
hauled," but that it corresponds to the *most favorable* position of the sail for
the given course — that for which the driving force is a maximum. It is
often the case that experienced yachtsmen upon the shrill command "full"
make the mistake of hauling in the jib flat instead of pulling it in only enough
to have it draw most effectively, as, for example, when the wind is from the
quarter. Before the command "full" is given, the man on the sheets should
be on the alert, with his hands on the sheet and his arms well stretched
awaiting the command, that he may not, as is usually the case, be taken by
surprise. Keep in mind that it is the duty of the man on the main sheet
to see that neither the mainsail nor the main boom comes in contact with
any part, pull or rigging, of another yacht, as also to call the attention of
the helmsman to any danger of collision of the stern of his boat with any
obstacle, mark, etc.

So-called "bad luck" is an expression that should be used most cautiously
in racing; otherwise you may be easily offended, should the winner of the
race begin to smile or shrug his shoulders upon some such remark or excuse
as: "Yes, if I had not had 'bad luck,' I should have beaten you easily."
Capsizing cannot be ascribed to bad luck, any more than the parting of a rope,
the breaking of a spar or much less an unfavorable tack can be offered as
an excuse for the loss of a race. It is quite similar with the start. A poor
start cannot be attributed to bad luck; it is a miscalculation on the part of
the skipper. This is the charm of racing; it is a game of chess of the highest
order with the chief difference that in a race you cannot rest your head on
your arms. It is a game, in which you must reckon out every move beforehand
and not only anticipate but also be prepared for the numberless attacks that
can or may be made, but with the disadvantage, that you do not have as
much time as you may like for your next move, but must be prepared to
parry at shortest notice the attacks not only of a single but of *several* competitors
and these under difficulties with which the latter may not have to contend.

The offensive is limited not to *one* but to numberless methods of attack
for one and the same situation, and there are just as many methods or possibilities of defence in the defensive. It can, therefore, happen that five attacks
may fail and a sixth must be attempted before your competitor, failing to find
a means to parry the attack or applying it a few seconds too late, succumbs;
then he is lost. That was of course "bad luck!" Although it may be impossible
to prescribe how you should start, there are, nevertheless, certain moves, which
the inexperienced terms "tricks," that can be employed to advantage by the
skipper who knows them. As in the case of a mathematical problem you should

not be in doubt as to the method to be employed for its solution — whether you should solve it algebraically, geometrically, arithmetically or otherwise — similarly there is for every direction and strength of the wind a socalled fundamental *theory for starting*.

Before we can proceed to the exact tactics or possibilities of starting, we must investigate certain positions of the boat, as an understanding of these is essential for the development of the different methods of starting. That special relative position of two boats to each other, that I have termed the

"Hopeless Position or Berth"

a subject, to which I have devoted months of study and a thorough knowledge of which is the fundament of all racing technique, is most important. I have designated this special case as "hopeless," because, provided the two boats are equally matched, the position of the one is absolutely hopeless, as there is no offensive that can be assumed by her with any chance of success; the boat is doomed, provided the other boat is properly handled and sailed. The apparently mysteriously fatal conditions for the boat in the "hopeless position or berth" are represented graphically in the diagram on the next page.

Let us first investigate the case, where boat I is *close hauled* and a few boat lengths ahead of boat II (cf. diagram). Under normal conditions it will be impossible for boat II to overhaul her competitor, boat I, as the former is in the so-called "hopeless position or zone." She is not only deprived of all means of assuming the offensive — with any chance of success, but she is so badly handicapped by the mere presence of the boat ahead of her, that we might compare her fate relative to her other competitors to that of a motor-boat running with only two of her four cylinders. If her skipper is not aware of this hopeless position at once, she will fall astern several boat lengths in the shortest time. This is due not alone to the so-called "back wind" from boat I, to which it is customary to attribute all such misfortunes, but to the prevailing conditions both in the air and in the water of the "hopeless zone," an exact knowledge of which is essential, that we may form a proper conception of the hopeless position, into which boat II has fallen.

The most hopeless position or zone conceivable, into which boat II can get, is that marked *a* in the diagram — directly in the wake of boat I. The harmful effect in this zone decreases as the distance from boat I increases; it is pronounced to a distance of several boat lengths astern the leading boat. It is caused indirectly, by the sails of boat I, which tend to *deflect* the wind from its original direction — in the diagram more to the left of the direction of the prevailing wind, as indicated by the lines of the air current, to the effect that the wind strikes the sails of boat II at a considerably *smaller angle of opposition*. The attention of the skipper of boat II is called to this phenomenon, familiar to every yachtsman, by the flapping or shivering of her sails, which makes it impossible for him to run as high as his competitor (boat I) ahead. What is to be done? After he has struggled a while in the wake of his competitor, trying in vain to point as high, he will realize that he is falling astern rapidly, whereupon he will probably bear off somewhat and attempt to better his position by giving his boat a better full. What is the result? His boat does not run faster; she becomes unsteady and her sails tremble; and finally, after making one mistake after another, he finds himself in the back wind of boat I — in the narrow zone that tapers to a point and is marked *b* in the diagram, several boat lengths behind his competitor; by this last manoeuvre he has sacrificed his weather berth, that is of such moment on a beat to windward. What will be his next move? He will probably bear off more and more, until he finally gets out of the back wind of boat I and into wind that is not materially disturbed by her, but not into undisturbed water. What is now to be done, should boat I also bear off more and run fuller? Boat

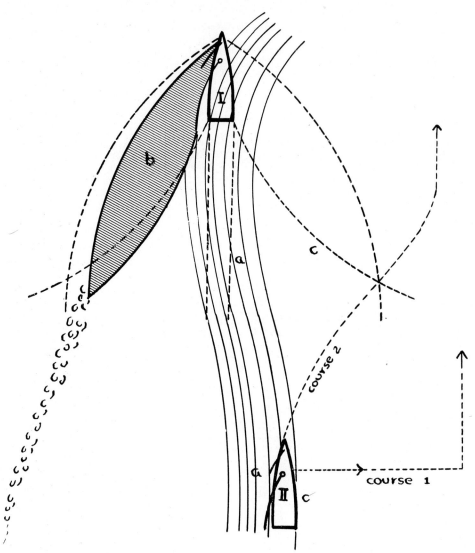

(The effect is well demonstrated in picture on page 174 by the difference of inclination of the five masts.)

Boat 25 Is in the "Safe-Leeward Position"—Boat 20 in the "Hopeless Position"
(Note the inclination of the masts.)

II is then again in the dreaded back wind of his rival and farther astern than ever; she may soon reach undisturbed wind but hardly undisturbed water, and can then finally find consolation only in the proverb: "Ut desint vires, tamen est laudanda voluntas," or as I once, in an examination, quoted it: "– – – est laudanda *voluptas.*" Upon which my colleagues smiled and the venerable examiner threatened me with dismissal in case of a repetition of such jokes. In the present predicament, however, the skipper of boat I will likely be smiling contentedly and the other skipper will probably have a long yarn to spin after the race about his "hard luck," and how it was impossible to avoid it, as the other boat was to blame for it.

Upon investigating *zone a* more thoroughly, we may discriminate between the following unfavorable *factors or influences* common to it:

1. *The deflection of the direction of the wind* already mentioned, to the effect that the wind strikes the sails of boat II following in the wake of boat I at a smaller angle of opposition.

2. *The presence of air filled with eddies* that have lost a greater part of their energy.

3. *The disturbed water* in the wake of boat I with its retarding effect on the speed of boat II, as confirmed in Part I (cf chapter on "Hydrodynamic Experiments").

In *zone b,* which, we may observe, at *short distances* astern the leading boat is to be regarded as the next most unfavorable position for boat II, the latter is subjected to the following retarding effects:

1. Being blanketed by the sails of boat I, or, at greater distances astern, of sailing in air filled with eddies.

2. The deflection in the direction of the wind similar to but not so pronounced as in zone *a.*

3. The bow and stern waves of the leading boat, the retarding effect of which cannot be underestimated.

Let us next consider an offensive method. What would happen, should we (boat II) succeed, by luffing at favorable moments, in reaching zone *c* (cf. diagram on p. 180)? We would accomplish little by this manoeuvre, as we should be still indirectly under the unfavorable influence of the deflection in the direction of the wind throughout zone *a.* We might by chance be able to break through the stern waves of our competitor, but we should then be doomed, being checked in our further progress by her bow waves, under the harmful influence of which, combined with that arising from the socalled "air cushion" or accumulation of air between the sails of our own boat and those of our competitor — to the effect that the negative pressure or suction on the leeward surface of our sails is disturbed, we should fall more and more astern, until our defeat were finally assured. However promising the prospects may appear, the attempt is doomed to utter failure, provided the two boats and their skippers are equally matched.

What next? Two alternatives may still be mentioned for the offensive, neither of which, however, offers much chance of success.

Should you fall into the hopeless position on a beat to windward,

    (a) split tacks *at once* with your competitor, as indicated in the diagram by course I, or

(b) attempt by *immediately* luffing to get the better of your rival, either through lack of attention on his part or by taking advantage yourself of some momentary favorable shift in the direction of the wind, running so high that you are able to break through to windward, if possible at the point of intersection of his bow and stern waves, as indicated by course 2 of the diagram. The intersection of these two waves is the most favorable point to attempt an escape, as according to the principle of interference their resultant (harmful) effect at that point is never greater than the sum of the two component effects and may, under favorable conditions, entirely vanish.

The best tactics are, however, to *avoid* falling into the passive, hopeless position by keeping quite clear of that zone and to parry all attacks of your competitor that might tend to that effect, *before* his attention may be directed toward you for that purpose, and, on the other hand, to make every possible attempt to secure that commanding position for yourself, that you may assume the offensive.

I must, however, state explicitly that the term "hopeless position" can be applied only to boats *close-hauled* — on the wind; *off the wind* the matter presents quite a different aspect.

Of the many possible variations of the hopeless position that are represented by the sketches on page 186, there is one particular variation included in this group that is of such importance, that it demands our special attention and thorough investigation; it is the so-called

"Safe Leeward Position or Berth"

which is represented, with lines of flow of the air, by the special diagram on the following page. The two boats A and B are lying close-hauled — on the wind, almost abreast and separated only by a few yards, having been brought into that relative position to each other by some manoeuvre that does not concern us further here. A is slightly ahead and *apparently* blanketed by B (cf. diagram on page 185). The uninitiated will maintain that B will overhaul A at once; the experienced skipper knows, however, that, even should his boat B be somewhat *slower,* he need have no apprehensions of being overhauled by his competitor. A knowledge of the advantage this position commands — for which reason I have designated it as the "safe leeward position or berth," offers, moreover, possibilities to boat B of *assuming the offensive.* Suppose the two boats meet on a beat to windward; boat B, being on the starboard tack, feels quite safe as she has the right of way; boat A comes ploughing along on the port tack, but with the uncomfortable feeling for her skipper that he must bear off — at the last moment, and let his competitor pass by. But suppose he has no scruples and comes to realize that, although he is on the port tack, he may master the situation; he heads his boat straight for his competitor, requests him kindly, should it seem advisable, to keep on his course and, just before the two boats are in danger of running foul of each other, throws his own boat quickly over onto the other tack — under the lee of his competitor. The latter has no doubt more headway and is travelling faster for the moment, but to the dismay of the uninitiated the two boats will soon be plying ahead at the same speed and, before one realizes it, boat A will be running faster and upon luffing somewhat will shortly have her competitor, apparently strange to say, in her wake. In this short interval boat B will have dropped from the "safe" windward into the hopeless leeward berth.

The secret or explanation of the above is to be sought in the deflection of the wind from its original path caused by the sails of the leeward boat A, which throw or guide the wind onto the leeward surface of those of the windward boat B and, what is most instructive and important, tend to *destroy the partial vacuum or suction along that surface.** A further *empirical proof* for the fact that it is the partial vacuum or suction on the leeward surface of a sail and not the (positive) pressure on its windward surface that furnishes the greater driving force! The chief condition for the success of the manoeuvre is that boat A should run well up under the lee of boat B before going about.

It is hardly necessary to observe that *after the shift of tack it is only the smaller boat,* which is capable of regaining her speed quickly, that is able to win the safe leeward berth with any degree of certainty on a turn to windward; even with these smaller boats the shift of tack must be made without the least hitch and the jib must be in and drawing the moment the boat is about. Should the boats be lying initially, as at the start, on the same tack in this relative position to each other, then the leeward berth in a beat to windward is always the preferable of the two, not only for the smaller racing boat but also for the larger yacht. The key to the situation is that the safe leeward position or berth can be regarded as won by the leeward boat only, when *her bow is still ahead of that of her competitor* to windward. The limiting case is that, where the two boats are neck to neck, as indicated in sketch E of the diagram on page 186 (cf. also the photographs of this chapter for example page 189). In this case the leeward boat may still be regarded as having the more favorable berth, but from the moment her bow falls behind that of the boat to windward the battle is lost, and in the next moment she is in the hopeless position.

All the variations that concern us in the investigations on the hopeless and the safe leeward position are represented collectively by the sketches on page 186, where the boat in the more favorable position or berth is colored white.

One of the most fatal positions for the boat in the windward berth is the variation represented by sketch G, as the boat to leeward is able not only to throw her back wind onto the leeward surface of the sails of her competitor to windward, but also, by hauling in her own sails very flat, to direct the flow of her backwind in such a manner, that it will strike the mainsail of the other boat in its first third, that is, according to our investigations in Part I, exactly where the suction effect is greatest. The boat to windward will thus be struck at her most vulnerable point, the driving force on her mainsail sinking from 100% to about 35% — to approximately $\frac{1}{3}$ its maximum.

Distant Action of the Safe Leeward Position

Although the behavior of the wind is most fatal to the windward boat only, when the two boats are quite close to each other, this does not imply

---

* The bow wave of the leeward boat is also thrown against the side of the weather boat and tends to impede the speed of the latter materially.

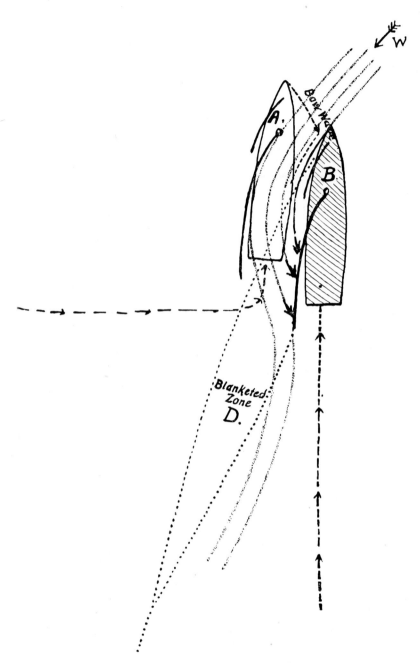

"The Safe Leeward Position".

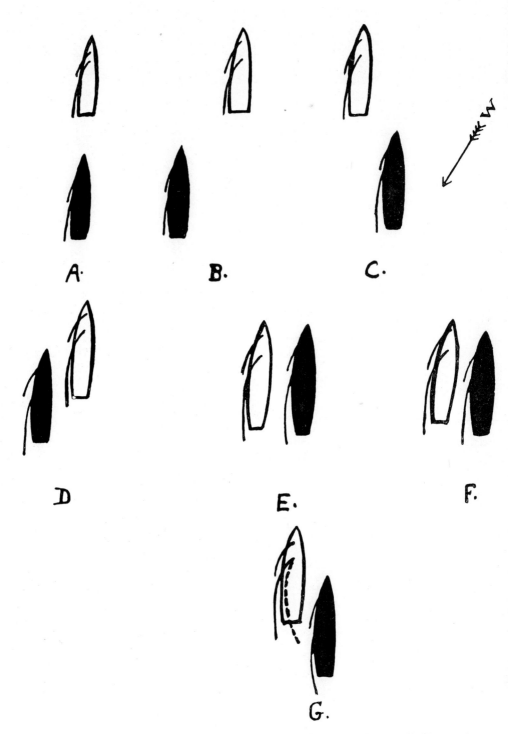

"Hopeless Position" A, B, C, D — *"Safe Leeward Position"* E, F, G.

"Safe Leeward Position"
(Note the different inclinations of the three masts.)

that its peculiar action does not still exist, when the distance between them becomes greater. Strange to say, this harmful effect developed by the boat in lee is perceptible to a distance of 100 yards or more to windward. This is confirmed both theoretically and empirically. Experiments made in *water* with most sensitive instruments have shown that the approach of a steamer can be registered to a distance of *several miles*. Not only the particles of water in the next proximity to its bow are shoved forward and thrust aside, but those at a distance of several miles in front of the steamer begin to move and to recede upon its approach. Then why should not this action that is propagated in the water to a distance of several miles also take place in the *atmosphere?* The comparison or analogy is, in fact, plausible, since all changes or motions are known to be relative; the same effect is produced, whether the steamer is in motion and the water remains stationary or the water is flowing and the steamer is anchored in the stream. The latter case is approximately realized by the wind and the sail of a boat; the air blows in the form of wind on to the sail, which in respect to the direction and speed of the wind remains practically stationary, is *obstructed* in its flow by the sail — in its close proximity, and *retarded in its speed* at greater distances from the sail or boat, as it approaches the latter.

Experiments with projectiles — bullets, have shown that when, for instance, a bullet is shot at a pane of glass, a hole is pierced in the glass *before the bullet arrives*. This surprising fact was discovered by means of slow motion photography, which showed distinctly that the glass was pierced by hard compressed masses of air propagated in advance of the flight of the bullet, the latter merely passing through the hole already made.

Upon examining the accompanying miniature photographs on page 191, we observe that the boat farther to leeward is heeled more; this may be regarded as a proof for the greater velocity of the wind to leeward. Especially when three boats are lying abreast high on the wind, this phenomenon is most pronounced, in that the boat in the weather berth sails more erect than the one in her lee, provided the situation of the two is not such that the latter is directly blanketed. On prolonging the lines of the masts of the boats in the photographs on page 191, we observe that they intersect below almost at one and the same point, radiating, as it were, like a fan from that point.

System for Starting

As a result of the above considerations and from a thorough study of the variations enumerated, I have worked out a system for starting that should insure to a certain degree a good if not the best start possible, provided nothing unforeseen happens.

Before proceeding further let me, however, call the attention of the reader to the conditions or factors mentioned at the beginning of this chapter, upon which not the method of starting but the start itself depends; — the various stages in its development are

I. The type of boat
II. The strength of the wind
III. The competition.

Aside from the individually more or less skillful manner in which the start is made — for no two persons will do one and the same thing in exactly the same way — there is a certain given start that can be adopted

188

Two Impressive "Safe Leeward Positions"
(U S 72 and U S 79)
See position E on page 186.

189

"Safe Leeward Positions"

Near and Distant Action of "Safe Leeward Berth".

quite systematically according to the *direction of the wind,* whereby we discriminate between five chief directions — with respect to the starting line, as designated below. I may observe at the outset that for all *on-wind starts* the best start is of greatest moment, and I maintain that, if one of every two races is won by the boat making the best start, eight out of ten races that are started *on the wind* will be won by the boat that crosses the line first — to the weather. You should, therefore, run all risks, even of crossing the starting line too early and of being recalled, in every race that starts *on the wind,* as here the best start enables you to force the "hopeless position" on your competitors and to hold them, even a faster boat, tack for tack in that position.

I. START: *Dead against the wind.* The wind is blowing at right angles to the starting line (cf. first sketch on page 194). Here the best start is most important.

You head your boat for the mark at the starboard end of the starting line and pass it as close as possible on the starboard tack, thus insuring for yourself the right of way. Although this start may offer great advantages, it is not, however, to be recommended, should you observe that *all* the other boats are choosing it, for they will be likely to get into close quarters at the starting mark with the fatal consequences that generally result from such straits. In this case choose in preference the *"safe leeward position"* and, running *close-hauled* well toward the weather end of the start, shoot over the line. You should not, however, forget that you must then start almost with the gun, that you may force the bow of your boat over the line ahead of your competitors to windward, as the "safe leeward berth" can otherwise turn out to be anything but "safe."

From another point of view the safe leeward berth may often be dangerous. The boats to windward may be running with *the wind abeam* at higher speed, in which case they will retain that accelerated speed for a while — after they have trimmed in their sheets upon crossing the line. This additional speed is often sufficient to enable them to overhaul other boats, in spite of their earlier start, that have started close hauled and reckoned on the advantage of the safe leeward position. It is, in fact, most remarkable how all boats that cross the line with such reserve speed forge ahead. It is due to the empirical fact that the pressure or driving force developed on a sail increases as the square of the speed of the boat; for example, suppose that a boat that crosses the line close-hauled at a speed of 2 miles an hour develops a pressure or driving force in her sails of 4 lbs. per square yard, then her competitor that approaches the start with eased sheets at a speed of say 3 miles an hour will be developing a pressure of 9 lbs. per square yard. Although the latter will lose that reserve speed slowly, she will be travelling not alone *that* much faster than the speed, which is due alone to her moment of inertia, but also *faster* by the additional amount that arises from the increased pressure on her sails in consequence of her higher speed. This extremely interesting fact is not universally known or, at least, not fully realized.*

II. START: *To windward,* but with the direction of the wind such, that

* We may experience the same phenomenon, if we seek to increase the speed of a small boat in light airs *on the wind* by rowing it somewhat. The accelerated speed is disproportionately **greater**. This is the reasons why motors are to be found on so many sailing vessels.

the first mark of the racing course can be fetched or almost fetched on a "reach" — here, as indicated in sketch 2 on the next page, on the port tack; * in which case the boats that approach the start on the port tack close to the more windward mark should easily pass those that start on the starboard tack more in the neighborhood of the other, more leeward mark, provided both groups remain on their respective tacks (cf. sketch 2). In spite of this apparent advantage that may be gained by starting on the *port tack,* and this accounts for the fact that most boats choose this start, we advise crossing the *starting line on the starboard tack,* but *as close as possible* to the weather mark. This start has the great advantage that, having the *right of way,* you can block the approach to the starting line for all boats on the port tack in the neighborhood of that mark, forcing them either to go about or to bear off under your stern. After crossing the line you must, however, go about as soon as possible, that you may blanket and overhaul the boats beating to windward on the port tack — those that have just passed under your stern.

III. START: *Wind blowing across the racing course.* We discriminate here between the two cases:

      A. The direction of the wind is parallel to the starting line (cf. sketch 3a).

      B. The direction of the wind makes a small angle with the starting line, such that it has a slight component directed against the course, as indicated in sketch 3b.

In both cases the key to the situation is the "safe leeward position," with the difference that in the former case you should start as far to leeward, *close to the leeward mark,* as possible (cf. sketch 3a), as you may thereby profit from the advantages of the leeward berth, provided you have started on the gun, and pointing higher, will be travelling faster than the boats more to windward, that have the wind somewhat more on the beam. The experienced skipper knows that our modern types of racing boat attain their greatest speed in moderate breezes when higher on the wind and not with the wind directly abeam, as is often supposed.

In case A an especially good start with regard to both speed and gun can be made by running up to windward along and close to the line and then by swinging off on to it with the gun. Here, having the right of way, you are often able to force another boat, that is approaching the start from any other direction, to start too early.

In case B you should, however, start as close as possible to the *weather mark* but directly in lee of the other boats that are bearing away for the mark to your weather (cf. sketch 3b). Then you need not press your boat to fetch the mark, but may let her run with a good full, taking advantage of your "safe leeward berth," which can be made still more formidable by luffing in due time. There is no danger that the boats to windward may run faster upon trimming in their sheets after crossing the line, as was the case in Start I, as they are obliged to bear off onto the mark — often running dead before the wind, and then under their greatly diminished speed to luff to such an extent at the mark, that the little headway they still have is entirely lost upon the sharp turn.

IV. START: *Wind abeam.* Here there are two possibilities, but the

* We take it for granted that the starting line, as is usually prescribed by the racing regulations, is laid at right angles to the racing course.

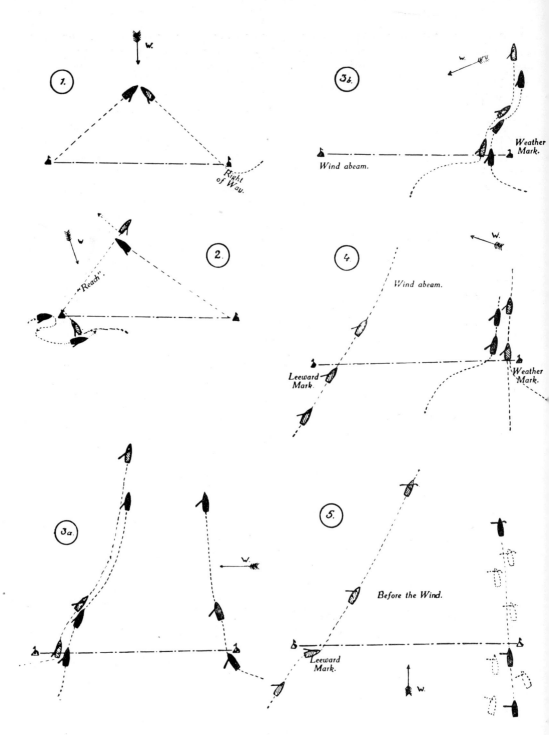

The fundamental Methods of Starting.

one only, the *start at the weather end of the line,* is that almost universally chosen. In this case the only boat that has undisturbed air is the one to windward, whereas all the others to leeward are blanketed and thus doomed in this hopeless position. Here you should, however, approach the line with the *wind on your beam* and not attempt to wedge your boat into the weather berth by bearing down on the mark before the wind, as her *speed* will thereby be so *greatly diminished,* that you run the risk of arriving too late, and the little headway she may still have will, moreover, be entirely lost upon the sharp turn (luff) at the mark. The other possibility is to start at the leeward end of the line; this should be duly considered, should you observe that the other boats are *all* preparing for the weather start, with the risk of getting engaged in luffing matches, whereas well to leeward you can choose your course quite clear of the others and, on trimming in your sheets and pointing higher after crossing the line, travel much faster. But this latter alternative should be chosen only, when the starting line is long enough and you can start to leeward *quite alone.*

V. START: *Dead before the wind.* In 80% of these cases the more favorable start is that at the leeward end of the line (if we may discriminate here between leeward and windward), since the wind on the leg to the first turning mark will be somewhat on your (weather) quarter and will thus enable you to trim in your sheets a bit and run faster. But the decision of the start to be chosen may depend on the important question: "How or rather where should I start, that my boat may be the inner boat at the first mark?" If this mark is to be passed to starboard and at no great distance from the starting zone, then your position at the start should be at the starboard end of the line, and, vice versa, if it is to be left on port, at the port end. Should your boat be lying on the outer side of the course with a short distance to the mark, you will seldom — at least in a large field, succeed in forcing her through the wind shadows of the boats in your rear and in reaching the other, inner side of the course for the purpose of winning the "inner position" at the mark.

We know that on a start dead before the wind it is not so essential to start with the gun, as the boats almost always arrive at the same time, neck to neck, at the first turning mark. The reason for this is that a faster boat, upon taking the lead, will be blanketed at once by those she has over-hauled; in this way the *speed* of the different boats is *regulated* more or less *automatically* and the whole field thus held together in a bunch (cf. photo-graph of "Seglerhaus Regatta" at end of chapter "Before the Wind"). The explanation for the phenomenon, that a boat a few lengths astern is not only harmful to the one or the other boat ahead but will haul up on the *whole* field, is, as we know from the laws of blanketing, that the driving force in her sails is *increased by about 15%* through the act merely of blanketing (cf. chapter on "Blanketing," Part I).

The advantage of the inner position at the mark is evident, as not only a few yards but often several boat lengths may be gained after the turn by forcing the "hopeless position" upon your various competitors. It can, there-fore, happen that a boat that runs well before the wind may, if sailed properly, win the race, even should she be slower than her competitors on the ensuing beat to windward.

Boat No. 11 Is in a Hopeless Position, Being Blanketed by 14 and Backwinded by 19. She Can Not Tack as 22 Has Right of Way.

(Note that boat 19 is sailing in undisturbed wind.)

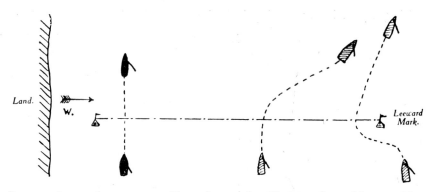

Start in Lee, when starting Zone lies under Shelter of neighboring Shore.

Another matter that should receive your most careful attention before every race is whether the wind conditions are influenced from the start being laid under the lee of a neighboring shore. In this case you must then naturally have recourse to quite other tactics; here you should start at the outer or leeward end of the line — well off shore, as indicated in the above sketch. As we have already observed, this position is, more often than is universally supposed, the more favorable one at the start. It also has the advantage that a premature start at the leeward end of the line may escape the watchful eye of the starters, as a boat in that position is often blanketed and concealed from their sight by boats that cross the line more to windward before the gun. Such an event is often alluded to in the report of a race in the form: "The leading boat must have slipped over the line somewhere."

After the technique for the start chosen has duly been decided upon and, while the second hand of your watch is indicating the last few seconds, be on the alert for the *starting signal or gun* — should the gun miss fire, watch the ball, as this then determines the start. (European method!)

Your boat shoots over the line. The good skipper lets his boat loose, at full speed, at once; this is a science in itself, known only to the few. How childish it sounds, when you hear some one say: "My boat is slow in getting under way." It is not the *boat* but the *skipper* that is slow in getting started. A good skipper will get a comparatively heavy boat started more quickly than a poor skipper a light one. It is a matter of "life and death" now — just now, to travel faster than the others, that you may get quite clear, even at the sacrifice of direct course.

C u r r y, Aerodynamics of Sails and Racing Tactics.

To get your boat started quickly, be guided by the following rules:

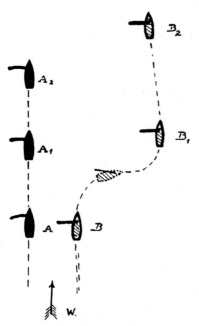

Method of starting Boat quickly.

1. Never run your boat dead before the wind in the *starting zone,* as she will lie with little headway, especially in light airs, but keep her on the beam or higher on the wind, as it is on this point of sailing that she attains her greatest speed.

2. Make use of the centerboard in the manner described in the chapter "Before the Start."

3. The steering technique: Suppose you are lying in a calm, with almost no headway, and a puff of wind sets in. Then, without the least regard for the racing course, quite indifferent as to whether you should have to run before the wind or with the wind abeam to be headed for the mark, luff up *even to 60°,* taking in your sheets slowly as you luff — during the period you are becalmed your sheets should be kept out rather more than is apparently necessary, and *then* bear off gradually in the direction of the course or mark. You will observe that by this manoeuvre you have got her started in the shortest possible time. Compare here the accompanying sketch.

The method of getting a boat started quickly, by luffing more or less according to the situation, is to be applied chiefly in light airs and should not be confounded with the more general technique of bearing off in flaws and luffing up in the intervals between them, when you are running on the beam in a stiff breeze; this general technique is treated in a later chapter.

On the wind you should start your boat in a flaw as follows: 1. The *moment* the flaw strikes your sails, ease the sheets — this tends to diminish the impact of the flaw, and at the same time bear off and run fuller. 2. Then trim in the sheets, *without* luffing. 3. Finally, luff up slowly, and you will perceive at once that you can point high and still run at maximum speed. This technique is applicable in both light and strong winds.

W. Colman

Scows on Lake Geneva

No. 11 is first boat to round the mark—No. 4 second and No. 88 third.

The

Beat to Windward

The Technique of Beating to Windward

On the assumption that the first leg of the course is a beat to windward, let us consider the technique of beating to windward; it is by far the most fascinating of all points of sailing and involves at the same time the greatest efficiency in the science and *technique* of sailing.

In consideration of the many difficulties to be overcome, before one may hope to succeed in sailing a boat correctly on the wind, it is not surprising that we repeatedly hear the complaint: "My boat is slow beating to windward." It may be that the one or the other boat of a certain class shows better qualities on the wind than the rest and that she will, therefore, travel somewhat faster, but it is, nevertheless, seldom realized that the difference in the *handling* of a boat on the wind amounts usually not to a few percent but, perhaps, to 10 or more percent. A safe criterion for judging the efficiency of a skipper on this point of sailing is the *"height"* he is able to attain and, when it is claimed a *boat cannot point high,* it is generally the case that this is not the fault of the boat, for whatever bad qualities she may have, there are surely two, when compared with other boats of her class, for which she cannot be made responsible; these are *"starting quickly"* and *"pointing high."* A good skipper will, in fact, always point higher or at least work his boat up farther to windward than his inferiors and, at the same time, travel just as fast, whereas the latter reveal their inefficiency by falling off.

In what, we may ask, does the science of pointing high and, at the same time, travelling fast on the wind consist? The answer is:

(a) In the proper handling of the tiller.
(b) In the proper trimming of the sheets.

Both apparently extremely simple and still most complicated!

On a beat to windward we may discriminate between the following *two methods of sailing a boat* — the choice depends on the type of boat, certain qualities that may be peculiar to her, and on the nature of the wind:

200

Beating to Windward

M. Rosenfeld

I. By watching the jib.

II. By watching the racing pennant.

Beating to Windward by the Jib

is customary on *yachts* with large fore-sails or balloon jibs especially in stiff breezes, that have a tendency to *shift* constantly.

The helmsman should watch the jib constantly and in light airs hold the sheet in his hand. He may or rather should ease the sheet at intervals in order to feel the wind, that its slightest veering from the quarter may not escape his notice. Many helmsmen are known to prefer to sit in lee, as from this position they are better able to watch and feel their boat, quite aside from the fact that this seat is the more comfortable one, especially when the boat is heeled, as one is not in constant danger of slipping down to leeward. Here the helmsman must, however, be *informed on the trim of the mainsail* by the man on the main sheet, whose duty it is to keep his eye fixed on both pennant and mainsail. This is absolutely necessary, as it can happen that the mainsail luffs, while the jib is full and drawing, or vice versa; or it is even possible that the upper part of the mainsail, especially of the Marconi rig, may be drawing in one direction and the lower part in the opposite — the pennant may, for example, indicate a light east wind above and the smoke of a cigarette a northeast or even west wind below. In such cases it is of course necessary to ascertain, which current is the stronger — the higher or the lower one, and to act accordingly; and, should the variation in the direction of the two currents be small, to take this into account and bear off somewhat. The peculiar feeling, often experienced even by the skilled helmsman, that *his boat is beating to windward badly on a certain day* is usually to be explained by the phenomenon that the wind is full of eddies and thus variable in its direction in the different layers of the air; in this case the only remedy is to *bear off and run fuller,* regardless of the direction of course, surely a most painful, but the only alternative!

As we have observed, the man on the main sheet should never fail to report to the helmsman the slightest change in the atmospheric conditions, as indicated by the pennant or mainsail, and this information, especially in a final struggle, should always be communicated in a low tone or whisper and repeated again and again, in some such form as "full — flapping — shivering — full — full — full — shivering — flapping — full — full —" etc. Under *these* circumstances it is the duty of the third man to assume the functions of the man on the main sheet and to inform the helmsman on all events pertaining to the competing boats, especially those in the rear, as, for example, A is in our wake — she is pointing higher — falling off — is again in our wake — is falling off badly — attention, she is coming about — etc. On a beat to windward the helmsman should seldom look aft, as a rule, only just before he intends to go about or make some other manoeuvre, for which an *exact knowledge of the situation* — of his own boat as of those of his competitors, is essential.

If the wind is too strong for the helmsman to hold the jib in his hand, he can make the sheet fast to the jib sheet cleat and rest his arm on it — on that part leading from the clew of the jib to the cleat, whereby he will be able from the tension of the sheet to form an idea of or feel the strength and direction of the wind. He can, for instance, by pressing his

Three International Class One Design, Close-Hauled in Long Island Sound. Neither Boat Is Blanketed

arm or hand on the sheet, that will yield somewhat to the pressure brought to bear on it, feel the flaw the *instant* it strikes the sail — at all events a second or two *sooner* than his attention would otherwise be called to its presence by the heeling of the boat. In this way he is able not only to luff up but also to bear off again sooner. The science of luffing and working a boat up to windward lies chiefly in luffing up and bearing off at the *right moment* — as *early as possible*. If you fail to take advantage *at once* of a flaw that sets in more from the quarter, there is little use in attempting to work your boat up to windward, as she will already be heeled over, sliding off and thus losing her headway rapidly. On the other hand, should

203

you luff too early, you lose your headway at once and will then find it difficult to get your boat running at full speed for the next minute or so.

According to the method just described of sailing by the jib the helmsman has recourse to the following means in working his boat to windward:

(a) To his eyes — in watching the jib.
(b) To the feeling imparted to his one hand by the tiller.
(c) To the feeling imparted to his other hand by the jib sheet.
(d) To the information communicated on the mainsail.

The handling of the tiller in its various details depends entirely on the type of the boat. The small centerboard boat can be steered comparatively freely, whereas the yacht, being much more sensitive, must be handled with the greatest care. Here many a sin is committed. The helmsman who is accustomed only to the smaller craft will, as a rule, behave like a fanatic at the tiller of a large yacht, jerking it round incessantly in both directions; this impedes materially the speed of the boat, as the slightest jerk, although it might be supposed, when judged by the little pressure that is brought to bear on the tiller, to give rise to a change of course that might be readily effected with little resistance on the part of the boat, works like a brake on her. In the case of a modern yacht with long overhangs, that swings on her short fin as a pivot with her long lever arms, the pressure that must be brought to act on the tiller to effect a change of course is extremely small; but, that the broad surface of her fin with its great resistance to the water may be brought to assume a new direction and that, in doing so, must be pressed like an inclined plane against the masses of water, is a matter that is seldom taken into account by the helmsman, because he himself does not feel the reaction on the tiller. As the slightest pressure on the tiller sets the long overhangs in motion, the helmsman is easily deceived and fails to realize that this slight pressure above gives rise to an enormous effect or resistance below in the water; this can be demonstrated by attempting to turn a board of the dimensions of the fin of a yacht, immersed vertically in the water, through even the smallest angle. The tiller of a 6 meter yacht should, for example, be held not in the palm of the hand but by two fingers only, and the arm of that hand should always be propped, as is customary in drawing a straight line. Moreover, the tiller should be held not in the middle nor ad libitum but at its extreme end, that the effect produced by the slightest motion may be reduced to a minimum; and, to insure still greater steadiness, you may rest the arm with which you are steering on your knee, holding and propping the wrist with your other hand.

On the wind, especially in a stiff breeze, the back-stays must of course be drawn as taut as possible; otherwise the mast will be bent forward (in the middle) by the pull of the jib, with the result that its luff becomes slack and the jib itself sags off to leeward, often to such a degree that it becomes quite impossible to sail by it.

Beating to windward by the pennant
is more or less customary on boats with small jibs and in winds that are *steady in both strength and direction.*

The helmsman watches the pennant and the mainsail and lets the man on the jib sheet report on the trim of the jib. On small boats the helmsman

204

may tend the mainsail himself, but on yachts this is not customary; it is also not customary to make the sheets fast on the wind, except on yachts in a heavy wind. In a stiff breeze it will be found extremely practical, especially on small boats, to let a third man tend the main sheet; in this case it is, however, essential that a certain harmony or understanding exist between the helmsman and the man on the sheet, as it is no easy matter to tend the main sheet correctly or, at least, to the satisfaction of the helmsman — to pay it off at the right moment in the flaws, that is, when a heavy flaw strikes the sail, to ease the sheet accordingly, that the skipper may gradually bear off and keep his boat travelling at full speed, and, as the flaw lets up and the boat is slowly luffed, to trim in the sheet at the proper moment. On a small boat in a heavy wind the following rule or order of action should be observed: *bear off and ease the sheets, letting the boat run as long as the flaw lasts; trim in the sheets and work up to windward, as the flaw is letting up.* On a yacht the reverse order should hold; as the sheets are made fast in this case, you will be obliged to luff somewhat during the flaw. With regard to the proper trim of the sails we have already observed in Part I that, generally speaking, you can trim closest and point highest with a small (centerboard) boat, when the wind is blowing at the rate of about 3 yards per second, and with a yacht, when its strength is about 5 yards.

The successive stages in the manoeuvre of *coming about or tacking ship* are the following: Luff your boat into the wind — the yacht more slowly than the smaller (centerboard) craft, and, at the same time, trim in the mainsail even midships, whereby you profit materially, as the sail is kept drawing to the very last moment of the turn and the turn itself is thereby greatly facilitated. Then let the jib sheet run; the jib itself will, moreover, continue to draw longer than the mainsail does, as it is pressed by the swing or rotation of the bow of the boat against the wind. As soon as you are on the other tack, bear off at once, at first rather rapidly, that your boat may get started more quickly at the same time easing the sheets, especially the jib sheet, for that purpose. Then after 5 to 15 seconds trim in the sheets and run as high as possible.

We proceed next to the

Tactics of Beating to Windward

We discriminate here between the following cases:

I. *You are clear of your competitors and can choose your course or tacks without regard to them.*

II. *You are being overtaken — for reasons unforeseen, and must assume the defensive.*

III. *You are in the lead but pressed by one competitor and must assume the defensive.*

IV. *You are in the lead but pressed by several competitors and must assume the defensive.*

V. *You are second or even farther astern and must assume the offensive.*

Case I: The simplest case is that, where you are unmolested by your competitors and able to choose the course or tacks you see fit; it is immaterial here, whether you are in the lead or far astern. In either case you should, however, be guided by the two long established rules:

I. *"Keep on the tack that will bring you nearer to the mark."* You

205

should not, for instance, at the beginning of a leg to windward make a long tack that may prove unnecessary (cf. sketches B and C of diagram below), for, in the first place, you cannot know how long you should keep on that tack, as you are unable to judge at a greater distance from the mark, whether you will be able to fetch it or not, when you finally go about, and secondly, should the wind veer more from the quarter, your competitors on the other tack may be able contrary to their expectations, to fetch the mark — without making an extra hitch, while you have been working unnecessarily up to windward. It can also happen in light, variable airs that the wind may shift or die out entirely, in which case the others will be well in front — nearer the mark, and eventually to the weather, whereas you have dropped far astern and, may be, to leeward. The same rule holds, when you cannot quite fetch a mark: You should not go about, until you have *reached or are abreast the mark,* as you will then be able to judge exactly how far you will have to run on that tack (cf. sketch A).

2. *"Choose your course according to the wind zones."* Should you discover a streak of wind within your reach, you may head for it, even should this change, of course involve a violation of the first rule. You must not be in doubt as to whether the streak of wind is due to a convectional current of air arising from an adjustment of temperatures, a phenomenon that is peculiar to the zone along the shore and is characterized by more or less *stationary* winds, in which case you *may steer for it,* or whether it is a forerunner of the wind prevailing in the upper layers of the air, that working downward and gradually spreading over the entire surface of the water will *soon reach the whole field of boats,* the one sooner the other later, to the satisfaction of the former and to the discomfort of the latter.

Case I.

Correct.	Wrong.	Wrong.
Starboard Tack not made till in immediate Neighborhood of Mark.	Starboard Tack too long.	Starboard Tack too short to fetch Mark on ensuing Tack.

Even then it may be advisable to head for the streak of wind, but in this case the saying holds: *"Never trust to luck — discover it first."* At all events, act either at once or not at all. *Never change your theory or the scheme* you have once decided upon. If you have bad luck in lee, do not attempt to work up to windward behind the others, but rather wait for the reaction or some favorable change, trusting to *some freak of the wind* for regaining your lead — or be doomed from *adhering to your theory.* A compromise is sure to be fatal. It is, in fact, remarkable how just the wind is in general, it favors first the one and then the other. If you are especially clever, you will say to yourself: "I must manoeuvre in such a way, that I profit from both streaks of wind, working ahead, first with the one, then with the other!" We shall treat this subject later more in detail.

Case II: *You are being overhauled — for reasons unforseen, and must assume the defensive.* Here we are possessed of those peculiar unsympathetic feelings familiar to every skipper, who first believed he was so far ahead that he was absolutely safe and then is suddenly forced to realize that the whole field is "close on his heels." The most experienced skipper will ask with grave mien: "What have I done wrong?" He may have made no mistake, but he was surely not cautious, for he should know from experience that it is seldom that one can gain such a lead, that one may choose one's course quite regardless of the others.

Let us assume we are well ahead — our competitors astern either in our wake or somewhat to the weather of it (cf. diagram below), and that on looking aft we suddenly discover to our dismay that our nearest competitor is pointing *extremely* high and getting, in addition, more wind. The situation may not yet be serious, as we still have a good lead; but, nevertheless, we begin to get uneasy upon observing that our competitor continues to point much higher than we can and is also favored by *one flaw after another more from the quarter.* The situation grows more serious, until finally our skipper realizes: "It is improbable that the improbable may never come to pass!" The moment has arrived when we would fall *astern* of our competitor, should we risk going about on the other tack. However painful the situation may have become, we should not even *think of going about* but, in spite of our ill luck, stick to the old saying;

"Never make a tack that will bring you astern of your competitor."

We cannot fare worse than we are faring at present, but we may fare better; should we go about now, our fate is sealed, and we acknowledge our defeat by the manoeuvre (cf. sketch A of diagram). But how can we be helped?

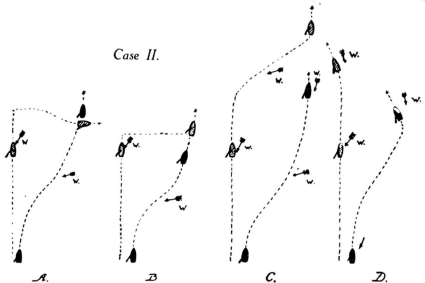

Case II.

A.   B.   C.   D.

Or can we help ourselves out of the fatal situation? We could, as is often the case, beseech the God of the winds to have mercy on us and favor us at least with the *second* prize. — But it often happens that the wind suddenly reacts and heads off our competitor to such a degree, that he must bear off on to his initial point of sailing, or it may veer to such an extent that both boats must bear off so much, that their former relative position is re-established — with our competitor in our wake (cf. sketch D). Another favorable moment is that we may get the wind more from the quarter somewhat later, while our competitor is obliged to bear off, as represented in sketch C.

But we may ask, is it not better to take no such chances, as those involved in the above defensive measures and to act in due time — at the right moment. It is, in fact, the one and only alternative, provided we can rely on our boat — on her good qualities, knowing that she is not inferior to the others under similar conditions and chances. The *moment* our competitor begins to point higher, we should go about at once — the sooner the better (cf. sketch B); but this manoeuvre must be made, at the latest, in due time to enable us to cross his bow, that we may come about on his weather and bless him with the "hopeless position." We sacrifice, indeed, by this move a greater part of our former lead, which we might be loath to do, had we the slower boat; in that case we should probably prefer to take the chances and trust to the other measures — those already mentioned above, for a successful issue.

Case III: *"You are in the lead but pressed by one competitor and must assume the defensive."* This is the most frequent case, as we know from experience, since you are bound to direct your attention, even in a larger field of boats, to the one nearest you and to *choose your course and tacks more or less with reference to her*. It is here that the science of sailing or rather racing can be developed to the highest degree of proficiency and that a spectator begins to follow the race with interest and apparent pleasure, being impressed by the enormous value of correct tactics, which make it almost impossible for the boat astern, even should she be the faster of the two, to overhaul the one in the lead. Many a skipper may think he understands and masters these tactics on the assumption that they can be formulated in the simple rule: "As leading boat on the wind blanket your competitor, that is, keep him always in your lee, (at least as long as he may not succeed in "breaking through!"), and tack the moment he tacks." This surely sounds like a plausible rule, but it really contains little advice, at least such as would always insure success, for there is no skipper whose designs could not be frustrated — an escape effected at some critical moment, should his tactics of defence be confined alone to those formulated in this rule. The reason for this is to be ascribed to the great variety of methods of defence that can be employed, between three of which we shall discriminate here. The manner in which these methods are to be applied, according to the case or situation in question, becomes clear from a study of the "hopeless position."

First Method of Defence

A. If your competitor is close on your heels, lay your course so that you bring him into your wake; it is here immaterial, whether the two boats meet on different tacks (cf. sketch A_2 of diagram on page 210) or are running neck to neck on the same tack (cf. sketch A_1). Only in the case where your competitor is approaching at full speed is it advisable to modify these tactics. As you always lose considerable headway in going about, your competitor might succeed in breaking through and escaping in lee: it is, therefore, better in this case for you to try to gain the "safe leeward position" by coming about beforehand, just before the two boats meet, directly ahead of your competitor. If you are successful in the attempt, you can then force him into the "hopeless berth." By this manoeuvre his fate is sealed, as, once in your wake, he will have to break through *first* the zone of wind deflected in its direction by your sails, the harmful effect of which becomes more pronounced the nearer he approaches (cf. zone or position a of diagram for "hopeless position" on p. 180), and *secondly*, should he attempt to bear off, also the zone of your wind-shadow (cf. zone or position b of same diagram); the result is: your competitor is materially handicapped, being at the mercy of two successive defensive measures always at your command, from which he is unable to escape. If the initial situation of the two boats is that represented in sketch AI a_1, b_1, or a_3, b_3) of the diagram, the boat in the lead — to windward, will have to run fuller in order to bring her competitor first into her wind-shadow and then into her wake. In this case it would be a great mistake for the leading boat to work up to windward and be contented alone with the harmful effect produced by her wind-shadow, as prescribed below by the second method of defence, since an experienced skipper could easily take advantage of a flaw, by bearing off to break through the pointed wind-shadow and to escape in lee. On the other hand, the leading boat must be pressed to the *last degree*, should her competitor attempt by pressing to get clear of her wake, for once the latter is out of it — to the weather, the situation becomes most serious for the other boat.

Second Method of Defence

B. *Should your lead be greater* (than in case A), *then force your competitor into the zone of your disturbed wind* (cf. sketch of "hopeless position" on p. 180 and sketch B of diagram on page 210)

If you can hold your competitor in this position tack for tack, it will be a difficult matter for him to make a favorable move; he should be kept to leeward, in the direction the wind is blowing, in which case you need entertain no apprehensions of a shift of wind, as the wind will always be blowing *from you toward him* and will thus reach him in the same condition, with its various shifts in direction and strength, only a few seconds later.

While the first method of defence enabled you to employ the defensive measures peculiar to both zones a and b of the "hopeless position" against your competitor, here, at greater distances to the weather, your more effective weapon is the disturbed wind of zone b. At such distances it would be a mistake to try to force your competitor into your wake, as he would then be running not in your wind zone but in one parallel to it, where the flaws might strike more from the quarter and thus enable him to work up to your *weather* and finally to escape to windward; this possibility is represented in sketch A of the diagram for Case II on page 207. It may, of course, often be difficult for you to hold your competitor in zone b of the eddies of your back wind; here you should be careful not to make the mistake of supposing

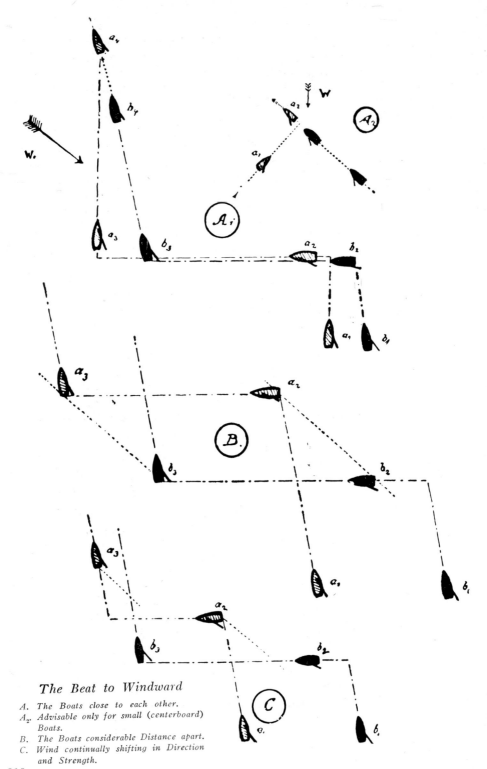

The Beat to Windward

A. The Boats close to each other.
A₂. Advisable only for small (centerboard)
    Boats.
B. The Boats considerable Distance apart.
C. Wind continually shifting in Direction
    and Strength.

Mainsail of 4144 is Blanketed. In Spite of It She Is Pulling Out in Front with Her Jib Due to Her "Safe Leeward Position"

Curry, Aerodynamics of Sails and Racing Tactics.

you are *blanketing him by directing your course according to the direction of the wind, as this does not indicate the real direction of your blanketing effect. Go by the direction of your pennant.* You will be able to recognize at once, even at *greater* distances from your competitor, whether he is running in the zone *b* of your disturbed wind from the fact that his speed will be materially diminished in that zone. On the one hand, in order to *keep* him at bay — by holding him in the zone of your disturbed wind, and, on the other hand, to increase your lead without travelling too fast — out of the prescribed course for that purpose, you should let your boat run at the same speed as that of your competitor by working up gradually to windward; this manoeuvre is not included among the sketches of the diagram. In this way you hold your competitor at bay and increase your lead at the same time. Should he attempt to break through the zone of your disturbed wind by running fuller, you also need only bear off more, and, by thus increasing your speed, you force him back into that unfavorable zone.

Third Method of Defence

C. If the wind is constantly shifting, always keep ahead and to the weather of your competitor (cf. sketch C of diagram on page 210).

These tactics have the advantage of insuring the greatest degree of safety for the boat in the lead, as it would be impossible for a competing boat to escape, even should she be favored by a *stronger wind and flaws that come more from the quarter.* We must, indeed, for the moment give up all hopes of harming our competitor seriously and of increasing thereby our lead materially, but in return we retain the two above mentioned defensive measures at our command. Should our competitor, due to some freak of the wind, succeed in decreasing our lead, he must still break through the zone of our disturbed wind — the first barrier to be encountered in an attempt to escape. Should the attempt prove successful, the second of the above mentioned defensive measures still remains at our command: we bear off, run fuller and force him into our wake. This mode of beating to windward is without doubt the safest, though not always the most advantageous, and should, therefore, be adopted by beginners in all winds in preference to the two other defensive methods.

Case IV: *"You are in the lead but pressed by several competitors and must assume the defensive."*

A. You have a good lead: Keep half way between the courses chosen by your competitors astern that you may blanket the one that seems to be getting nearer (cf. sketch on page 213).

If, for instance, two competitors are pursuing you and both are equally distant astern, then work your boat up to windward on a course that lies *half way between the courses* they are steering. You can then, at any moment, change your course and bear over toward the one that appears to be closing up on you; that is, you direct your course more toward the quarter, from which the greater danger is imminent; in which case you will always be in a position, should it prove necessary, to throw your boat directly ahead and to the weather of your more dangerous competitor, thereby barring his course before it is too late (cf. sketch on next page).

212

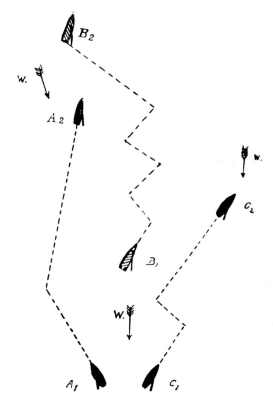

B. Your lead is short: The problem of defence becomes more difficult, as your lead is diminished and the number of your pursuers increases, especially when they approach on different tacks or split tacks and diverge in two groups in different directions; for you must then decide between the two groups, *against which one of the two you should assume the defensive — which you should blanket.* This is perhaps the only or gravest predicament encountered in a beat to windward, one where the most experienced skipper is often at a loss to know how to act and need make himself no reproaches, should he finally be overtaken by the one group, after having frustrated all attempts of the other to overhaul him; for it was impossible for him to know at the critical moment, which of the two tacks would be the more favorable one.

In this embarrassing situation, where you have to decide which boat or group of boats you should hold at bay, there is no rule that can be offered, only the good advice: *Hold the group whose course or tack seems to you the more favorable; or assume the defensive against the group, in which your most formidable rival is competing.* To choose the middle course would be a grave mistake, as, by failing to take advantage of the defensive measures at your command to injure the one or the other group, you may be beaten by *both.*

Case V: *"You are second or even farther astern and must assume the offensive."* It is, of course, an extremely difficult matter even to suggest any offensive tactics that may be employed in this case, after we have already disclosed the various effective measures of defence that are always at the command of the leading boat; but, nevertheless, an offensive should be undertaken, even should your competitors all be *most* skilled and experienced skippers.

Let us first assume the simpler case, where the skipper of the boat in the lead is not familiar with the defensive tactics at his command on a beat to windward, as formulated above; here one may be guided by the universal rule: *"Do always exactly the reverse of what the boat ahead of you is doing."* In other words, always choose the other tack or split tacks with her at once. The chances are then equally divided between the two boats and the probability thus one to two that you may decrease the lead of your competitor or even cross his bow the next time the two boats meet. You should avoid by all means falling into his wake, for, once in his wake, you are in a most hopeless situation; you are obliged either to struggle in vain in the hopeless position, or, should you be farther astern, to run under *similar wind conditions,* and in either case your fate is sealed from the very beginning.

We now proceed to the more unsatisfactory case, where our competitor is thoroughly familiar with all the defensive tactics of beating to windward and checkmates at once any manoeuvre we may attempt — he does exactly what we do, tacks when we tack, etc. — in other words, he frustrates every attempt on our part to escape. Can anything be done? On the one hand, we may hope our competitor will make some slight tactical mistake sooner or later — he has only to go about a few seconds too early or too late — and we are saved — we have succeeded in breaking through. On the other hand, we should do everything in our power to annoy an experienced competitor in carrying out his defensive tactics — by laying all sorts of snares for him; but first of all, we should sail our boat most carefully, taking advantage of every flaw that comes more from the quarter, and try to work up to windward out of his wake; or, what is even more promising, we may bear off considerably and, giving our sails a good full at the same time, attempt to break through in lee. From the knowledge that the form of the wind shadow is conical, we may assume that it will be no very difficult matter to break through this zone of disturbed air at a somewhat greater distance to leeward, where it becomes *much narrower and tapers gradually to a point.* To effect this we bear off and let our boat travel at full speed, until we have broken through this narrow zone and are quite clear of our competitor;

In Zone of Eddies

then we trim in our sheets and try to run higher and work our boat up to windward, sailing her with greatest care and all means at our command on a beat to windward. In this manner we may then succeed in working our boat slowly to the front and reaching finally the "safe leeward position," as indicated in sketch 1 of the diagram below.

I wish to lay special stress on the following point or rather advice that holds not only for the preceding case but quite in general: Should you succeed in bringing your boat to the front by only a few yards, although you may lie one or two yards to leeward of your competitor, you should press her to the extreme, even at the sacrifice of speed for the moment, in order to force your competitor into your wake (cf. sketch 2 of diagram below).

As a third and last method of offence, the only remaining and final alternative that can save the situation, should your competitor manoeuvre correctly and frustrate all your attempts, as formulated above, to break through, I may recommend the following: *"Keep shifting tacks until your competitor gets tired of following suit and finally lets you escape — on the one or the other tack."* It is an extremely amusing sight to watch two boats shifting from one tack to the other in quick succession; by this manoeuvre the *leading boat only* is endangered — in two respects: she is handicapped so seriously with regard to her other competitors by this constant shifting of tacks that, unless she changes these tactics of her own free will, she may in the mean-time be overhauled by a third boat, whereas the pursuing boat is enabled, by shifting from one tack to the other at free will, in correct form and at such opportune moments that she retains her headway after the shift, to draw up gradually on her rival and perhaps seal her fate, before the latter has succeeded in carrying out all the defensive measures required of and forced upon her at most inopportune moments (cf. first sketch on next page).

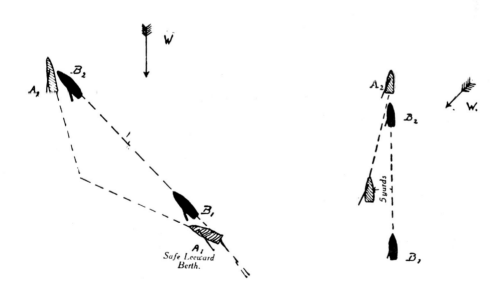

215

Meeting of Two Boats on Beat to Windward

The powerful weapon on a beat to windward is the "starboard tack," as it has the right of way over the port tack. Once in a position to make use of this weapon and force your competitor to go about or bear off under your stern, you should win the race; it is most decisive, when made proper use of — at the critical moment.

You can, for instance, prevent your competitor from rounding a mark in the manner desired by approaching him on the starboard tack and forcing him about; if he should be just to leeward of you and on the same — starboard tack — but *not quite able* to fetch the mark, he can not go about, as you have the right of way; he is thus obliged, in order to avoid a collision, whether it suits him or not, to remain on the starboard tack, passing *to leeward of the mark*, and may be forced a considerable distance beyond it, before he can make the necessary hitch — on the other tack — that will enable him to fetch and round the mark (cf. sketch A on next page).

The situation may be such that your competitor is approaching the mark on the port tack. In this case he must give way to you, as you have the right of way, and he may not wedge himself in between you and the mark, but must bear off and pass under your stern (cf. sketch B).

However important the starboard or right of way tack may be in general, its value will seldom be so highly appreciated by the skipper, who is familiar with the manoeuvre of

"Going About in the Lee" *

of a competitor and realizes the advantages resulting from this manoeuvre, if carried out correctly. This means of meeting and assuming the offensive against a boat approaching on the starboard tack — by a counter manoeuvre — which is sure to result in gaining the lead, has already been mentioned in the section on the "safe leeward position" (cf. pp. 183-191). A more detailed description of how the manoeuvre should be carried out is, therefore, justified here. I may observe, the premises for a successful issue of *this manoeuvre* are that the boats in question be *small (centerboard) boats* and not yachts, as the latter are too sluggish in getting started after the shift of tack.** The manoeuvre itself should be carried out in the following manner: We are approaching on the port tack, our competitor on the starboard, and our courses are such that the two boats would collide, if they continued on these courses. Now, we do not bear off, as most skippers without exception are accustomed to do, and pass under the stern of our competitor, but we keep on our course till the last moment, go about quickly close under his lee, gain thereby the safe leeward berth and with this formidable weapon at our command force our competitor into the hopeless position. I have made this manoeuvre at least 100 times in races of recent date and invariably with success. The chief condition for a successful issue of the manoeuvre is, however, that the *bow of your boat should not be behind that of your competitor's* after you have gone about and have filled away on the other tack (cf. first sketch of diagram on page 218).

The conditions are, however, quite different in the case of yachts and,

---

* This manoeuvre is confined to the smaller or centerboard craft.

** And the danger of collision being too great. (See Racing Rules.)

as already stated, it is only under *most exceptionally favorable* ones that the manoeuvre should be attempted by a larger yacht. If you come about directly in the lee of your competitor, the latter will probably plough by you to windward like a steamer, while your own yacht will be struggling in vain to get started, and, before you realize it, you will find yourself in the "hopeless position." And you will hardly fare better, should you be able, due to a slight lead, to just cross the bow of your competitor, and should then go about directly, with the intention of blanketing him, as indicated in sketch B on the next page; for, by the time your own yacht gets started again — after shift of tack — your competitor will probably have slipped through her blanketing zone, and you will find yourself dropping astern yard by yard — in spite of your weather berth — due to the unfavorable action of the air cushion caused by the sails of the other yacht in the zone, in which you are sailing, the harmful distant action arising from her "safe leeward berth."

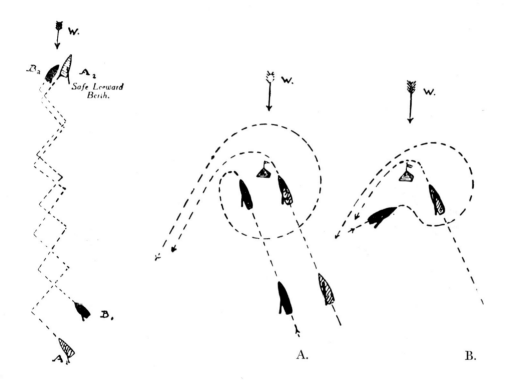

A.   B.

Sketch A on page 219 represents the correct manner in which you should manoeuvre with a yacht in the present case. On the general assumption that we are somewhat in the lead, we come about — in spite of the fact that we should be able to cross the bow of our competitor — about 30 to 50 yards to leeward of the course he is steering. This insures us a sufficient lead in the direction of our new course, a greater part of which we may expect to lose due to our reduced speed from coming about; but this sacrifice is willingly made for the favorable berth. The most unfavorable position ensuing from this manoeuvre is that where the two yachts are lying neck to neck, after we have regained our speed. Under normal conditions we may, however, exclude the "hopeless position" even here and reckon, by pointing gradually higher, to work up slowly to windward of our competitor and finally to subject him to our commanding "safe leeward berth." Even should we not succeed in accomplishing this, our ensuing position is not only quite undisturbed but, due to the distant air cushion action of our sails, the more favorable one.

Among the many other cases, where two boats may meet on a beat to windward, the following may be briefly mentioned. Suppose through some manoeuvre — after the rounding of a mark or "breaking through" in lee — we find ourselves, boat I, in the relative position to our competitor, boat II, indicated in the second sketch of the annexed diagram. According to our above views on the tactics of beating to windward we must *expect* to

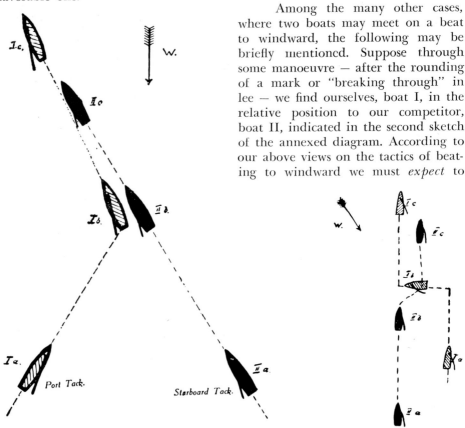

be attacked by our competitor at any moment, for the course we are steering is such that we are exposed to imminent danger. We must, therefore, go about on the other tack just as soon as the first opportunity offers a chance of our crossing our competitor's bow (cf. sketch, position Ib). By this manoeuvre our situation is saved and we are in a position (Ic) to make use of the tactics of beating to windward set forth in Case IIIA, first by blanketing our competitor and then by bearing off and forcing him into our wake.

218

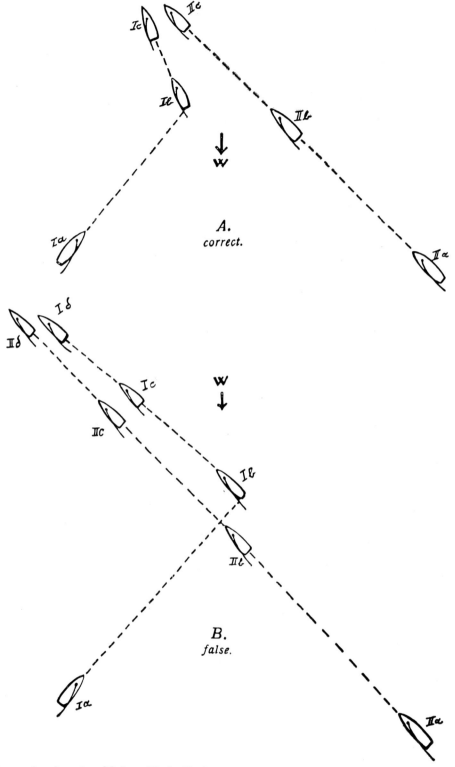

A.
correct.

B.
false.

Curry, Aerodynamics of Sails and Racing Tactics.

Rounding a Mark

The rounding of a mark is an act in itself that demands a certain amount of both skill and practice. The skipper who is able to round a mark with the correct technique will always gain a few boat lengths every time he makes this manoeuvre. The most common mistake made by the inexperienced skipper is that he turns the mark too sharply and thereby robs his boat, especially if a yacht, of her whole headway. It is seldom the case that a good skipper describes too large a curve at a mark. The question is: How may one round a mark in a comparatively sharp curve and at the same time not materially diminish the speed of the boat? This is demonstrated best by the manner in which the driver of an automobile takes a sharp curve. If he wants to take it at a good speed without being thrown off the road, he will drive his car, upon approaching the curve, close to its outer side and then swing off gradually in a long flat curve, that brings him *close* to its inner side at the point, where the curvature of the road is greatest, and across it again close and parallel to its outer (opposite) side, as represented in the last of the accompanying sketches. The same technique should be applied by a skipper in rounding a mark. Suppose we are approaching a mark before the wind or on the beam, then we should bear off somewhat from the mark just before we reach it, that we may be able to describe the ensuing curve in the form prescribed; to which effect we should run as close to the mark as possible on passing it, as indicated in sketch A. But we must be especially careful in case of currents and in light airs not to run too near the mark — to avoid fouling it.

An *exception* to the above is the following: *One or more competitors are close on our heels and the next leg is a beat to wind-*

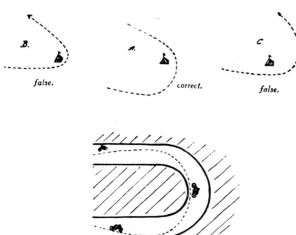

B. *false.*

A. *correct.*

C. *false.*

Rounding a Mark.

ward. In this case there is danger that the other boats that are approaching the mark before the wind or on the beam may attempt to wedge themselves in between us and the mark by a sharp turn; this we can frustrate only by describing a sharp curve at the mark, such as is designated in sketch B on the preceding page as "false." Even should we *still be clear* of the boat directly astern, we must round the mark in a *sharp curve* and after the turn luff up quickly and press our boat (boat I of the

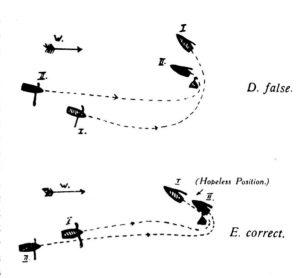

D. false.

(Hopeless Position.)

E. correct.

accompanying sketch E) to the extreme, at least for the first few seconds (cf. also photograph on next page); otherwise it may happen that, while we are rounding in a graceful curve (cf. sketch D), our competitor makes a sharp turn at the mark and immediately runs up to our weather — a fatal manoeuvre, for which there is no counter manoeuvre on our part. In this case the disadvantage of the sharp turn will always be more than counterbalanced by our weather berth, which may mean the "hopeless position" for the other boat. (However watch also that your competitor does not break through in the lee!)

The second important factor in rounding a mark is a correct handling of the sails. You can not only retain the headway or speed of your boat but even augment it in the case, where you are approaching the mark before the wind or with the wind a beam, by tending your sheets correctly, that is, in such a manner that a certain unison always exists between the trimming in of the sails and the curve described by the boat; the former must correspond exactly to the turn, such that the angle at which the wind strikes the sails is never, not for a second, less than 15 or more than 20 degrees. It is, of course, extremely difficult to tend the sheets in such a manner, that the sails are kept under *"maximum pressure" during the whole turn.* As the man on the sheet is misled by the slow turn in a light wind to trim in the sails *too soon and too fast,* to the effect that the boat is close hauled long *before* the turn is finished, similarly in a stiff breeze it will be found almost impossible to get the sails in fast enough. The more common mistake is probably the former, especially as the jib sheet, which is seldom run through blocks, is generally taken in with a *single* pull or jerk during the relatively slow turn, instead of being pulled in *slowly and carefully.* In a *heavy wind* the solution lies almost exclusively in the skill or rather celerity of the man on the sheet. For how can the sails be trimmed in, almost midships, during a turn, for which hardly two or three seconds are required? The following suggestions may be of service in tending the sheets:

221

J 226 Rounds Mark in Sharp Curve and Runs at Once High on Wind, Forcing Pursuer Into "Hopeless Position"; Otherwise There Is Danger That Latter May Pass to Windward

(1) The main sheet of a *yacht* should be tended by two men, if possible one on each end of the sheet; in the exceptional case, when there is no third man at our disposal, the jib should be taken in *before* the manoeuvre, in order that the man on the jib sheet may assist in tending the main sheet. The sheet should be hauled in hand over hand with your arms well stretched, as in this manner you are able to grasp a longer piece of the rope than with your arms bent. This method of hauling in or hauling yourself up a rope is the one that is customary and most successfully employed by the rope climber; but you must be especially careful not to miss your grip. As the tennis player or golfer must keep his eye fixed on the ball and not look off or up, *until* it has been struck by the racquet or club, similarly the man on the main sheet, when hauling it in quickly in the above manner, must follow every grip of his hands along the sheet most carefully — with his eyes. Then it will not happen that he misses his grip, which is so often the case, when he is anxious to work fast. The above also holds for the halyards, when the sail must be set quickly. *In heavy winds, not only on a yacht but on a small (centerboard) boat, the man on the jib sheet or a third hand, but under no circumstances the helmsman, should help in tending the main-sail in turning a mark.*

(2) In the case of a very quick turn you may make an exception to the general rule and begin to haul in not only the jib but also the mainsail shortly *before* you reach the turning mark.

(3) The helmsman should be guided by the momentary position of the sails and if necessary lengthen the turn somewhat, *until* they have been hauled in.

Let us now return to the technique of rounding a mark and consider the case, where we are approaching it *on the wind,* as represented in the accompanying sketch F. The path to be described depends here upon the momentary speed of the boat; it should naturally assume a sharper form at the beginning of the turn as it is generally the case that we have had no reason to work our boat unnecessarily to the weather and are, therefore *just* able to fetch the mark. Then the curve should be *lengthened* — the turn itself made less sharp, *after the mark,* as indicated in the sketch.

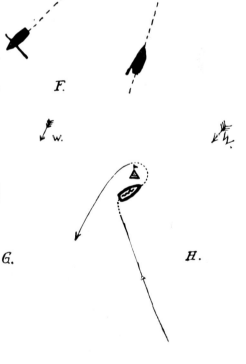

F.

G.

H.

223

What is to be done, if we *cannot quite fetch* a mark on a beat to windward? It is always a great mistake to try to force your boat round a mark by pressing her; the general result is that she loses her headway to such an extent that she slides off more than she goes ahead, and you are finally obliged to make a tack at the last moment. Even should you succeed in getting your boat over onto the other tack, you will find she has lost all her headway and that it is most difficult to get her started again (cf. sketch G on preceding page). The result of such a manoeuvre is, even if successful, the loss of at least several boat lengths; if not successful, as is oftener the case, it ends in misfortune — in your fouling the mark and being disqualified.

Here the only possible alternative of rounding the mark, without an extra tack — or rather two, is the following: Steer your boat as high on the wind as possible, but "full and by," *without pressing her,* and head either straight for the mark or for a point a few yards to *leeward of it;* and in the last moment, upon reaching the mark or the point just to leeward of it, throw her into the wind, let her shoot up to and beyond it with her sails flapping and then bear off sharply round it (cf. sketch H).

Should it happen that you are not quite sure in which direction the mark is to be rounded — on the starboard or port, there is no reason to despair, for in this predicament you need only round it in *both directions,* first in the one and then in the other direction — first on the port and then on the starboard, as indicated in the accompanying sketch.

The most important role played by a turning mark is in the various manoeuvres called forth, when a whole field of boats or a greater part of them reach it in a *bunch* — in close quarters. Here the first question

A.

Boats not overlapping (Wedging in between Boat ahead and Mark not allowed by Racing Regulations.

B.

Boat in Lead on ensuing Leg, not having been overlapped at Mark. (Wedging in between her and Mark not allowed.)

C.

Boats overlapping. (Wedging in between Boat in Lead and Mark allowed.)

to be put is: Are we overlapping or not? That is, are we clear of the boat ahead of us or not? We are "overlapping," that is, we are not "clear of" her, if our relative positions are such, that it is impossible for us either to luff up or to bear off without fouling her, as indicated in the last of the above sketches. The racing regulations stipulate that only in the case, where you are overlapping, that is, where you are not clear of your competitor ahead, may you wedge yourself in between him and the mark and with that intention call for "room," provided, however, your competitor has not already altered his course for the purpose and in the act of rounding it (cf. the three sketches).

In the chapter on "The Start" we have already observed, how important it is to acquire the inner position at a mark, especially on a leg before the wind. It is clear from the above considerations that this vital question of whether we may succeed in acquiring the inner berth at the mark depends alone on our ability to overlap the boat ahead of us or to prevent being overlapped by one astern, as the case may be, before we reach it. We should, therefore, make the greatest exertions till the last moment before the turn to establish an overlap on a boat ahead or to prevent one by one astern. It is here that only a few feet may decide the issue and perhaps the race in our favor.

Suppose we are approaching a mark before the wind. We should then always be guided by the rule of choosing the course that will assure us the inner position at the mark; should our competitor still have a lead of one and a half boat lengths, we may appear to be doomed to turn the mark on his lee quarter — in his wake. Our task is, however, to *establish an overlap at all costs — even at the last moment*. We can succeed in the attempt only by letting our spinnaker stand and draw till the last second, after our competitor has perhaps found it advisable to take his down; our spinnaker must catch the last breath of air that wafts us on toward the mark and must not be taken in till we are in the *act of turning it*.

As *leading boat* we should manoeuvre in a similar manner, should our competitor astern attempt to establish an overlap at the last moment, keeping all our sails set and drawing till and into the turn. It is just these situations, which are of such *vital and decisive moment*, that are seldom properly comprehended or that are, at least, generally undervalued by the inexperienced skipper.

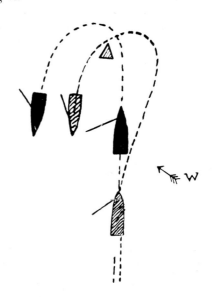

Let us imagine ourselves once more in the situation of the *skipper, who has hoped to establish an overlap* on the boat ahead and is finally forced to realize that his expectations are not to be fulfilled; in this case we are apparently obliged to bear off from the mark and to round it under the stern of our competitor, with the sad prospects of the ensuing situation — the "hopeless position," etc. But even here there is still a possibility of acquiring the lead, provided we have realized in *due time* that we could not expect to establish the desired overlap. To this effect we proceed as follows: Shortly before the mark we hold off well toward the outer side of the course — to windward of it, as represented in the accompanying sketch, so that we may be able to finish the greater part of our turn *before* we reach the mark; we can then run close up under it, passing it high on the wind and with our course already laid for the next leg. On the other hand, our competitor, who is somewhat

German Championship Races of 22 sq. m. Centerboard Class, Berlin, 1926

Leading Group: J 278, 363, 365, 306, 331. Middle: J 371, 303, 330, 250, 267, 302, 270, 366.
Rear Group: J 268, 289, 336, 334.

Photograph of Same Race Taken One Minute Later, Showing Order of Rounding Mark

Note that Boats formerly to leeward—on inner Side of Mark, reach it first. (278 rounded first, 363 second. See page 226.)

Hohmann, Berlin

ahead and laying his course straight for the mark, does not begin his turn till he reaches it, so that the greater part of the turn will have to be made after he passes the mark. The result is that there is *plenty of room* between him and the mark for us to round or rather to pass and that, after we have both laid courses on the next leg, we are to his weather perhaps to such an extent that we may soon acquire the lead. Even should we be somewhat farther astern, we are at least to windward of our competitor and have thus evaded being forced into the "hopeless position." This manoeuvre is most likely to succeed, when the boats have to jibe at the mark (cf. sketch on page 225).

Another method of overhauling a competitor before he reaches a mark is the following: Let us suppose he is heading straight for the mark with *the wind abeam;* we luff somewhat, in order to disturb his wind; this he cannot, of course, allow, and he must, therefore, have recourse to some counter-manoeuvre; he is obliged to luff also — according to the rule: "Always keep your competitor astern in your wake, especially on a course off the wind." The next question is whether we shall continue to luff or not. The skipper astern generally makes the mistake of luffing for only a short time and then bears off onto his former course — for the mark, without having accomplished anything. Here the correct manoeuvre on our part brings about the very situation, where we can lay a trap for our competitor, into which he

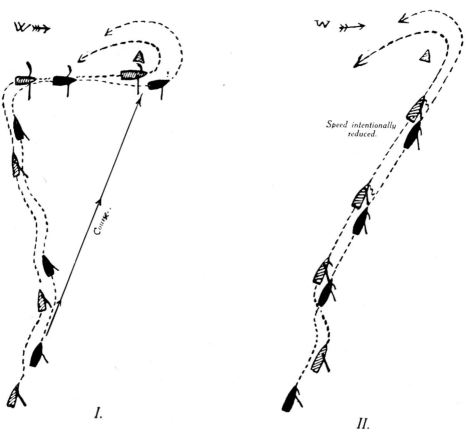

Speed intentionally
reduced.

Course.

I.

II.

is most likely to fall and from which he is seldom able to escape. We *continue* to luff, accepting the luffing match offered, whereas our competitor can hardly act otherwise, if he hopes to retain the inner position at the mark. What happens then? The next observation to be made is that our competitor begins to get extremely uneasy and nervous; naturally, he is in a dilemma, for he must bear off *sooner or later,* if he has any intention of rounding the mark. "Why?" would the novice ask. For the simple reason that the moment he bears off toward the mark he is lost; in the meantime, *the course on beam has become one dead before the wind,* and on the latter the boat with a short lead is doomed — she is blanketed completely; for, as we know from Part I, the harmful effect produced by blanketing is most fatal to a distance of twice the length of the mast. The further success of the manoeuvre is, of course, based on the assumption that our spinnaker is clear, can be set in a moment and is then kept up and drawing till the very last second. In this manner our competitor is soon overhauled, and upon our call for "room" at the mark his fate is sealed, for he is forced there into the outer position and on the ensuing leg into the "hopeless position" in our wake (cf. sketch I on preceding page).

As sequel to the above I will now disclose the counter-manoeuvre for the boat in the *lead,* the safest defensive method at our command for holding at bay a competitor close on our heels on any course off the wind.

In order to avoid a long luffing match, we luff *at once* so high, that our competitor astern finds it advisable to attempt to break through to leeward. He is likely to fall into the trap we are laying for him, unless he realizes at the moment that, even should he be successful in the attempt, he can hardly expect to break through our wind-shadow on the short run to the mark. Let us assume, however, that our competitor falls into this trap and bears off sharply to leeward; we follow suit at once and, before he realizes his situation — close under our lee quarter, his fate has been sealed; he has fallen into the trap laid for him, for the climax of the manoeuvre is reached: our competitor can no longer pass us to leeward, nor is he able to luff up under our stern and run up to our weather, which would be the only manoeuvre we could recommend in consideration of the proximity of the two boats, for his boat is *not clear* — she is, as it were, *made fast* to our lee quarter. As our competitor is handicapped by being blanketed, he may perhaps hope to get clear again by thrusting the nose of his boat around under our stern to the weather at some opportune moment. But this should also prove futile, for we as leading boat and, at the same time, in the inner position run correspondingly slower — *purposely.* This case belongs to those exceptional ones, where one must retard the speed of one's boat. We regulate our speed by letting the jib shiver or flap at intervals to such a degree, that our competitor can get clear of us under no circumstances; he is caught and is helpless, till we reach the mark, and there he is administered the bitter pill of the outer position with the "hopeless berth" as sequel (cf. sketch II on preceding page).

Another excellent method of defence to save, for instance, a *prolonged luffing match* at the last moment is the following: we know that it is not on the beam nor during the luffing match that danger is imminent, but that it is on the ensuing stretch before the wind that one's fate is sealed. We should, therefore, get our spinnaker clear, without attracting the attention of our competitor, and see that it is set and drawing the *moment* we bear off before the wind. Our pursuer, whose whole attention is concentrated on the luffing match, has probably made no preparations for setting this auxiliary sail, and, in the meantime, before he succeeds in getting his spinnaker out and drawing, we may have slipped out of his grip.

Finally, let us investigate the following situation: Suppose, through some manoeuvre, we — the light boat, find ourselves in the situation represented in the accompanying sketches A and B — a few boat lengths only from the mark; we are, in fact, so near it that it is too late and, moreover, in violation of the racing regulations to enter into a luffing match or the like with our competitor on our weather quarter, for our initial situation

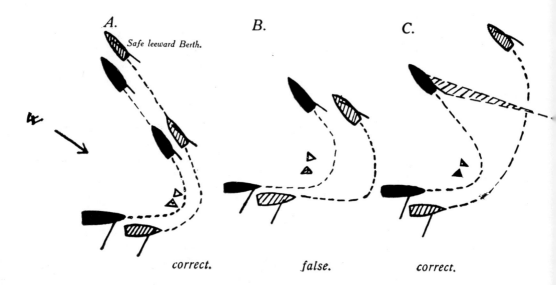

is such, that we are not quite clear of him. The former sketch shows the correct tactics or course to be chosen — that should insure us the lead, and the latter the wrong manoeuvre, that seals our fate at the mark; in other words, the situation can be saved only by giving our competitor, upon his request for room, only so much as is *absolutely necessary*, thereby forcing him hard on our weather quarter. Our somewhat longer turn at the mark is thereby shortened; we naturally lose a few yards of our short lead, but seldom so much that we do not succeed in retaining the "safe leeward berth" after the turn (cf. sketch A and photo on opposite page).

Sketch C differs from the two preceding ones in that the overlap is greater, whereby all offensive measures are excluded for the moment. In this case the only alternative is to bear off and run at as high speed as possible, until we have broken through the wind-shadow of our competitor, and then to hold up to windward.

*37 Is Holding Her Lead by Staying Close to Her Competitor While Rounding
the Mark—Applying "Safe Leeward Position"*

Wind Abeam

We discriminate here also between technique and tactics. If we are sailing alone and undisturbed, it is then solely the technique of attaining the greatest speed that concerns us, but if we are racing against other boats, tactics play the first role, and our course is directed entirely with this in view and is thus more or less prescribed.

The Technique

We imagine that we are running with the wind abeam and unimpeded by other boats, and we put the question: What can be done to increase the average speed of the boat to a maximum? The old school doctrine to "steer a straight course for the mark" was in consideration of the former types of boat and the agreeable, almost indifferent way of sailing in those days surely not to be discarded. But the new school advocates the doctrine: "Rather return to your mooring than keep on a straight course." This advice is a result of the new technique, which has gradually developed from the excellent on-wind qualities of certain modern types of racing boat. The rule runs: *"Bear off with the flaws and luff in the intermediate intervals — when the wind subsides."* That is, one bears off to leeward with every flaw, in order to be able to run that amount higher, when the wind lets up. This method of steering a course off the wind is applicable to all winds, light or strong, and should be given the preference to the old method, especially in a strong breeze. The reason one gets ahead faster by this method the reader may already have surmised. If we assume that in light and moderate breezes our modern boats travel faster on courses somewhere *midway between wind abeam and close-hauled* and not with the wind *directly abeam or freer,* we may conclude that the increase of speed developed higher on the wind during the intervals between the flaws more than counterbalances any loss in speed attained by a slight change of course during the flaws. In other words, whereas with our modern racers we run at a comparatively slow average speed on a straight free course (according to the old school), we may increase that speed materially by steering a zig-zag course; for we lose little or almost nothing by bearing off in the flaws, because the boat cannot travel faster than at a certain maximum speed, as the wind increases in strength, whereas, when the flaw lets up, then,

232

M. Rosenfeld

Breaking Through to Windward

233

by pointing higher, that is, by running on the course on which our boat then attains her greatest speed — one midway between wind abeam and close-hauled, — we are enabled to get the boat started again much quicker and, in spite of the lighter breeze, to increase her speed materially. For a boat *steered strictly on a straight course* remains sluggish during the wind pauses.

The second essential advantage of this technique is that, by bearing off with a flaw, we remain in its zone of effectiveness *longer;* and also, by running up more to windward — toward the next flaw, during the pause between the two, we reach the latter all the *sooner.*

To these two principal advantages, in the case of *very strong winds* the following may be added: Let us imagine that a very heavy flaw sets in; whether we luff or remain on our course, the boat is pressed over on her side and thus tends to run up into the wind of herself; this retards her speed greatly. After the passage of the flaw we must then bear off again, even still more before the wind, on our course, and on this point of sailing the speed of the boat is materially reduced. Under the present conditions we should however, pay the sheets *well out,* sail the boat *as upright as possible* and let her shoot before and with the wind at full speed; we force her, as it were. In the pauses between the flaws the distance we have borne off to leeward is more than regained on the ensuing course higher on the wind, on which the boat is enabled to travel correspondingly faster.

But suppose that the wind is blowing quite steadily, i. e. is not at all flawy; here, as an exception, we may *steer an approximately straight course,* although I recommend even in this case a slight, hardly perceptible serpentine path, as one increases the speed of one's boat by occasional opportune luffing, the acceleration acquired thereby continuing to act long after one has begun to bear off again.

As second rule for a course on beam may be stated:

(a) *Sail the boat as upright — as little heeled, as possible, especially the smaller (centerboard) racer and*

(b) *Shift the crew somewhat aft.*

With the exception of some scows, which may be somewhat heeled, as their wetted surface is thereby reduced, all boats, large and small, should be sailed upright. In a strong breeze, therefore, rather let the sails flap, thereby keeping the boat in an upright position, than let her heel over too much by giving her to good a full. This holds especially for narrow, slender boats — the meter R-yachts, and is often overlooked. In order to form a correct conception of the *disadvantages* arising from the heeled position of a boat, which should be familiar to every yachtsman, let us enumerate here the most important.

1. In most cases the boat swims on a less favorable water-line, one on which she was not constructed, with the following disadvantages as sequel:

(a) a less favorable form of hull under water,

(b) a greater wetted surface,

(c) an asymmetry in that part of the surface of the hull that is in the water whereby the forward part or point of the approximately streamline form of the wetted surface is shifted more to windward, the rear part more to leeward. This is the explanation for the tendency of

234

a boat to luff when heeled. Towing experiments, which were undertaken on the Havel river, showed that all the boats were harder to tow, when heeled than when held upright.

2. The wind produces a component force that is directed *downward* in consequence of the inclination of the sail from the vertical. This component force or pressure is imparted to the boat and presses her only deeper into the water, thereby increasing her displacement considerably.

3. It is not the entire surface area of the sail but only its projection on a plane at right angles to the wind that is called into action.

4. Wind a beam and, in fact, on any free course, that part of the sail, which is next to the surface of the water, is partly blanketed by the hull of the boat, especially in the case of a hanging boom, and the drive developed thereby, due to the fact that the velocity of the wind decreases toward the surface of the water, diminished (cf. chapter on "Wind").

5. The favorable effect of the arching of the sail is reduced, especially on the wind, in that the path of the wind no longer coincides with the direction of the arching, which is approximately parallel to the boom, but now is directed partly upward over it.

6. The boat drifts to leeward in consequence of the lateral inclination of the centerboard from the vertical, whereby its effectiveness is greatly reduced.

7. The steering effect produced by the rudder is no longer proportional to the pressure that is brought to bear on the tiller, but decreases with the heeling of the boat; the more the boat heels, the smaller the steering and the greater the retarding effect, until, at 90°, the former entirely disappears, since the blade of the rudder, which was originally vertical, has assumed a horizontal position and thus fails to produce any lateral pressure, which alone directs the course of the boat. To rectify this shortcoming one would have to construct a rudder that would always stand vertical, whatever the position of the boat may be.

8. The boat assumes a tendency to *luff* for the reason stated under 1, which must be counteracted by the rudder at the cost of speed.

There are only two reasons that can justify the skipper in letting his boat heel somewhat. They are:

(a) In an extremely light wind that he may keep the sails swinging out in their proper position — just full and by. (Especially the jib.)

(b) That the hull may take the waves better. As large waves (without wind) have a harmful effect on the speed of the boat, this can be avoided by shifting the live ballast to leeward or even toward the bow of the boat.

Regarding the distribution of *weight,* we know that in running free, it should be shifted as much as possible *aft,* as all boats tend to bury their noses on this point of sailing.

The Position of the Centerboard

The solution is simple: Have as little centerboard in the water as possible, but under no circumstances so little that the boat will drift. While one of the crew should be charged with the tending of the centerboard, regulating it according to the momentary direction of the wind or of the latter to the course, the helmsman must from time to time take bearings on the land to determine, whether or not his boat is drifting to leeward. Even the slightest lateral drift is most detrimental and generally very much underestimated.

The amount of centerboard to be given is, however, dependent not solely on the *course* but also on the *speed* at which its surface is being moved through the water, as more particles come in contact with the surface of the centerboard of a fast boat (in a given time) than with that of a slow one. For we know that the more sudden the blow to which water is subjected, the more incompressible it becomes, since the particles of water require a certain time to yield to the pressure that has been brought to bear on them; this surface or frictional resistance increases with the square of the speed (pressure). This phenomenon becomes most palpably apparent, when one, for example, holds one's hand in the water on the side of a motor boat that is running at high speed. However, one will try this experiment only once, for the hand may get badly injured or even broken by the enormous resistance of the water.

From these observations it follows that *the greater the speed of a boat, the more may the surface of the centerboard be reduced.*

Accordingly, the centerboard should, if possible, be tended like the sheets in every flaw; but whether one should take such pains or not, the individual case must decide. The reason why we lay so much stress on having the centerboard down as little as possible on a free course is not solely that the wetted surface, and hence the frictional resistance may be reduced, but chiefly that the center of gravity of the lateral plane, that is, the lateral support of the centerboard, may *wander aft,* whereby the *tendency of the boat to luff is lessened* and may, in fact, entirely disappear. It thus follows that we should direct our attention toward a sufficient and prompt hoisting of the centerboard, especially on a boat with a pronounced weather helm. On the other hand, the larger the jib, the more must the centerboard be lowered.

The Position of the Sails

As previously mentioned, there are two prevailing opinions on this point. The one contends that a sail should be trimmed so that it is *just* full and no more; the other demands a somewhat closer trim. So long as the boat is balanced, that is, remains approximately on her course with her rudder midships, I tend toward the point of view I have advocated and also proved in the theoretical part of this book, namely, that every form of sail requires a given (different) angle of opposition to the wind for the attainment of maximum drive, which, in turn, is dependent on the relation of length to breadth of the sail. We have seen from the experiments in Part I that we may carry a high, narrow Marconi sail at a smaller angle (about 20°) to the wind than the gaff-rigged sail, as it develops its greatest efficiency at an angle of opposition to the wind of about 22°, whereas, with the lower and broader gaff rig, we must trim in the sail much closer, as this form develops the greatest drive at an angle of opposition to the wind of about 38°.

The secret of the technique of sailing with the wind abeam lies in preventing the current from being broken off, i. e. in keeping it streaming along the sails.

If we gradually luff, when sailing before the wind, we notice that at a certain position of the boat to the wind her speed suddenly increases considerably. This occurs at the moment when the eddies in the lee of the mainsail disappear and the air current streams along the lee of the sail. Normally this phenomenon appears not with the wind abeam, but somewhat closer-hauled — to windward or high on beam, because the position of the jib, in the former case, is not yet favorable to an undisturbed streaming of the air along the lee of the mainsail. The chief reason for using outriggers or other devices for holding out the leech of the jib is to enable the air to stream along and, as nearly as possible, parallel to the mainsail, instead of spilling onto it.

In sailing with the wind abeam, the real contest is with the air current itself, and the helmsman who can prevent this current from the jib from being broken off, will always have a great advantage over his competitors. The fact that, when sailing on the wind or high on-beam, but not with the wind abeam, the air current automatically streams along in lee of the main-sail (the local disturbing effect of the mast is not taken into account here), is of greatest importance for both the tactics of attack and those of defense and in many cases also for the method of starting.

The popular "starts in lee" high on-beam, with the wind abeam and also before the wind, enable one to haul in the sheets in running up to windward. The smaller angle of opposition to the wind resulting from this manoeuvre allows the air current to stream along the sails instead of breaking up into eddies.

For the same reason, a good skipper will bear off in flaws with the wind abeam or before the wind and luff in the intervals.

Any experienced skipper will recollect with regret the cases — especially on legs before the wind or with the wind abeam, where his competitors astern have overhauled him due to the accelerated speed acquired by trimming in their sheets. This accelerated speed is chiefly due to the fact that the air current streams along the sails of our competitor, whereas it breaks off in the lee of our sails. This is demonstrated graphically in the adjacent sketch. There can be no doubt as to which boat will reach the mark first. Boat B, of course!

In *light* airs the above might even be expressed by the equation: distance to leeward = ultimate lead, i. e. one acquires a lead equal to the distance one was initially in lee of one's competitor.

These conditions change, of course, as the wind increases and are dependent on the type of boat.

It is generally known that the great advantage gained by a continuous shifting of the sheets lies in the possibility of trimming the sails according to the wind, without changing one's course. A further advantage of the mobility of the sheets, that is not generally realized but often instinctively made use of by many yachtsmen, is that *the maximum pressure on the sail is achieved, not when the sheets are being eased, but when they are being hauled in.*

Aside from practical observation, this fact is confirmed by the following experiment made in the wind tunnel:

A square plane develops its greatest pressure at an angle of between 38 and 42° to the direction of the wind. According to whether one approaches the critical angle from greater or smaller inclinations one attains a higher or a lower pressure on the plane. Starting with the plane parallel to the direction of the wind (a = 0°) and increasing the angle of opposition to it, one reaches a high driving efficiency. On increasing this angle cautiously over 40°, one finds the greatest drive at 42°. After that the drive rapidly decreases!

Starting with the plane perpendicular to the direction of the wind, one can decrease the angle even below 40°, without materially increasing the drive.

If one places the plane at an angle of 40° and then turns on the air current in the tunnel, one may get a high or a low pressure.

The same observations hold for arched planes with a ratio of 2 : 1 and 3 : 1 at angles of between 15 and 20° to the direction of the wind.

On comparing these planes with our sails, we now understand why the increase of pressure on hauling in the sheets is greater than that obtained by letting them out, if they were trimmed too close. In order to obtain the maximum pressure, we often let out our main sheet entirely, only to haul it in again. This proceeding is constantly being repeated. One suddenly eases the sheet and then slowly hauls it in, thus feeling the point of maximum pressure. If the air current is broken off in the lee of the sail, the development of drive sinks rapidly, and the only way of getting the current to stream along the sail again is by letting out the sheet entirely and then slowly trimming it closer.

When sailing in light airs, the sheets are eased before the arrival of a flaw, so that they may be hauled in when the flaw sets in. Similarly, the *quick starting* of a boat is facilitated by this manoeuvre. One luffs in a semicircle and slowly trims the sheets closer. The difficulty lies in keeping the sails beyond the critical angle and yet coming as close as possible to the latter, i. e. in keeping the air current streaming along the sail as much as possible. One must not be discouraged, if one does not succeed in this method of tending the sheets the first time.

The position of the jib on a free course is also a subject of dispute. Some maintain that the jib must be trimmed closer in a stiff breeze in order to reduce the pressure on the rudder. This may often be correct; but I have, as a matter of fact, experienced the contrary; I have even found that a larger jib made the boat more inclined to luff. This was due to the fact that the boat lay over more on her side, whereby her bow was pushed up more to windward than the pressure of the larger jib was able to press it off to leeward.

On these points I am of the opinion that every one must draw his own conclusions — for his own boat, for only one's own faith makes one happy. On the other hand, it is certain that in a heavy wind too large a jib tends to press the bow of a boat into the water, and that one must *ease the jib sheet as much as possible* in order to counteract this fault.

A frequent question with respect to the handling of the tiller in a heavy sea is the following: Should one attempt to counteract with the helm the yawing of a boat off her course or not? My experience is that one should make every exertion to hold the boat on her course and not let her yaw, because she is otherwise thrown against the masses of water of each wave with her whole side. If the waves are approaching more from the quarter, it is advisable to *bear off somewhat with every wave in its direction*.

238

The live ballast on a small (centerboard) boat is the man on the jib sheet, whose function it is to keep the boat properly balanced; he should hold her as erect as possible by shifting his weight constantly and quickly — not suddenly, anticipating all violent movements or oscillations of the boat; he should be lying on deck and well up to windward, *not when but before* the flaw sets in. The more the course approaches one on the wind, the more he may allow the boat to heel.

Tactics

The contest on a free course is comparatively simple, as we do not have to reckon with so many possibilities as on a beat to windward, having, on this point of sailing, on the one hand, as leading boat a single tactic and, on the other hand, as aggressor only two recognized methods of offence at our command.

It is, however, surprising how hard it is to overtake a boat in the lead on a free course, and, in as much as we may not ascribe the difficulty to a material disturbance of the air, it would appear that the prime reason for it

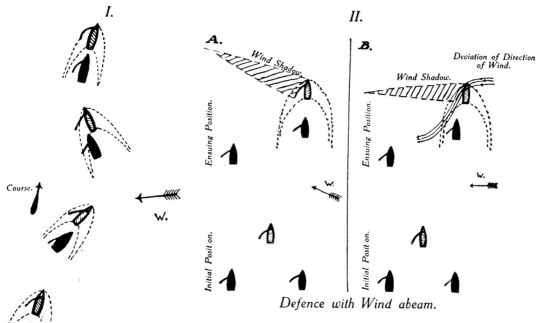

Defence with Wind abeam.

is to be sought in the water. Here especially we find it confirmed how difficult it is to break through the bow and stern waves of a boat in the lead, and I do not think the retarding effect of these waves can be overestimated.

The Defensive Tactic

for the boat ahead is to *keep the pursuer always in her wake,* so that the latter will always be running in the zone of most disturbed water; if our pursuer should attempt to pass us to leeward, we need only bear off — so

239

far as this may appear compatible with our course and is not in violation of the racing regulations, and blanket him; should he try to slip by to windward, we offer him a luffing match with the prospects of the "hopeless position" or, at the very worst for us, the "safe leeward position." By this manoeuvre our opponent is held within the bounds of our wave sector or fan (cf. sketches on foregoing page).

We parry every move of our pursuer by doing just what he does — with the least possible loss of time; and we must, therefore, not lose sight of him even for an instant, for, in a moment of inadvertence on our part, he may bear off abruptly and break through in our lee or else luff up and take us under his sails before we can prevent it. It is for this reason that many helmsmen like to be kept posted by the crew on the course of an opponent, in order that they may be able to devote more attention to the helm.

In the case of *several pursuers,* one directs one's chief attention, as on a beat to windward, to the one nearest, that is, one steers a course midway between those in pursuit and, always ready for action, tends toward the group that appears to be drawing nearer (cf. sketch II A, page 239).

The tactics with the wind directly abeam (sketch II B) differ from the foregoing only in that one works a little more up to windward, in order to insure the weather berth, should the wind suddenly head one off; in this case the deflection of the wind also plays a most important role — to the advantage of

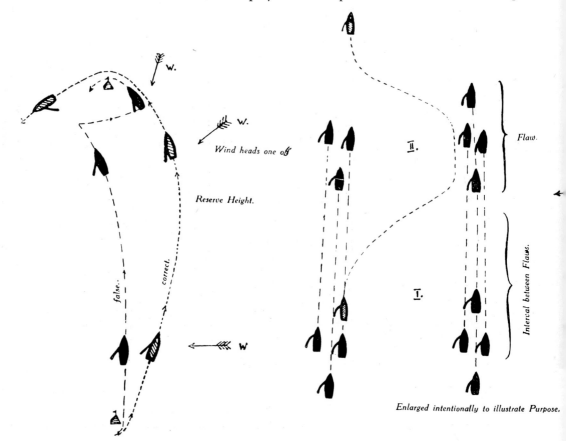

W.

W.

Wind heads one off

Reserve Height.

II.

Flaw.

Interval between Flaws.

I.

false.

correct.

W

Enlarged intentionally to illustrate Purpose.

The Last Boat Attacks Correctly

the weather boat — in the lead. For this reason — an eventual veering of the wind more from ahead, one never steers a leg, where the wind is blowing directly abeam, or a "reach" absolutely straight, but *always in such a curve* that one insures at once a certain *reserve* weather berth, that one may easily fetch the mark, should the wind head one off later (cf. first sketch on page 240).

In a light wind, as indeed in general, the saying holds: "*Never depend on luck — discover it first.*" If, for example, we observe that in a flawy breeze the boats to windward are drawing away in a favorable streak of wind, we should not, for instance, luff up immediately and try to run over toward them, as we would *surely fall astern*. Wait, rather, until the streak of wind works down to leeward, for, by the time the boats to leeward begin to catch the breeze, those to windward have already lost it, and equilibrium is often restored.

But the most advisable thing to do is to work up to windward during the quiet intervals between the flaws and then to bear off to leeward with the flaws — as soon as they set in; in this way one runs first with one and then with the other group (cf. second sketch on page 240). These are similar to the general tactics recommended for a course with the wind abeam, only that the changes of course are in the present case much more pronounced, as we are concerned here with streaks of wind that spread out over the surface of the water—of

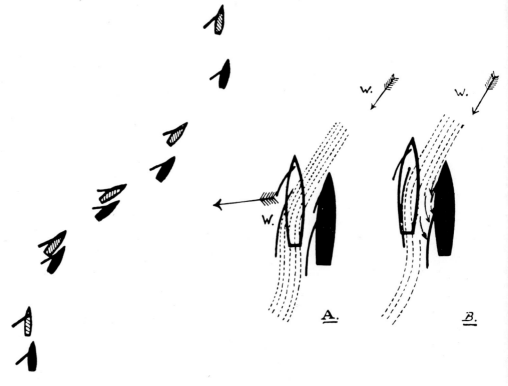

Normal luffing Match.   *Luffing Match during Safe Leeward Position.*
                                 A. Sheets eased.   B. Sails trimmed midships —
                                                                       more effective.

Curry, Aerodynamics of Sails and Racing Tactics.

which we should seek to take full advantage, and not with separate flaws. But the chief means of defence on a course off the wind is, as we know and have already mentioned, the

Luffing Match,

the climax of the contest. Although it presents rather a strange sight, when two boats undertake a solo journey in an apparently most senseless direction, luffing desperately away from the course, yet even this characteristic sort of contest loses its charm for the connoisseur, for he knows that the *leeward boat must eventually win the match,* unless some unaccountable mistake is made by her skipper. But this does not signify that the skipper of the boat in the less favorable, windward position should assume that his contestant to leeward may *not* make a mistake.

Let us now consider what trivial mistakes may suffice to turn the tables, or, in other words, what is absolutely essential that the *boat to leeward* may win the match. The rules I am laying down here hold, of course, only for equally good boats and skippers.

1. She must run up close enough under the lee of her opponent.
2. She must luff so high that she is not blanketed; but she should not shoot into the wind, as the relative inertia (weight) of the two boats may be decisive for the issue; it is, for example, seldom the case that a heavy weather boat gets the worst of it upon shooting into the wind.
3. The manoeuvre must be carried out smoothly; sudden or sharp movements of the tiller should be avoided, especially with yachts.
4. The disturbance of the suction effect on the sails of the boat to windward may be further increased by *trimming in the mainsail* of the boat in lee *extremely flat,* even midships, that the backwind off her mainsail may be guided to a still greater degree onto the leeward or suction side of the sails of the other boat (cf. above sketches A & B on page 242).

If the leeward or luffing boat manoeuvres according to these rules or principles, there is not much hope for the boat to windward. The latter then has only two alternatives that may be tried under certain circumstances.

If the windward boat is able to work so far ahead that a blanketing may be expected at any moment, then, in order to force it before it is too late, she can bear down somewhat on her opponent (cf. sketches on next page). She wins thereby the missing yard or so and forges ahead just so far that she can force her nose *in front of* that of her adversary. She blankets the latter and wins thereby the coveted position (cf. sketch A). But, should she not be successful, in spite of bearing off her course, or, in other words, should the missing yard not have quite sufficed to bring about the blanketing, then the manoeuvre has miscarried and should not have been undertaken, for the adversary is in a position to make use of his "safe leeward berth" (cf. sketch B). The decision as to whether this attempt will succeed or not, depends on the relative initial position of the two boats. If the boats are neck and neck at the time, then the game is won; but if the boat to windward is only the shortest distance behind, it is lost.

The second alternative — the last and only hope for the weather boat, is that, upon a prolonged luffing match, the final stretch to the mark changes from a course on beam to one before the wind. If the skipper of the weather

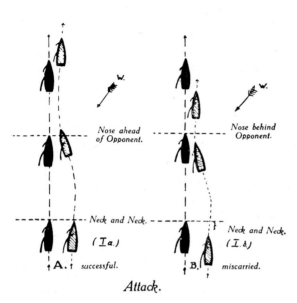

Nose ahead
of Opponent.

Nose behind
Opponent.

Neck and Neck.

(I a.)

Neck and Neck.

(I. b)

A. *successful.*

B. *miscarried.*

Attack.

boat realizes this in time and has given orders to get the spinnaker clear and ready to be set, without attracting the attention of his adversary, then, the moment the two boats bear off for the mark, he can run down on the latter with everything set and drawing. Note, therefore, that in every luffing match, that lasts any length of time, the *spinnaker manoeuvre is decisive* (cf. chapter on "Rounding a Mark").

As a warning to the *windward* boat we may observe that *she must not foul her competitor to leeward, for the racing regulations stipulate that the latter may continue to luff until she is in such a position that her bowsprit or stem would strike the windward boat abaft her main shrouds.* This is to be interpreted in the sense that, although the leeward boat may not luff further, she is, nevertheless, allowed to *continue on the course she was steering at that moment.* Most yachtsmen are, however, too fair and sportsmanlike to take advantage of this rule or privilege, and consequently the general opinion prevails that the weather boat must luff, that is, must avoid fouling the leeward boat, *only so long* as the stem of the latter is *not abaft* the main shrouds of the former. This is, however, false, as the leeward boat *still has the right to foul the boat* on her weather, provided the former is simply continuing on her previous course, however high on the wind she may be pointing. Under these circumstances the slightest foul by the windward boat, even should her boom merely touch any part of the other boat or her rigging, results in a disqualification of the former.

True sportsmen will surely take little interest in this sort of hair-splitting and any skipper should be ashamed to win a prize by *taking advantage of a racing rule* that was made with the intention only of avoiding collision. It should also be unworthy of a true sportsman to enter a protest against a competitor, who, under normal circumstances, would have passed under his stern on the starboard tack but, due to a sudden flaw that set in somewhat fuller and caused him to luff, just touched the stern or perhaps only the rudder of the other boat; similarly it is unsportsmanlike of the leeward boat to try to bring about a foul in a luffing match by *suddenly* luffing or bearing off.

I maintain that a skipper, who is familiar with the racing regulations and well routined, could get rid of half of his competitors in a race simply by protests, if he directed his efforts strictly to that effect. The judges should not uphold protests that are founded on fouls in a luffing match or in exceptional (limiting) cases of the right of way on a beat to windward, for, in 95% of such cases, the foul is intentional on the part of the one and a surprise to the other skipper. Upon the filing of a protest the leading motive of the judges should be: "Was the position (speed) of the protesting boat affected by the foul unfavorably to such a degree that the *final result* of the race was influenced thereby?" in support of which they may "discourage all attempts to win a race by other means than fair sailing and superior speed and skill" — from § 1 of Racing Rules of I. Y. R. U.

The skipper who is frank with himself will admit that in many of the protests he has entered he was morally in the wrong, and as honorable men we should prefer rather to lose a race and win a moral victory than to win by means of a protest. But as there are men who, in their exaggerated sense of justice, see marks fouled by other boats, when no such contacts have taken place, or who even feel justified, *after a race, in entering protests on measurements,* and as there are, in fact, so-called yachtsmen, who indulge not in yacht racing but, realizing the lack of their own ability, in splitting hairs, one must, unfortunately, learn to sail against these doughty cavaliers also. But one need not be afraid of such men, and one should not disdain to pay them back immediately in their own "coin" for their immoral "justice," for one can win even with the despicable weapons in these mutual contests, as the protest adorer is always the less clever sailor. Anent this, I permit myself to warn and to recommend as follows:

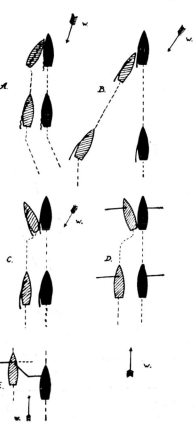

If in a luffing match the leeward boat succeeds, by a sudden, sharp turn of her rudder, in hitting her opponent in front of her main shrouds, *the latter is disqualified,* even should she be standing with her sails flapping in the wind (cf. sketch A).

If the leeward boat luffs quickly and excessively high, when her bow is still in front of *the main shrouds* of her opponent, and thereupon, after falling somewhat astern on that course, should foul the latter, *the weather boat is disqualified* (cf. sketch B).

If the leeward boat bears off suddenly and sharply and thereby hits her opponent with her stern, which swings out to windward, *the latter is disqualified* (cf. sketch C).

If two boats are sailing *quite peaceably* side by side before the wind and the boat with her sheets to port suddenly bears off hard to leeward and thereby touches her opponent with her stern, *the latter is disqualified* (cf. sketch D).

If, on a run before the wind, the blanketed boat suddenly tautens her rear or back stay and thereby touches her opponent's boom, which is swinging over her, or, in hauling in her spinnaker boom, hits a stay of her opponent, *the latter is disqualified* (cf. sketch E).

These are only a few examples of many, where the sword, the emblem of justice, reigns supreme.

But now let us finally take leave of this unedifying subject, the art of protesting, and return to our theme, the art of regatta sailing.

The Attack on a Free Course

It has already been observed how difficult it is to overhaul a boat on this course, and the various methods of attack have been mentioned above in the treatment of the defence — the "breaking through" both to leeward and to windward. To leeward we encounter the waves, as indicated in the sketch below and we have also to reckon with the deflection of the wind and the danger of being blanketed. To windward the only impeding element is the disturbed water. Therefore, in a race one generally tries to break through to windward instead of to leeward. But when one is well in the rear or contesting with several boats, one usually attempts breaking through to leeward (cf. sketch on page 247). When a number of boats are all making up to windward — away from the course in a series of luffing matches, then it is advisable to bear off to leeward and to steer the shorter course to the mark. In either case the minimum distance to leeward should be four mast lengths from one's competitor, to windward one mast length, as otherwise, in the latter case, the socalled "air cushion" formed on the sails of the boat to leeward will be felt, and, on the other hand, an eventual blanketing may be undertaken most effectually at that distance (cf. chapter on "Blanketing"). At the beginning one lays one's course as accurately as possible between the bow and stern waves of the boat in the lead.

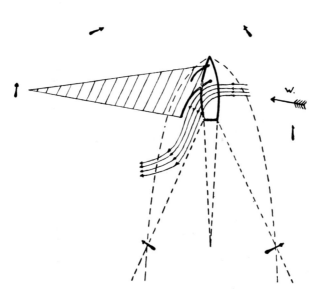

Attack with Wind abeam according to Theory.

Another reason, why we should undertake the attack *not from the wake but on either side of it,* is indicated in sketch A on opposite page. In this manner we are able to cast our wind-shadow on the sail of our adversary to leeward even at a considerable distance to her weather.

Sketch B shows how the attack is to be carried out in lee. This method of breaking through is one of the most difficult but, if successful, one of the most satisfactory weapons we have at our command in the tactics of modern racing. As in the technique *before the wind,* which is

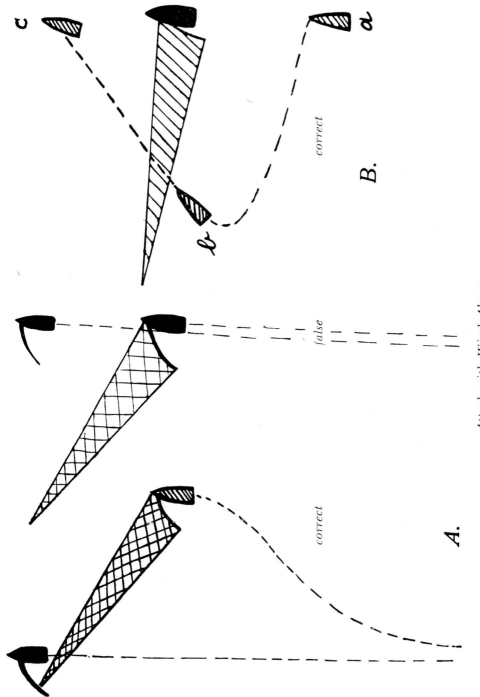

c

b

a

correct

B.

false

correct

A.

Attack with Wind Abeam.

One breaks through Wind-Shadow in lee by luffing and running at accelerated Speed. (B.)

treated in the next chapter, we work slowly to leeward at opportune moments — during the flaws (cf. position b), and then attempt, by most careful
sailing, to approach the outer or pointed end of
the wind-shadow of our competitor. The difficulty
encountered in this manoeuvre lies in the fact that
only the most experienced skipper is able to judge
exactly, when he has reached this dangerous zone.
Then comes the critical moment for action on our
part and the next minute must decide the issue —
whether we have succeeded in breaking through or
not. We luff, trim the sails closer and let our boat
run — at the highest possible speed, through the wind-
shadow of our competitor (cf. sketch B, page 247).
The course we are sailing is, as we know, the one on
which we can develop the highest speed — "high on
beam." The accelerated speed at which we were already running before we entered the wind-shadow
should carry us through this zone — provided the
manoeuvre is carried out correctly; in other words, the
stored up energy we have acquired should just suffice
to carry us through the narrow, harmful zone of our
competitor's wind-shadow. But the contest is only in
its initial stage; the harmful cone or wind-shadow
is still *close* on our heels and the slightest mistake

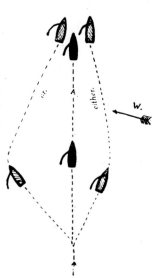

*Attack with Wind abeam
according to Practice.*

is sufficient to throw us back into it. We, therefore, continue on the same
course or rather point of sailing and strive to reach the "safe leeward position,"
running with our sails full and drawing on the fore edge of the wind-shadow
and thereby closing up slowly on our rival; and the successful issue of this
final manoeuvre, the winning of the "safe leeward berth," decides the contest
all at once in our favor. I have applied and developed this method of attack
in preference to all others, and there is no other weapon of attack that has
had such a fascination to me. The attack proves unsuccessful, if one luffs
too soon, that is, if one is not close enough to the outer, rear edge of the wind-
shadow, for one is then running too near to one's rival, that a complete
breaking through may succeed. If one luffs too late, that is, after one has
already entered the wind-shadow, then one is doomed to remain within its
confines, as the required accelerated speed cannot be attained in this harmful
zone. This manoeuvre should only be attempted with a very fast type of boat.

While the success of the above manoeuvres depends principally upon
the nature of the wind and the possibility of taking advantage of the various
flaws, there is still another method, which is independent of the wind and,
at the same time, ought to be one of the most feared by the boat in the
lead; it is the socalled

Apparent Attack

We work up as near as possible to our rival and try to make him
nervous by running close to him. We pretend to be preparing to break
through in his lee and first bear off sharply directly under his stern. In order
to defend himself, he must follow suit. We immediately change our tactics

and luff, attacking him to windward. He also luffs hastily, for it is high time, if he realizes the danger to windward. We perform these provoking manoeuvres several times; in this manner we gradually close up on our competitor, for, from the fact that he begins to change his course a few seconds later than we do, his change of course has to be a more sudden and abrupt one, in order to correspond in its final effect to ours. In other words, we are cutting off the corners of the course and, as we are thus covering a shorter distance, we must be hauling up on him. Similarly, a dog, chasing a rabbit, overtakes him best, when the latter runs in curves, while the pursuer follows a straighter path. We finally draw up so near on our rival that, with clever steering, we are able to pass him at a favorable moment. Naturally, this death blow is generally dealt, when we are *on his weather*.

Briefly summarized, the technique and tactics to be employed with the wind abeam are the following:

Technique
1. Bear off in the flaws and work up to windward by luffing in the quiet intervals.
2. Sail your boat as erect — as little heeled, as possible.
3. Tend the sheets most carefully.
4. Tend the centerboard accordingly.

Tactics
5. Defence: Hold your adversary in your wake, doing whatever he does.
6. Attack: Pass your opponent at a considerable distance to leeward, if you are farther astern. Avoid luffing matches. If you are close on his heels apply the "apparent attack," sailing a zig-zag course, and break through to windward.

Apparent Attack.

249

All Sails Drawing with Wind Abeam

Before the Wind

It will surprise many to learn that this so apparently simple, harmless course is, at the same time, both most interesting and most complicated. This is due chiefly to the difficulty of the technique, which differs so materially for every course before the wind, that one always appears to be confronted with a new task. As some musicians possess an absolute ear for tones, that is, can name every tone they hear or, more exactly expressed, are able to count unconsciously with their ear the number of vibrations of that tone, similarly the racing man must possess or acquire a certain feeling for speed, by means of which he can at once recognize, whether his boat is running only a few inches per second faster or slower, as the case may be. He must be able to feel, how much he can increase the speed of his boat by a change of course, and he must also recognize, when his boat is approaching the socalled "dead point," to which I shall refer later. This technique, simple in itself, becomes complicated on account of the difficulties encountered in performing the various manoeuvres correctly.

The *tactic* is not much easier, since it affords but a grim game due to the small chances for a successful issue; for here, more than on any other point of sailing, the boat astern has the upper hand.

That the good qualities of a boat before the wind play an inferior part here, will be doubted only by those to whom the intricacies and the diverse characteristics of this course are a closed chapter. The skill of the skipper is the decisive factor before the wind, and the boat herself, in spite of her good qualities, as the form of hull, etc., is quite helpless and under no circumstances to be held responsible for the final outcome.*

The Technique

Practice has shown that boats run badly dead before the wind and that, compared to the speed they attain on other courses, they seem to stick to the water, except in a strong wind. Our task then is to avoid this — quasi perceptible sticking, the socalled "dead point." One might make the simple suggestion: "Sail the leg with the wind abeam." It is true that the boat will

---

* Even a small centerboard boat or a lugger can often, under certain circumstances, hold a large yacht on a run down the wind. The only factor with reference to the boat that has any influence on speed is her weight or indirectly her "wetted" surface; light boats are somewhat faster. But in one and the same class the differences in weight are so small that even this factor plays hardly any rôle.

generally run faster on this point of sailing, but it is seldom the case that one reaches the mark sooner, as one has to cover a considerably greater distance. The attempt may, of course, sometimes prove successful, but if one wishes to get at the root of the matter, one is confronted with serious difficulties, which appear to differ for every individual case. It is only the experienced skipper, who will be able to draw the conclusion, after most careful study, that it is chiefly the strength of the wind that is the decisive factor for the technique to be chosen on this course. It is, therefore, most natural that two general theories have been developed, of which the one is just as wrong or just as right as the other, if they are to be regarded as general rules.

The advocates of the one theory steer a straight course for the mark, while the others sail the leg in zig-zags — criss-crossing before the wind, by jibing over first onto the one quarter and then onto the other and running a certain distance with the wind on that quarter.

As the eventual ill success of the latter method is, as already observed, to be ascribed to the longer distance to be covered and to repeated jibing, we may ask: How can we get rid of the disadvantages of this technique without renouncing its advantages? How may we develop a technique for this course before the wind *without* jibing and *without* lengthening the distance to be covered? On this basis I have built up a technique for moderate winds, the development of which was, as in most cases, a matter of mere feeling.

Moderate Wind Technique

Criss-crossing in light and moderate breezes may be executed as follows: Let us imagine that we have to sail a leg dead before the wind and that we are not molested by any competing boats — pure technique. And let us suppose that the course starts with the rounding of a mark: This is rounded smoothly in a long, drawn out curve and the ensuing course is begun, not dead before the wind, but with the wind somewhat on our port *quarter,* as represented in the first sketch on the next page. The boat is kept on this course until she has, in the first place, attained her maximum speed and, secondly, until her spinnaker is set and drawing. Then we bear off on the straight course for the mark. We thus introduce our criss-cross course down the wind, and our next task is to continue it with as small deviations as possible from the direct course. This is not so simple, the choice of a course that deviates only a few degrees from the straight line to the mark and, at the same time, avoids all those "dead points," that "lying dead" on the water, which continually threaten the boat, as it were like an iron sceptre. To accomplish this we proceed according to the following principles:

1. *During the flaws press the boat down to leeward.* As the "dead point" becomes perceptible, when the boat is running before the wind in a light breeze or, especially, when the wind falls for a moment on the lee of her sails and *gradually* subsides, even should we be running dead before the wind and it should begin to increase in strength, we should utilize every opportunity, as it increases, to run down as far to leeward as possible, that we may overcome the "dead points" later by luffing during the quiet intervals. The exact manoeuvre is as follows: The wind increases slightly or a flaw sets in; first, we luff somewhat in order to get the boat started, then we bear off sharply (with the flaw), similarly as in the technique applied with the wind abeam, and *strive to run down to leeward as much as possible during*

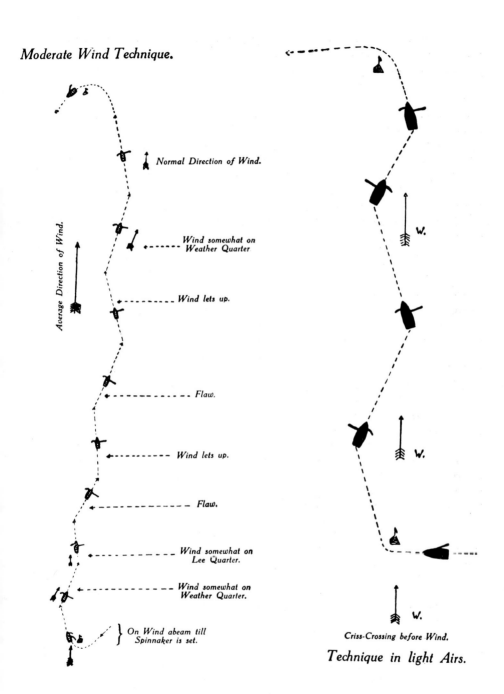

Moderate Wind Technique.

Normal Direction of Wind.

Wind somewhat on
Weather Quarter

Wind lets up.

Flaw.

Wind lets up.

Flaw.

Wind somewhat on
Lee Quarter.

Wind somewhat on
Weather Quarter.

} On Wind abeam till
   Spinnaker is set.

Average Direction of Wind.

W.

W.

W.

Criss-Crossing before Wind.

Technique in light Airs.

the flaw, without impeding our speed materially. The puff then passes by. If we allow the boat to lie for only a few seconds on her present course, she becomes "dead" at once. Therefore we luff and, thereby putting new life into her, proceed with the wind striking slightly on our quarter, until the next flaw permits us again to bear down to leeward (cf. first sketch).

2. Let us next assume that the wind is changeable, not only in its strength but also in its *direction;* then the course is determined by the further principle: *Press down to leeward, when the wind strikes on your weather quarter.* In as much as we know that it is not absolutely necessary to run with the wind exactly abeam to increase our speed, but that it suffices, if the wind comes only *slightly from the quarter,* we should not, at first, take too great advantage of this favorable shift of the wind, but we should bear off somewhat to leeward. Then, if the wind shifts directly aft, we can luff a bit and run again with the wind *on our quarter,* taking advantage of the reserve leeward position just acquired. On the other hand, if we had continued on a straight course for the mark during the shift of wind from the quarter, we should now have to lay our course dead before it and run at a greatly reduced speed.

However the case may be, one must avoid under all circumstances letting the wind fall even to the slightest degree on the lee, of the sail, and one should not defer jibing at once, when one is no longer able to luff as required by this technique. As we may avoid jibing, on the one hand, by working down to leeward at the proper time, on the other hand, we should not postpone this manoeuvre for a second, should the wind keep changing in its direction to such a degree, that we cannot discriminate between windward and leeward. In such cases we cannot, especially in a light breeze, haul the sail over from one side to the other often enough.*

But in yachting circles there is, strangely enough, an exaggerated aversion to jibing, which is quite unjustified, provided the wind is variable in direction and is *not too strong.* True, a clumsily executed or superfluous jibe may cost an entire boat's length, but most yachtsmen do not realize that a boat can fall just as far astern, when the wind shows only the slightest tendency to strike the outer side of her mainsail first for even half a minute.

To summarize, the predominating thought in our technique of running down before the wind in light and moderate breezes is to strive by all means to work down to leeward, undertaking the necessary manoeuvres to that effect at *favorable moments,* when our speed would be only slightly diminished, that we may then profit materially from the ensuing course with the wind more on our quarter by luffing.

In competition with another boat there are exceptions to the above rule; in such cases, aside from the technique, the following tactical principles should be observed: *Bear off in unimportant moments, in order to be able to increase your speed by running higher on the wind later in such critical situations as upon approaching a mark; and luff in critical moments, in order to decide an issue, even should you be obliged to bear off considerably later, as the latter is of little moment, provided you command the situation.* This is most important at the start.

Technique in Light Airs

The more the wind decreases in strength, the more pronounced should be the manner in which the criss-crossing before it is executed; in very light breezes this manoeuvre should be accompanied by repeated jibing. In light

---

* In a calm a boat is shoved forward every time her sail is shifted, provided it is taken in with a jerk and let out slowly; this mode of propulsion is termed "rowing with the sail." Similarly, in light airs one can work a boat forward on the wind by tacking superfluously with the rudder, that is, by moving it in the same manner through the water. These tricks are, however, in violation of the racing regulations.

airs boats become so sluggish dead before the wind — as though they could never overcome the "dead points," that they reach the mark sooner by criss-crossing before the wind and shifting the spinnaker constantly (letting it swing well forward), in spite of the longer distance and the frequent jibing which is less detrimental in this case.

The choice of every technique is, naturally, largely governed by the nature of the wind and is, in fact, often entirely dependent upon it.

We may, moreover, suggest that the helmsman should often stand up during these criss-cross manoeuvres and take a general survey of the distance surroundings from some elevated point, that he may lay his main course according to the prevailing wind streaks observed.

In a Strong Wind

Keep on the straight course. That is, we should have recourse, if possible, to the technique employed in moderate breezes, but we approach the *straight course* more and more as the wind increases. On yachts the tiller should be tended with the greatest care and all unnecessary deviations from the *straight course* avoided.

In order not to complicate matters, I have purposely omitted one important point in the treatment of this subject — the technique, and that is that the course to be chosen depends also on the form of the *mainsail.* Upon recalling the fact that a low, gaff-rigged sail develops a much greater drive with the wind abeam than the high Marconi sail does, it follows that we *should tend more toward the criss-cross course, when running before the wind, with the former than with the latter rig.* The technique is practically the same for both rigs, only that we should choose the straighter course with the higher rig.

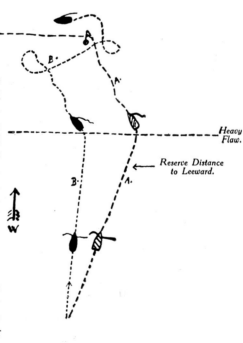

In Stormy Weather

Here technique must renounce all claims on finesse, and we should be satisfied, if the principal requirements of the boat are fulfilled. First of all, avoid jibing, as the danger of capsizing or carrying away the mast is greatly increased by this manoeuvre, especially if not properly executed or it takes one by surprise. It thus follows that we should take every opportunity that presents itself to work down to lee-ward as much as possible (without jib-ing) and that this should be our pre-dominating thought, *as long as* it is pos-sible; for, should the wind continue to increase, it may become absolutely out of the question for us to keep the boat before the wind — on her course. But if we have been success-

Heavy Flaw.

Reserve Distance to Leeward.

ful in working down to leeward in the meantime, we may perhaps be able to luff just enough — with the wind more on our quarter or on the beam, to reach the mark (cf. sketch on page 255, course A). On the other hand, if we keep on the straight course for the mark, the ensuing path we are *forced* to steer due to the fierceness of the wind may drive us to the weather of it, and our only alternative of finally reaching it is either to jibe or to run up into the wind and go about onto the other tack and then to perform the same manoeuvre a second time at the mark (cf. sketch, course B). And this is equivalent to losing the race, as we know only too well from experience.

It is also my duty to call attention here to the common phenomenon of the burying of the bow or nose of a boat on this course — before the wind; it is justly feared, as it can easily culminate in capsizing the boat — with ensuing somersault; it may be prevented in two ways: Either shift the weight (crew) aft, especially on small boats, and let no one go forward unless absolutely necessary; in which latter case — of emergency — one man at least should be sent aft for the time being. Or, if, for any reason, the shifting of weight should be impossible or prove insufficient or ineffective, one should pull the boat's nose out of the water sideways in every flaw by luffing suddenly — by a series of jerks of the tiller; but this is applicable only to yachts, as small centerboard boats generally capsize when handled in this manner.

In a storm the tiller of a small boat must never be belaid. One must be on the alert, as the boat may unexpectedly start to jibe, due to a sudden shift of the wind; any such tendency must be observed and parried immediately. If the tiller is not free for only a few seconds — if, for example, it is restricted in its freedom of motion by one of the crew — this may prove fatal.

Who has not experienced that the boat, all of a sudden, begins to lie over more and more to windward, in spite of the fact that she is held on a straight course? This is always a sure sign or warning that the mainsail is let out too far. The head of the sail, especially of the gaff rig, sags out far to leeward and thus develops a force that acts not alone in the direction of the course but also at right angles to it — to windward — and presses the boat over in that direction. It is customary to counteract this heeling to windward by shifting a member of the crew to leeward, but the correct remedy is to trim the mainsail closer.

Small boats as well as large ones often yaw so in a storm that the mainsail threatens every moment — on every sea — to swing over to the other side. Though the crew may *work with* great dexterity by continually shifting their weight to *counteract* this yawing, the helmsman may have an extremely difficult task steering; he may be compared with a tight rope walker: he balances the boat, as it were, on a narrow, straight line in the direction of the course, *on neither side of which* he may, for reasons, already mentioned *luff or bear* off in the least; but, on the other hand, if he *does not luff or bear off,* he may lose his balance, "fall off," in fact and *land* on his head — in the *water*. But let us observe that luffing is always the more dangerous of these two alternatives in critical moments; it generally means a capsize.

The Position of the Sails

There is little to add about the tending of the mainsail, but one matter deserves our special attention on this point of sailing: *In light winds the mainsail must be let out as far as possible.* As the technique of steering on this couse demands that one should employ all one's skill to prevent the wind from striking the sail at right angles, which implies a course dead before the wind, one must strive here, by letting out the mainsheet even farther than may appear possible, to increase the angle at which the wind strikes it, should it be only 5° or less. Only a few degrees may decide, whether the wind will be able to glide off the leech of the sail, allowing the on-coming wind to replace it, or whether an air cushion is formed on the sail, which blocks the flow of the on-coming wind on it and thus promotes "dead points" (cf. diagrams on next page). We should not, therefore, be satisfied, when the man on the main sheet exclaims: "The sheet cannot be payed off any farther" or "the main boom is already pushing against the stay." As a rule, it can always be let out a *little* farther, and it is just that *"little"* that may suffice to increase our speed materially. Even should the spreader press against the sail, the danger that it may tear a hole in the duck is hardly to be taken into consideration.

The Dead Point

It is obvious from the diagrams on the next page where the cause of the harmful effect of the "dead point" is to be sought. As we know from Part I, the pressure on the windward side of a sail, before the wind, is always greater than the suction on its leeward surface. If the wind strikes the sail at right angles, the air cushion already mentioned is formed, and the center or zone of comparative rest (cf. also p. 106) lies where the two currents of air meet or rebound upon each other (cf. diagram A on next page). On the other hand, if the angle at which the wind falls on the sail is only a few degrees more than 90° (cf. diagram B), the air cushion vanishes with the exception of a small remnant; and the suction is also intensified, since the return currents of the eddies on the lee of the sail are weakened.

The conditions become still more unfavorable, if the wind falls on the sail *from lee* (cf. diagram C). Here a large air cushion is formed on its windward side, which extends from the mast, where it is most pronounced, to the middle of the sail, and further a smaller one, the center of which is determined by the dividing line, along which the main current is deflected to the right and to the left in its general direction of flow. Consequently, the wind rebounds against *two* air cushions and loses the greater part of its intensity. The suction is also weakened by the relatively strong return currents of the eddies on the leeward side of the sail and thus does not succeed in contributing much to the pressure or drive developed on its windward surface (cf. diagram C, dead point No. 2).

In the attempt to prevent the wind from falling on the sail from lee, one must realize that with many sails the pennant does not always indicate the exact direction of the wind, but that it tends to stream out *more to windward,* being, as it were, deflected in that direction by an invisible force; it is apparently subjected to a current of air that is directed from lee, although the wind itself may be falling on the sail at right angles or even somewhat from windward. The deflection of the pennant, which is especially noticeable on sails with a high-peaked gaff, where the *pennant flies on the side of and*

257

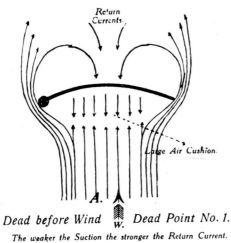

Return
Currents

Large Air Cushion.

A.

Return Currents.

Small Air Cushion.

B.

Dead before Wind W. *Dead Point No. 1.*

The weaker the Suction the stronger the Return Current.

*Wind somewhat on Weather
Quarter.*

The stronger the Suction the weaker the
Return Current.

(Cross Section through Middle of Sail.)

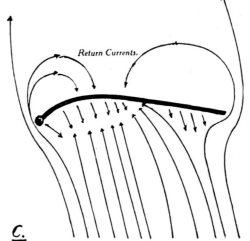

Return Currents.

C.

*When Wind strikes
Sail from Lee.
Dead Point No. 2.*

←— ··· *2 Air Cushions.*

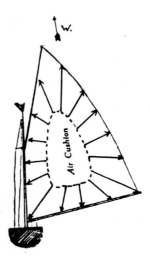

W.

Air Cushion

*Lines of Flow of Wind on (wind-
ward Side of) Sail — Deviation
of Pennant to Windward ¡to Side
opposite Sail¡.*

258

close to that spar, is due to the fact that the wind streaming off the sail toward the pennant is deflected by this secondary current of air (cf. sketch on page 258). On the other hand, with the high Marconi sail, where the pennant flies at the highest point of the rigging, no deflection occurs.

The Allotment of the Work

must be carefully thought out for every manoeuvre and the manoeuvre itself rehearsed accordingly. Especially in a *heavy wind* it is advisable to discuss thoroughly the different stages of every manoeuvre with the crew beforehand, that no essential part of it may be forgotten. Should a manoeuvre miscarry, it may be the fault of a single person and, as is often the case in the majority of manoeuvres that are executed too slowly, the mistake is that, where a hand is wanted, there is *none* and that four or five hands are all striving to do *one and the same thing,* for which one would suffice. As in an operation every assistant should co-operate in his thoughts with the surgeon and consider beforehand, which knife or instrument he is to hand the operator, similarly every member of the crew should think over the different stages of the manoeuvre, before it takes place, and, at the same time, try to take into account all eventualities — as the skipper himself must do — that he also may be prepared for them.

It has already been observed that in working to windward the crew should remain as long as possible *"up but down,"* as the expression runs, that is, well "up" to windward, but "down" on the floor of the cockpit or on the deck of the boat, so as not to offer any unnecessary resistance to the wind. In a strong breeze the command thus runs on yachts: *"Flat on deck;"* and in small boats; *"Close together."* In this way the resistance the crew offer the wind is considerably reduced.

We now proceed to the execution of the different manoeuvres, and we suggest that the following fundamental principles be observed by the crew:

1. Always do the most important thing first! To recognize at once the most necessary thing — in proper succession — is often not so simple, and this is only understood by one, who has sailed considerably alone and has accustomed himself to thinking independently.

2. Before shackling a sail on to a *halyard,* be sure that it runs clear; nothing is more annoying than to find everything tangled, after one has attempted in vain to set a sail.

3. The chief thing is to get the sail *drawing* as soon as possible, not to clear or make fast its sheet. This is a point which is often overlooked by the beginner. For example, if the sail is flapping, one does not first cast the sheet off the cleat and then haul it in, but one *first* trims in and *then* casts off. Similarly, it does not matter whether the spinnaker guy has already been led aft or not; the sail must *draw,* and, even if there is a tangle, one can hold the boom with one's hand; *when everything is drawing,* one can then direct one's attention to the belaying of the sheets and getting things clear — and one then has *time for it.*

4. It is not absolutely necessary that the crew have great bodily strength; it depends more on *how* that strength is used. A weak, but agile man, who employs his strength at the right moment and with correct technique, accomplishes more than an untrained man with double the physique.

5. Belaying the sheets and casting them off quickly must also be practised. The socalled "head turn" is made only with the halyards, never with the sheets; the halyards remain belaid and it does not matter, if a "head turn" gets so taut from being wet, that it often can be loosened only with great difficulty; but with a *sheet* this may prove fatal, and one should rather take several simple turns around the cleat than run the risk of not being able to loosen a hitch — at shortest notice.

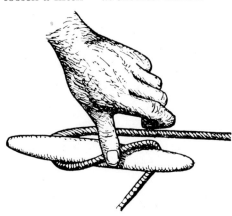

The best method of making a sheet or halyard fast is to lay it first diagonally across the cleat and then, in order to increase the friction, to press it with the thumb or palm of the other hand against the cleat (cf. accompanying sketch). In this way any rope may be held fast for the moment and, even under great tension, it is not likely to slip. Thereupon the rope is wound around the cleat once or twice and drawn taut. This is the *quickest and surest* way of belaying. Before the wind, especially in a strong blow, it is most important to have the (weather) back stay fastened with absolute *security*, and this simple and quick method of belaying it is of great service. It should, moreover, be noted that in hauling in a sheet, that is under great tension, one should never take hold of it directly behind an eye, block or even the cleat to which it is to be made fast, on account of the danger of pinching one's hand in this auxiliary device, if the sheet should unexpectedly slip or one should not be able to hold it. Therefore, beware of a yacht's sheet in a storm.

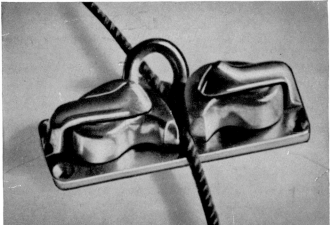

"Bulldog Jam Cleat"

A most satisfactory device for fastening sheets is the "Bulldog Jam cleat" (see photograph), it is manufactured by the Narragansett-Yacht-Fittings at Providence, R. I.

The Spinnaker Manoeuvre

Generally speaking, the spinnaker is usually set too late and, above all, much too seldom. Unaccountably a certain fear prevails of "risking" a spinnaker manoeuvre, because it may prove to be superfluous. But I wish to state that

260

a cleanly and carefully performed spinnaker manoeuvre — provided the wind is not too strong — can never do any appreciable harm, whereas a race may be decided by getting the spinnaker set a few minutes sooner than one's competitor — at a critical moment — should it prove expedient.

But here we should, in general, be guided by the following rules or principles:

As leading boat:

"*Refrain from a doubtful spinnaker manoeuvre, should your pursuers not undertake it,*" but, on the other hand,

"*Set your spinnaker if the others do, even should this be against your own judgment.*"

As pursuing boat:

"*Try every manoeuvre, rather a false manoeuvre than none at all; — everything the other boat does not do is correct for the boat astern.*"

It is very desirable to have two spinnakers; the ordinary one, of very light material, for light airs or a blow and a large, socalled "parachute" spinnaker * for fresh winds. In a light breeze the latter would drag in the water, but, as the wind increases, it will fill out grandly, not only forward, but especially *on the sides.* In this way nearly double the sail may be carried to advantage.

Setting the Spinnaker

The spinnaker boom should always be stowed under the *after* and not under the foredeck, as is generally customary but most impractical, for in the former case one only need to shove it in one direction to get it on deck; the ropes, which are attached to the spinnaker and must be led aft, can then never get caught or tangled, as the sail lies in the open cockpit, not under deck. If stowed forward, the boom must first be hauled out from under deck, then forward again onto it, with the usual result, that the helmsman is hit by the end of the boom with deadly accuracy in the face and, at best, has to be satisfied with a well-meant "Excuse me!"

On a *free course or with the wind abeam, just preceding a run before the wind,* the spinnaker should be hoisted *just before the mark is reached.* As one rounds the mark, the spinnaker boom is shoved out, and the sail begins to draw at once.

It is different, if the *mark is approached on the wind;* the retarding resistance of the wind forbids an early hoisting of the spinnaker, and one should not begin to set it, until *after* rounding the mark. But, with a good crew, the time needed for this manoeuvre should not exceed ten seconds (on small boat).

Allotment of the Work for a Crew of *Three*
First Part of Manoeuvre

The man on the jib sheet goes on deck with the spinnaker and shackles it to the halyard — see that the halyard runs *abaft* the bifurcation of the jib sheets! He takes the spinnaker sheet, which should always be made fast to the sail, between his teeth or steps on it with his foot. Sheet, spinnaker guy and halyard are not to be confounded. At the same time

The man on the main sheet shoves the spinnaker boom forward onto the deck, leads the *guy* outside the main and back stays aft and hands it to the helmsman — the only thing the latter has to do is to hold it. The man on the main sheet now hoists the spinnaker; at the same time the man on the

* First used and introduced to America by the author.

jib sheet holds the sail, spreading it out with its rope leech outward.

Second Part of Manoeuvre

The man on the jib sheet pushes the spinnaker boom out and holds it in its proper position, indifferent as to whether the guy is being tended or not. It should be shoved out in such a manner, that the sail gets no back wind; this can be avoided by pushing the boom out not exactly at right angles to the boat, but *always inclined somewhat forward*. In setting the spinnaker as well as in shoving out the boom, the man on the jib sheet should always work with his face toward the bow, i. e. he should stand *behind the* spinnaker *boom* and *keep his eye on the sail* and not in front of it looking aft.

For the socalled *"secret manoeuvre"* the order of succession is naturally quite different. No one goes on deck at first. The sail is shackled onto the halyard below in the cockpit, so as not to attract the attention of one's competitors; everything is prepared quietly and without unnecessary commotion.

Allotment of the Work for a Crew of *Two*

The man on the jib sheet shackles on the sail, hoists it and, in order to prevent it from being caught by the wind and blown off deck into the water and, at the same time, that he may be able to pull it up with both hands, lets the spinnaker slide up *between his arms;* he then pushes out the boom and tends the sheet.

The helmsman pulls up the centerboard and holds the spinnaker guy.

Tending the Spinnaker

We designate as a faultlessly tended spinnaker a sail:

I. That never once falls in nor gets back wind.

II. The whole surface of which, never only part, always draws.

III. The surface of which always presents the greatest attainable arching to the wind.

IV. That always draws in the direction of the course sailed.

From these fundamental requirements we can realize how difficult is the tending of this sail, which must, as it were, be served constantly in such a manner that a maximum efficiency is developed. Many an experienced skipper may have a series of glorious victories to his credit, without having ever appreciated the *true value or actual power* of the spinnaker.

The falling in of the sail can be avoided, that is, its maximum driving power can be attained only, when it is served by one man *alone,** who tends both sheet and guy; as with a balance with its two arms or scales, he strives continually to improve the position of the sail by correct adjustment of the two ropes. These two reins of the spinnaker are tended according to the following principles:

I. One strives to pay out the *sheet* as much as possible, in order to enable the spinnaker to fly. Two advantages are gained, when this can be accomplished: The wind off the spinnaker no longer falls on the lee of the mainsail and the jib is clear — not blanketed — and also draws (cf. sketches B & C on page 264).

II. One pulls in the guy as far as possible, but only so far that no back wind falls onto the lee of the sail, in order that the boom may stand as nearly

___
* On small boats.

262

Parachute Spinnakers

"Before Wind."

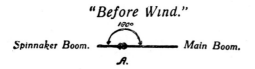

Spinnaker Boom. — — Main Boom.

A.

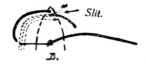

Slit.

B.

Correct.
*(Funnel Effect — Wind off
Spinnaker streams onto Jib.)*

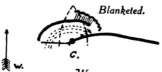

Blanketed.

C.

W.

Wrong.
*Wind off Spinnaker spills onto Main-
sail — Jib blanketed, also Spinnaker
partly — Suction reduced in Mainsail
— Air Cushion in Spinnaker.*

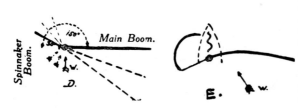

as possible at right angles to the course, i. e. that the driving force may act as much as possible in the direction of the course (cf. sketch A).

At first sight it may seem a paradox to haul in the guy to its limit on the one side and to let out the sheet as far as possible on the other. And yet the art of tending the spinnaker lies precisely in a compromise between these two endeavours. We can, in fact, remain true to the above four fundamental rules very simply, if we tend the spinnaker according to the following principle or order of precedence: First, let out the sheet — dead before the wind — until the clew of the spinnaker lies just in front of or against the luff of the jib, whereby a narrow *slit* is formed between the spinnaker and the jib (cf. sketch B). In order to accomplish this, the guy is let out considerably at the same time. The sail begins to fly.

Then haul in the guy slowly, as far as possible — without letting the sail *fall in*.

The slit between spinnaker and jib cannot always be brought about on account of lack of wind. An especially simple manipulation to assist the spinnaker to *fly* and at the same time to prevent the falling in of its leech during the intervals between the flaws without having recourse to the *guy* — letting it out — is to *lift the outer end of the spinnaker boom;* for this purpose, on yachts, a man is sent forward on deck. The sail will then not fall in, when the wind lets up (cf. sketch on next page).

The reason for having a slit between spinnaker and jib is an aerodynamic one; it introduces the action of the socalled "funnel" effect between spinnaker and jib, which increases the suction of the jib on the one hand

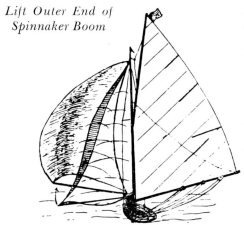

Lift Outer End of Spinnaker Boom

and reduces the size of the air cushion on its windward surface on the other, since the air streams off the spinnaker through the slit, which serves as a vent, and so allows the influx of fresh wind onto it. In spite of the slit, or rather perhaps on account of its presence, a part of the wind off the spinnaker is thrown onto the jib, which fills out in consequence, whereby it is utilized a second time by the latter sail (cf. sketch B on preceding page).

With the Spinnaker Shifted Forward

The position of the spinnaker boom is, of course, dependent on the direction of the wind; dead before it the boom should lie in the prolongation of the main boom, i. e. at right angles to the keel of the boat (sketch A, p. 264), but with the wind veering only a few degrees toward our weather quarter it should form an angle of about 30° with the prolongation of the main boom, i. e. the latter should still be carried at right angles to the keel, whereas the spinnaker boom should be shifted forward about that angle (30°) (cf. sketch D). The reason for this is that the comparatively flat mainsail draws better or develops a greater drive, when the wind falls on it obliquely than at right angles, whereas the spinnaker with its larger arching develops its maximum drive at an angle of about 90°.

Let us now investigate the reverse case, where the wind veers more toward our leeward quarter. If, for any reason, we are compelled to endure this veering of the wind — for example, one avoids jibing just before reaching a mark — one should not refrain from hauling in the spinnaker boom considerably over the line at right angles to the keel of the boat; at the same time the spinnaker sheet should be let out to a great distance (cf. sketch E, p. 264).

With regard to the handling of the spinnaker in a heavy flaw, in which the spinnaker boom, especially when shifted forward, is lifted to such an extent that it threatens to clap or jibe over to the other side — onto the mainsail — *do not luff, but bear off!* Remember this! Even if the wind is blowing a hurricane, keep on your course until this auxiliary sail has been taken down — at an opportune moment. If one luffs, then everything flies off and away, the spinnaker flaps round in front of the fore stay and off to leeward, the boat lies way over on her side and, if one happens to be on a *small centerboard boat* and does not capsize, one can, as the Austrians say, "incidentally" congratulate oneself. So, if we wish to keep the spinnaker drawing and the boat quiet or if anything is unclear on the foredeck, we bear off dead before the wind.

The Trim of the Boat

Before the wind as with the wind abeam a boat should be sailed *"upright."* One may even tip the smaller (centerboard) craft a bit to windward, that the center of effort (gravity) of the mainsail lie higher. The mainboom is thereby lifted somewhat out of the lowest layers of the air — next to the surface of the water, where the wind is known to decrease appreciably in velocity (cf. Part I). On the other hand, in stormy weather, one lets a small boat lie over somewhat *to leeward,* as the danger of capsizing to windward is greater than to leeward. The same holds also for a yacht, whose boom threatens to clap over to windward at any moment. In a dead sea, the mainsail should be held fast, that it may not swing to and fro, and, especially on boats with flat overhangs a man should be sent forward to lessen the pounding.

The distribution of weight: Strangely enough, the majority of our yachtsmen are of the opinion that, before the wind, the weight must be aft; hence the command: "Every one on the stern." But this is wrong. The idea of weighing down the stern has been erroneously adopted from the meter boats (the 6-12 meter R-yachts). These narrow breasted boats settle or bury so at the head from the pressure of the wind, as well as from the great weight of their sails and rigging, that they can be balanced only — before the wind, by shifting the whole crew aft. But the conditions for our modern racing boats are quite different. The modern boat must without exception be laid on her nose in running before the wind. Thereby her stern is lifted out of the water, the water line aft becomes more pointed or tapering and the boat is not held fast to the water from the harmful suction effect astern. Whoever doubts this should try to row a tender or skiff with a heavy man sitting in the stern!

The Position of the Centerboard

In order to form a clear conception of the manner in which the centerboard should be tended, let the following experiment serve our purpose: Two boats, one with her centerboard pulled quite up, the other with hers let entirely down, are sailing the same stretch before the wind side by side. We find, to our surprise, that both boats reach the goal at about the same time, that is, they boat attain the same speed. How is this to be explained? According to current opinion, one would expect the boat with the centerboard pulled entirely up to be the faster of the two. The reason that both boats ran at the same speed is that *neither* carried her centerboard in the correct position. We gain the impression, on the one hand, that too much board appears to be far from so harmful as one is accustomed to suppose, and, on the other hand, there can be little more doubt that it is also not advantageous to have the board pulled up entirely. The circumstances are these: The less centerboard in the water the better, *provided the boat does not drift — slide off to leeward.* If we are dead before the wind and steer an absolutely straight course, then the centerboard may be hauled up entirely. But how often is it the case that the wind strikes the sail exactly at right angles for any length of time? Extremely seldom! If the wind veers only a trifle toward the quarter, the boat with no board in the water will drift or slide off to leeward. This drift, even if it be ever so small and hardly noticeable, retards her speed more than we are accustomed to suppose.

Using Spinnakers on a Reach

267

From the above considerations we may conclude as follows:

I. On starting on a stretch before the wind, we first set the spinnaker and then, upon the conclusion of this manoeuvre, pull up the centerboard, for the latter is the less decisive factor.

II. Before the wind, the centerboard should generally be *half or three quarters way up,* and only very seldom — practically never, should the last quarter be taken out of the water. One judges, the amount of centerboard to allow indirectly from an exact determination of the direction of the wind. One follows the course of the boat from a range taken on the land and assures oneself every few minutes, whether she is drifting or not. The centerboard may then be pulled up gradually, as long as one does not detect the slightest drift. To sum up: It is a less mistake to carry too much board than too little.

III. Just before the end of the spinnaker course, first lower the board and then prepare to take down the spinnaker. The former will then not be forgotten, and it does not matter, if the whole surface of the board is in the water a few minutes sooner. It is also better, in consideration of the excitement incidental to the ensuing manoeuvre, to have the centerboard down in time.

IV. In jibing or in coming about, you should have sufficient centerboard in the water. If you are expecting a luffing match or the like, see that the board is well down in *due time.*

Technique of Jibing

Attention should be called here to the differences in the execution of this manoeuvre in light and in heavy winds.

Jibing in light breezes: The mainsail should be jerked in with *great strength and speed,* with *all the ropes* of the sheet in one's hands, and *not* taken in — slowly, by hauling in the sheet through the blocks. On the other hand, it should be let out *very slowly* — on the other side. This gives the boat a shove forward, similarly as the jerking of the tiller to one side with a slow return midships imparts a forward motion to the boat. *The centerboard should be at least half way down* when jibing.

Jibing in a strong wind: Haul in the mainsail by pulling in the sheet through the blocks. When it is half way in, corresponding to wind abeam, hasten the jibing by bearing off a bit (cf. sketch on page 270). The result is that the sail will soon come over, without one having to wait until it is pulled in midships (cf. sketch, positions b). Now follow two important points, on which the complete success of the manoeuvre depends. First, pay off smoothly and quickly, whereby the sudden pull to which the sheet is subjected from the swinging over of the sail is greatly diminished. Secondly, *bear off* as much as possible (cf. sketch, positions c). The boat is thus prevented from being pressed way over on her side and consequently from being thrown unnecessarily off her course into the wind (cf. sketch, positions d). The centerboard should be half or even the whole way down, as also the blade of the rudder.

Jibing in a light wind: The allotment of the work and its order of succession for *two men* are the following:

1. *Cast off the jib sheet;* this is important, as otherwise the spinnaker may get entangled in it. Lower the centerboard.

W. Colman.

Scows on Lake Geneva.

I 40 is in leading position.—I 17 can not break through in lee in spite of her larger spinnaker.

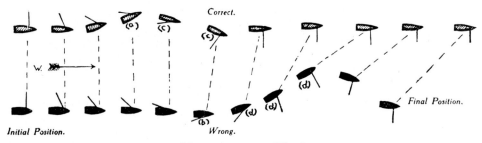

Correct.

(a) (c) (c)

W. (d)

(b) (d) (d)

Initial Position.

Wrong.

Final Position.

Jibing in strong Wind.

2. The helmsman takes charge of the mainsail; the man on the jib sheet casts off the spinnaker sheet and guy, swings the spinnaker boom *up abaft* the jib, lets it down on the other side, without trying to pull it aft, and then holds it in place *without* tending the sheets.* *Simultaneously* the mainsail is brought over; and thereupon:

3. The sheets are tended and, finally, the centerboard is pulled up, but not entirely.

Jibing in a strong wind:

1. Cast off the jib sheet and lower the centerboard.

2. Upon the spinnaker sheets being cast off, the man on the jib sheet swings the spinnaker boom up abaft the jib, lets it down on the other side directly in front of the mainsail, adjusts the sail and makes the sheets fast. In this way the spinnaker, being blanketed by the mainsail, is easily set and adjusted in the *"wind-shadow"* of the latter (cf. sketch below).

3. Then — but not before — the mainsail is taken in and swung over to the other side in the customary manner (cf. above), and the spinnaker, being already set, begins to draw at once. Meanwhile the man on the jib sheet tends the back stays.**

4. Pull up the centerboard.

In jibing around a mark the jib should be hauled in (on the other side) and *trimmed for the ensuing leg before* the manoeuvre.

Taking Down the Spinnaker:

1. Cast off the guy.

2. Let the outer end of the spinnaker boom swing forward, and then shove the boom aft between mast and stays into the cockpit. Lower the sail *into the cockpit.* The time required for this simple manoeuvre should not exceed five seconds. There is, therefore, no reason for not letting the spinnaker

Jibing in Strong Wind remain set and drawing until just before the turn.

* For brevity, when referring to both sheet and guy, we use the expression "sheets."

** On jibing a yacht, the weather back stay must be made fast *before* any pressure is brought to bear on it. On a smaller centerboard boat it should first be wound round the cleat only once, as the most important thing after the jibing manoeuvre is to get the crew *lying out on deck — up to windward,* at once; upon the successful conclusion of this critical manoeuvre, the back stay may be carefully belaid.

This concludes our discussion on the technique of running before the wind, and the principal points may be summarized as follows:

     I. Press down to leeward at opportune moments.

    II. Let the mainsail entirely out — as far as the sheet permits.

   III. The spinnaker should be tended by *one* man, carefully and correctly (small boats).

   IV. Keep the boat erect — as little heeled as possible.

    V. Let down enough centerboard — rather too much than too little.

   VI. In ordinary winds do *not* shift the weight aft.

Tactics

It has already been observed that the tactics on a run before the wind are of an irksome, bitter nature for the leading boat, as she is doomed to be overhauled, unless she is at least four or five boat lengths ahead. Even when the lead is greater, the sword of the pursuer still sways over the head of his victim. Is there any helmsman who sails his boat before the wind *in the lead* with pleasure and a feeling of ease? What skipper has not had the experience of being overhauled, the whole field running up on him at full speed in a flaw, that enables them not only to overcome an enormous lead but also to rush by and beyond him? Who does not recall that otherwise so agreeable but under such circumstances so thrilling sound, the rumbling of the bow waves of an approaching opponent? One lies defenceless awaiting the fatal blow, only to come to grief in the turmoil of one's aggressors with the painful thought of having gained in vain a lead that has required hours of hard work.

What is to be done? What offensive measures remain at our command? Certainly, in this case we cannot maintain our good lead, that is out of the question, but we may contest it, *that is possible*. However, since the cards are, as we have observed, very unequally dealt in this game, let us, in pursuance of our tactics, imagine ourselves at once in the position of the attacked and assume the defensive. A few general facts should, however, be premised.

1. Provided the two skippers are equally matched, the pursuer has the advantage.

2. The blanketing zone extends to four mast lengths, that of the disturbed wind to a greater distance. (In a light breeze the former distance is somewhat less.)

3. The windward position is, generally, to be preferred. At all events, the inner position at the turning mark is a fundamental requisite and a decisive factor.

4. Avoid fouling the mark either with the hull or sails of your boat.

5. If the run before the wind should be the last leg of the racing course, note whether the finish is *at right angles to it*.

6. If tactics require it, do not refrain from giving up the lead for the time being.

7. Do not lose sight of a third boat in your fight with a second and, should the former close up on you, prepare to conclude that fight at once.

In the following treatment of a fight between two boats alone, we discriminate between the *ten principal or familiar cases* (cf. sketches I-X on pp. 274-277):

Case I: Defence (Sketch I, p. 274)

Our pursuer holds his course, blankets and gradually draws up on us. We luff up somewhat to avoid being blanketed. If, in spite of this manoeuvre, our competitor travels faster than we do and passes us, we hold close to his leeward quarter, in order, if possible, to be able to lay our boom across his stern and incidentally blanket him. In this situation a breaking through in our lee is quite unlikely. But we must not lose sight of our opponent for a moment, because, if he gets his bow clear, he can shove it up suddenly under our stern to windward — an attack that is difficult to parry, if discovered too late. If our opponent holds his course, remaining in our lee, he will lose the race under normal circumstances.

In the racing regulations there is a paragraph which reads: "A yacht is not allowed to leave *her proper or correct course*, in order to prevent an overtaking yacht from passing her to leeward." In my opinion this paragraph is not justifiable, because it gives the overtaking yacht a further advantage and is contrary to the sporting idea that "contest is the essence of boat racing." On the other hand, however, it is not so very difficult to evade this stipulation, as it lays special stress on the expression "proper or correct course" and, in my opinion, the "proper or correct course" is the one which *wins* the race. But even if we do not interpret the regulation in this sporting sense, the expression "proper or correct course" is an extremely vague and elastic one.

The German interpretation (translation) of this racing regulation appears to differ materially from the original — the English text, which reads: "An overtaken yacht must never bear down on a yacht passing her to leeward (on the same side as her boom), but the leeward yacht must not luff until clear."

Case II: Attack (Sketch II, p. 274)

On the part of the overtaking boat the attack is carried out as follows: On the assumption that your opponent steers a straight course for the mark or finish, blanket him, directing your own course exactly according to your racing pennant. The blanketing effect extends to a distance of at least four mast lengths — of your own boat. In this manner you haul up gradually on your competitor, running in his wake until you have quite closed up on him; it is here that the blanketing begins to work effectively, that is, most detrimentally for the blanketed boat. At the last moment, just before you become unclear, you luff and shove the nose of your boat up around the stern of your competitor's, but your boom should *still be hanging* over the deck of the other boat; just before it threatens to foul her back stay, you luff again, this time quickly, and let your boat shoot by her to windward. But even then your victim should not be allowed to escape, for your mainsail is still blanketing his *spinnaker*.

As soon as you have worked so far ahead that your main boom is in danger of fouling the spinnaker pole of your competitor, you luff once more, the third time, and shoot by at full speed to windward; but be careful of a foul, as your competitor will surely take no precautions to avoid one. The other boat is so handicapped by having been blanketed — at least partially — up to the last moment that considerable time will have to elapse, before she can recover and get started again.

Case III: Defence (Sketch III, p. 274)

Our pursuer blankets us. We run up to windward to get clear. He luffs too, cuts off the corners of the course and thus gradually hauls up on us. We continue to luff until we have brought him into the "hopeless position." He cannot break through to windward. The situation is not, however, as simple as it may appear, as one has to direct one's tactics according to two points of view. On the one hand, one must not luff too little, as the overtaking boat might be able to break through to windward, and, on the other hand, one must not luff too much, as otherwise one might be obliged to sacrifice one's whole lead unnecessarily, which is to be measured by the distance to the mark or finish. Suppose now our competitor, who has not succeeded in breaking through to windward, tries a second very dangerous manoeuvre. With a sharp turn he suddenly bears off, in order to break through to leeward and run straight for the goal — note this for the attack. If we do not discover this — his intention — before he has begun to carry out the manoeuvre, then it is already too late. We must *expect* such a manoeuvre and be prepared for it. The main sheet, which has already been taken in, not by hauling it through the blocks, but with all the ropes in the hand at once, is let out again quickly and the boat is swung off to leeward simultaneously with our competitor's and at the same speed. If we succeed in this manoeuvre, the ticklish game is won, and, as we are partially blanketing our adversary, we reach the goal first, provided, however, we are able to keep on the same tack, that is, provided we are not forced to jibe on account of having crossed the *axis of the wind*.

Case IV: Wrong Defence (Sketch IV, p. 275)

In the preceding case the game is lost for the boat in the defence the moment *the axis of the wind* is crossed. It ensues as follows: Both boats luff as in case III. Our aggressor falls somewhat behind and gets clear of our stern; he then swings the nose of his boat suddenly off to leeward and *jibes*. However cleverly and quickly we may follow suit, by the act alone of jibing — and in this case we are obliged to do so in order to lay our course for the mark — we become the *leeward boat* and the game is lost!

Case V: Correct Defence (Sketch V, p. 275)

How should the attack be parried in such a case as the preceding? The pill is a bitter one — but healing. Most will recoil from swallowing it, because nothing is harder for a skipper than to sacrifice purposely even as little as a single yard of his lead. But so it must be in this case. The fight, which can be won with certainty, is to be conducted as follows: One takes the greatest pains to note just when the axis of the wind is crossed. Therefore, one should be constantly taking bearings on the direction of the wind with respect to the mark — in the case of a finish with respect to the more weather mark. As soon as both boats reach the axis of the wind — provided our aggressor has not already swung off to leeward — then, from that moment, our situation improves, as we are the attacked, and it continues to do so the more we can entice him off the course to the mark, that is, the further we can force him over the axis of the wind. The manoeuvre itself is extremely simple: We let our aggressor catch up on us, waiting until *he is no longer*

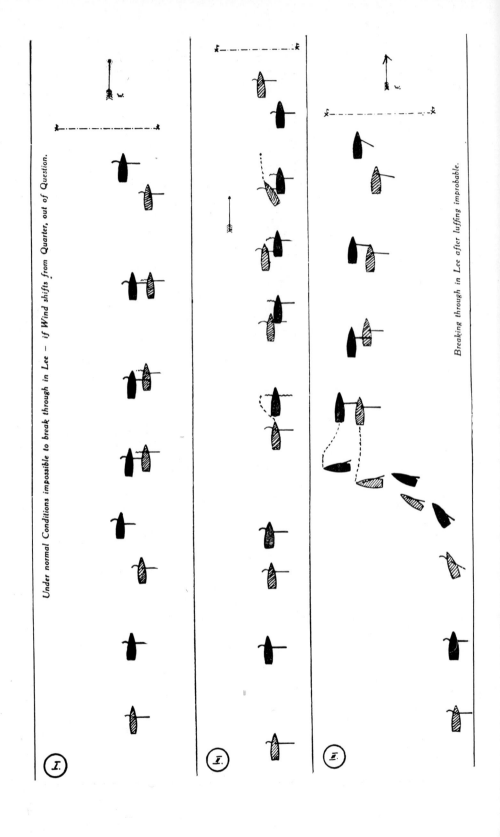

I. *Under normal Conditions impossible to break through in Lee – if Wind shifts from Quarter, out of Question.*

II.

III. *Breaking through in Lee after luffing improbable.*

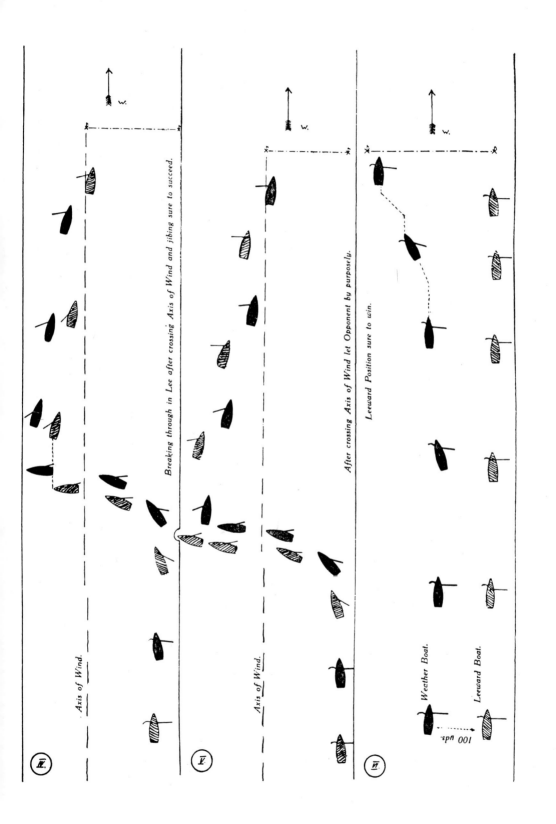

IV.

Axis of Wind.

W.

Breaking through in Lee after crossing Axis of Wind and jibing sure to succeed.

V.

Axis of Wind.

W.

After crossing Axis of Wind let Opponent by purposely.

VI.

W.

Leeward Position sure to win.

Weather Boat.

Leeward Boat.

100 yds.

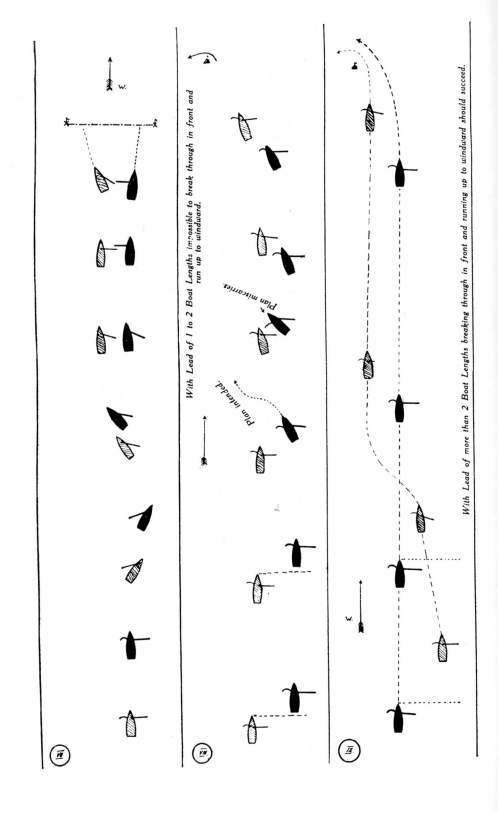

W.

With Lead of 1 to 2 Boat Lengths impossible to break through in front and run up to windward.

Plan miscarries.

Plan intended.

With Lead of more than 2 Boat Lengths breaking through in front and running up to windward should succeed.

W.

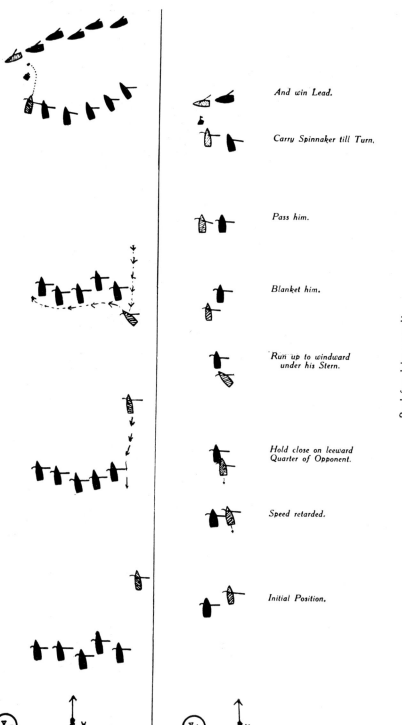

And win Lead.

Carry Spinnaker till Turn.

Pass him.

Blanket him.

Run up to windward
under his Stern.

Hold close on leeward
Quarter of Opponent.

Speed retarded.

Initial Position.

Read from below upward!

clear of us, so that he may not be able to swing off under our stern and break through in our lee. Proud of having overtaken us so easily, he is unlikely to give this possibility a second thought, quite aside from the fact that we could frustrate the least intention of such a move on his part by not allowing him to *escape* from the overlap already established; in other words, he cannot swing off under our stern without fouling us. Should he, however, fall astern somewhat, in order to avoid the overlap, we also need only retard our speed correspondingly. This situation, which we have brought about *purposely,* after having crossed the wind axis, becomes the more favorable for us the longer we are able to maintain it. If, on the one hand, we have forced our aggressor, as weather and overtaking yacht, to establish the overlap, having slowed up, if necessary, to hold him at bay, we should, on the other hand, resort to all legitimate measures to make it as difficult as possible for him to overhaul us *too soon.* Not until he has finally succeeded in the attempt, which we shall hardly be able to *frustrate,* should the following manoeuvre be undertaken: We bear off, jibe and hold a straight course for the mark; we are in the lead and to windward, and our prospects of winning the race are most favorable.

Case VI: (Sketch VI, p. 275)

The two boats are running neck and neck but so far apart that the windward boat cannot reach her rival to leeward, without running considerably off her course. Therefore, it would not be advisable for the former to try to attack her competitor to leeward, because she would be obliged to jibe and would, moreover, fall so far astern before she reached the wake of the latter — due to the greater distance to be covered — that it might be doubtful, whether the ensuing blanketing would prove effective. Now let us suppose the boat to leeward steers a straight, the shortest, course to the mark, that is, she runs straight for the leeward mark (cf. sketch VI). As windward boat, we can win the run in two ways. Either we can steer straight for the weather mark with the wind somewhat more on our quarter, whereby, it is true, we must cover a greater distance, but we travel so much faster on that point of sailing, that we may, nevertheless, reach the finish sooner. Or — and this might be the better, although somewhat more difficult technique, we make a compromise between *greater speed and shorter course, that is,*

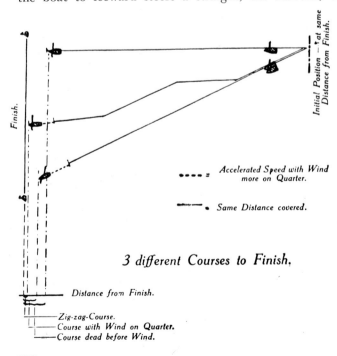

- - - = Accelerated Speed with Wind more on Quarter.

———• Same Distance covered.

3 different Courses to Finish.

———— Distance from Finish.

———— Zig-zag-Course.
———— Course with Wind on Quarter.
———— Course dead before Wind.

Initial Position — at same Distance from Finish.

Finish.

278

we luff at intervals, in order to accelerate our speed, and then bear off again, in order to run on the shorter course with that accelerated speed. By taking exact bearings on our rival, we can ascertain whether we are travelling faster than he is on this latter course. Not until that acceleration has been spent and we observe that both boats are running again at the same speed, do we repeat the manoeuvre. We luff again somewhat; the boat recovers her agility, that is, she begins at once to run faster. Upon attaining the desired acceleration, we bear off again slowly onto the shorter course. This process off luffing and then bearing off, resulting in a change in direction of course of about $10°$, is repeated at intervals until the finish is reached. For a better understanding of this technique the schematic drawing on page 278 may serve, in which three different courses are represented; the equal distances are shown in the black lines, the remaining portions of the two longer courses covered in the same or even shorter time, that is the distances gained due to the accelerated speed on these two courses, in dotted lines.

Case VII: Attack (Sketch VII, p. 276)

Let us now imagine we are closer to our rival, either next to him, or in his wake; in this case we assume the offensive. We attack at once by blanketing. Our opponent assumes the defensive and jibes. As counter-attack, we jibe also, cut off the corners, draw up on and blanket him again. As counter-defence, our opponent jibes again. We jibe too at once, keeping him blanketed. This is repeated several times. Thereupon he gives up the struggle and bears off on the straight course for the mark. But thereby he sacrifices his weather berth. If both boats have their sails on the same side, we blanket our opponent, until we can take advantage of a flaw to shoot by him at full speed. Our victory is then assured.

The second time our opponent jibes, as indicated in the drawing, we may be able to blanket him, but only for a short time, as the two boats soon diverge. In this case the success of the manoeuvre is doubtful, but the boat, that has the wind more from the quarter, has the better chance to win.

Case VIII: False Manoeuvre (Sketch VIII, p. 276)

Let us imagine ourselves in the position of the leeward boat and that our opponent is about one or two boat lengths astern. On the supposition that we are on the last leg of the racing course, there would be no reason for us, under normal circumstances, to change our course, as we should maintain our lead to the finish, provided our opponent does not try to blanket us, which need scarcely be feared, because he would have to jibe to do so. But the situation undergoes a change, if the run is not the last leg of the course but ends at a mark, which must be rounded, as indicated in the sketch. Then the solution is: "Inner position." To attain this, we work up slowly to windward, for we must acquire the inner berth at the mark, that we may be able to blanket our rival upon turning up to windward. The beginning of the manoeuvre seems to succeed smoothly enough, until our sail runs into the blanketing zone of our competitor's. We were perhaps of the opinion that we should be able to break through this zone with little difficulty, but this is *not the case;* we soon realize that we have been deceived. The speed of our boat decreases more and more and, before we can reconsider our situation, our plan has failed. We are subjected to the blanketing action of our opponent that increases from second to second and, gnashing our teeth, we must witness how he shoots by us to windward. Now, where was the mistake in our calculations?

Judging by feeling alone, one would think that the tip end of the blanketing cone might be easy to break through, that is, that it could be broken through quickly. But what we have overlooked is that the windward boat has to luff up only a trifle, in order to shift her blanketing cone to the side, causing it to *travel in the direction of our course,* so that we are *continually* lying within its baleful influence and have to *contend with the blanketing four or five times as long* as we first supposed.

Case IX: Successful Manoeuvre (Sketch IX, p. 276)

Experience has taught that the attempt to run up to windward under the sail of a competitor succeeds only, when *our lead amounts to more than two boat's lengths.* This case is represented in sketch IX.

Case X (Sketches X, a and b, p. 277)

The minimum lead of two boat's lengths will not be sufficient for breaking through to windward, when one is running in the lee of several competitors. Here a lead of five or more boat's lengths is required, and it should be undertaken only to gain the *inner position* at a turning mark. To run *through such a blanketing fan* is exceedingly difficult and, unless one has a sufficiently long lead, there is only *one alternative:* Sacrifice your lead, retard your speed and run in *behind* and up to windward of the whole field. Here one always has the automatic compensation, upon bearing off before the wind again, of being able to run at accelerated speed in undisturbed wind; the lost ground may, in fact, be regained from the accelerated speed attained alone from the suction effect produced by the sails of the other boats to leeward. Note, therefore, that *even, when one is well in the lead, a leeward position at a short distance from the turning mark must be given up at once.* Let us briefly repeat how the manoeuvre is to be performed with one or more opponents (cf. sketch X a and b). Retard your speed purposely, work up alongside your nearest opponent, and, the moment you are clear of him, run up to windward under his stern and blanket him, doing it as quietly as possible, that he may not be aware of your intention. This manoeuvre is repeated, until you are to the weather of the whole field. The inner position at the mark is thereby gained, with the result that you acquire the lead at the turn (cf. photograph on page 282).

Before leaving the tactics before the wind, let us consider one more case, which, it is true, seldom occurs but the knowledge of which may prove useful at times. On a run before the wind, suppose the wind changes quite unexpectedly, heading off the boats in the lead to such an extent that they have

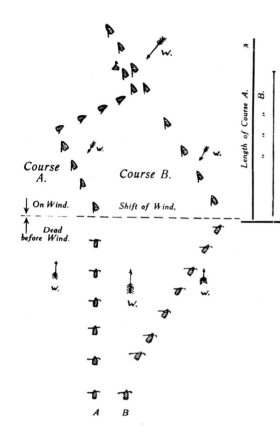

Course
A.

Course B.

On Wind.

Dead
before Wind.

Shift of Wind,

W.

W.

W.

W.

W.

W.

A   B

Length of Course A.   B.

to beat to windward. If we are far in the rear, how should we manoeuvre that we may take advantage of this sudden shift of wind? — As soon as we notice that the group in the lead begins to run close-hauled, we change our course in the direction that will bring us farthest up to windward upon finally reaching the wind that heads us off. We gain three advantages by this change of course: First, the weather berth, just mentioned, upon the shift of the wind; secondly, we run for a longer time with the more favorable, still prevailing wind; and thirdly, we travel at greater speed on this course — with the wind somewhat on our quarter. The accompanying drawing represents two boats, A and B, which observe at once this shift of wind in the leading group. A keeps on her original course, but B holds well off of that course — to the right in the drawing — and runs with the wind more on her (starboard) quarter. Both boats run into the head wind — indicated in the drawing by the broken line — at about the same time and must then beat to windward. But now B is well in the lead, as the distance to be covered by her is shorter.

Fight "for Inner Position" at Mark; "Mephisto" [J 239], Winner of "Seglerhaus" Challenge Cup, Wannsee, 1925, Rounds First.

Precautionary Measures

Sailing in Rough Weather

should be treated in a section for itself, as in a storm, where all finer technique and tactics have to be left out of consideration, the leading question is: How can one weather it? In the ensuing let us, therefore, imagine ourselves on a boat of one of the *smaller* (centerboard) classes, fighting the storm, and let us discuss the most important questions which arise in this connection.

How to Parry a Flaw

A. Watch the approaching flaw and its various characteristics, observing the effect produced by it on the boats to windward — that are struck by it first.

B. Watch the flaw carefully before it strikes you and determine its direction of propagation from the direction and intensity of the curling and darkening of the water. In a storm, every flaw should be observed beforehand — as it is propagated over the surface of the water — in this manner.

C. Bring your boat at once in a position to take the flaw, i. e. parry it *before* it strikes her sails. It is often necessary to luff beforehand, that the flaw may not strike the sails too full, but the amount you should luff must be determined by the direction of the wind in the flaw. Sometimes one has to luff very quickly, with a *jerk*, especially on a yacht, as the flaw develops its greatest intensity, when it first sets in. On the other hand, the most dangerous situation for the boat is that where she is struck by the flaw with flapping sails, as she is thrown over on her side much more easily, when she has little headway; for we know the stability of a boat increases with her speed. The heeling tendency of the boat is much greater during the short interval from the moment the flaw strikes her sails till the pressure imparted to them has been conveyed, in the form of speed, to her hull, and it is generally within this critical interval that she capsizes. Therefore, we should parry a flaw of longer duration fuller, a short stormy burst of wind, which lasts only a few seconds, higher on the wind.

D. After the flaw has already struck the boat, the most important thing is to determine, when it will *develop its maximum intensity,* and to reserve the various methods of parrying it — these are letting out the sails and luffing or shooting up into the wind — for this most critical moment. But here luffing is to be recommended only, when the *boat is well under way*. In this case, an upset is unlikely.

E. Therefore, the most essential thing in a flaw is to keep your boat *running*, giving her a good full; in other words, risk driving her at full speed and do not luff, until you think the critical moment has arrived. If you have erred in your judgment by anticipating this moment of maximum intensity and have already parried the flaw, then your boat begins to lose her headway and the increasing velocity of the wind will drive the helpless craft to leeward and may soon upset her. Your only safe recourse — but this is applicable only for a short time, luffing, should, therefore, not be resorted to, until you are on the point of capsizing and sure that the wind will subside by the time the boat has come to a standstill.

The safest course, that is, the course on which the boat stands up best, is that with the wind *abeam*, because it is easiest to keep her running on this point of sailing.

A flapping of the *entire* sail, especially of the jib, should be avoided until the critical moment, alone on account of the unsteadiness, to which the boat is subjected, and the retarding effect which accompanies it. A flapping of the entire sail is, moreover, likely to cause a tear, whereas a sail which is only partly flapping will never tear. *In a race the jib should always be kept close-trimmed during the flaws,* (but that does not mean that it should be made fast) and every flaw should be parried with the mainsail alone. This is a technique that has been thoroughly tested and to which I should like to call particular attention. By this technique the boat acquires a certain steadiness in her forebody and does not keep luffing of her own accord; she also retains her speed, even when the whole mainsail has to be let out and flaps.

F. It is absolutely requisite that the helmsman on a small boat convinces himself every few minutes that the main sheet runs clear, so that it may be eased easily any moment. The main sheet should not lie in the immediate neighborhood of cleats, blocks or other obstacles, as it may get entangled or jammed, with the usual result that the boat capsizes. *If the main sheet gets fouled* and the boat consequently upsets, *the fault lies not with the main sheet but with the helmsman.*

G. Just as important as letting out the sheets at the right moment is taking them in again immediately after the flaw has been parried. This is in order to increase the speed and, apart from the advantage to be gained thereby over one's competitors in a race, to acquire the additional stability due to increased speed for the next flaw. If one person is tending both helm and main sheet, he will have to hold the sheet between his teeth every time he pulls it in with his one hand, for he must not take his other off the helm under any circumstances. Many a helmsman helps himself out of the predicament by steering for the time being with his foot, which is often quite advantageous, when the boat is so heeled that he should lean far out to windward; this is practically the only alternative of getting both hands free to tend the main sheet. The crew service is technically complete on small racers only when a third man and not the helmsman tends the main sheet; but, as it is necessary to have perfect accord between the tending of the helm and that of the main sheet, such distribution of work is difficult and must be thoroughly practised. If one is compelled to sail a boat *alone*

Cup Defender, "Enterprise"

in a strong wind, it is better to make the jib fast and manoeuvre with the mainsail alone, than vice versa. To be sure, in a storm this method has its shortcomings and, if it is impossible to lower the sails, let the jib flap and try to keep the boat from capsizing by running with the wind abeam. But, if it is possible to strike the sails, *lower first the mainsail and then the jib,* and not vice versa. Note this!

The same measures for the parrying of flaws hold also for yachts, with the exception of the tending of the sheets. Normally these are made fast; but in a storm, especially with a yacht that is not sufficiently decked in or in the case of one that has not been thoroughly tested, the main sheet should be kept in hand.

Danger of Sinking

is far greater than is generally supposed. On a heavy-weather boat, the sheet of the balloon jib must never be made fast in a storm. Although there may be no danger of the boat's capsizing, there is always the risk of a halyard parting, or the sail may tear or the mast may be carried away — generally where the jib halyard block is made fast to it. As on the smaller centerboard boat we should ease the main sheet as the wind increases; the same holds in a heavy sea, in which a boat would otherwise pound herself to death. Therefore, one should note the following: *If, in spite of the greatest exertion on the part of the helmsman to bear off in a flaw with the helm, the boat does not react but shoots up into the wind, this is always a sign that the mainsail is trimmed in too close.*

Let us next discuss briefly a few *possible impossibilities,* of which

Capsizing

deserves our special attention.

The reader will justly remark that theory differs from practice here most decidedly. Theoretically, capsizing is out of the question with faultless handling of boat and sails, but practically it appears to be more than possible. And still, if we premise a certain amount of forethought and caution, and exclude capsizing from a slow swamping of the boat — during a race — then capsizing ought to be avoidable as such, provided, of course, the handling of both boat and sails be faultless.

Let us consider the case, where the boat gradually fills with water. A craft, which is not fully decked in, is continually washed by the waves in severe weather and gradually fills with water. It is hardly necessary to observe that we should begin our struggle with this so dreaded, often invincible element as late as possible, not until a few moments before the preparatory gun. Before the start one should sail "dry," but during the race to sail "dry" is to sail badly. Now, how shall we keep as dry as possible before the start?

We luff in the trough of every wave as much as possible. As we begin to ascend, we bear off *sharply,* that our boat may not bore into the next crest with her nose. As we slide down on the other (windward) side of this wave, we luff up at once and let our boat run down its crest to the next wave, thereby accelerating her speed. By bearing off on ascending the crest of a wave, we offer our broadside to the impact of the on-coming masses of water, whereby the whole body of the boat is lifted evenly and not, as would otherwise happen, partly lifted and partly washed by the wave (cf. diagram

286

on this page). This technique, however, should be exactly reversed, if we are at sea in a small boat and trying to ride the large breakers; here we steer straight for the breaker, cutting it at right angles with the bow of our boat. This difference in technique is due to the prevailing conditions or to the purpose in view; at sea one has to avoid being upset and entirely swamped by a powerful combing breaker; but on landlocked bays and lakes this thought need scarcely trouble us, as the essential point here is to keep *as dry as possible.*

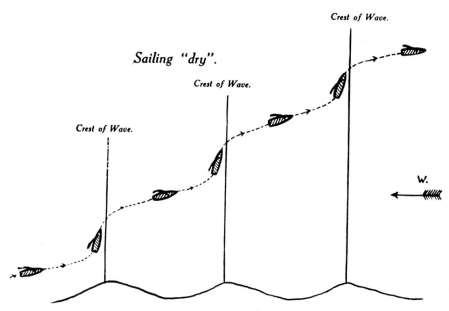

Now let us allow our fantasy to wander further. The race lasts several hours, the waves throw the little craft hither and thither and partly dash over and into her — for, in competition with our rivals, the technique of keeping dry must go overboard. Our boat gradually fills with water, until it reaches the cockpit floor and the floor boards begin to float. True, the man on the jib sheet is bailing continually during the *intervals between the flaws* with a bucket fastened to a long handle, so that, although he is sitting well up to windward, he can reach the water in the bottom or rather chine of the boat with his bailer. But even this precautionary measure may not suffice after a while. What is accomplished by hard work is suddenly quite undone by a single wave. More and more water collects in the boat. The helmsman may have chosen his course such that he will soon be able to run up under the lee of the land, but it may occur that this plan, correct enough in itself, cannot be carried out. The boat is already lying so deep in the water, that the next flaw may put her lee rail so far under, that with relatively little heeling the craft overturns, due to *no fault* of the crew; a most depressing finish, especially when one is in the lead, to have to succumb to one's only *two* remaining adversaries — wind and water!

But how is one to avoid every danger in such a case? Let us imagine that the boat is on the point of capsizing. The sails have already been let out entirely. Still a final attempt must be made to save the situation. The

287

Starboat in a Blow

E. Levick

man on the jib sheet, perhaps the helmsman too, *jumps out onto the center-board*. If the boat rights, then this acrobatic feat has succeeded, but if she does not, after repeated attempts to right her, then her fate is sealed, at least as regards the race.

The chief dangers which one seeks to avoid upon capsizing are:

1. Falling down to leeward and especially onto the sails. The latter is an especially unpleasant situation, as the wet duck of the sail sticks to one's body and deprives one of every freedom of action.

2. Getting one's feet entangled in the ropes.

On an overturned centerboard boat, that floats, one can climb up quite easily over the planking, as she turns over, onto the side that is out of the water — not too difficult, even for a woman.

Hereby the first danger may have been evaded, but a second is threatening: We are in danger of *re-capsizing*. The sail, which shortly after capsizing generally lies on the water, is suddenly caught by a flaw and lifted; the boat rights herself and, with a quick turn, the whole rigging slaps over to the other side. Those clinging to the upper side of the boat are plunged into the water and have to climb up over her deck to the other side, that they may not be buried under the boat or her sails; in the attempt they may congratulate themselves, if they do not get entangled in the rigging or ropes and drawn down under water. To forestall this re-capsizing, after the first overturn, a man should at once place himself *before the mast*. This position is in itself not only the best, as in the case of recapsizing one does not get buried under the sails but is able to jump back and forth between the mast and jib, but it also enables one to render a re-capsizing impossible, by simply *stepping on the mast* and pressing it down, should it threaten to right itself.

289

This danger averted, our next thought is our belongings. Valuables must be made fast to one's body or the boat at once. Also floor boards, oars and other boat trappings should be sought and secured. The next thing is to "unrig," provided there is no reason for sparing our strength — in case the judges' boat or some other craft is already coming to our rescue. Generally, in order to tow a capsized boat, the sails have to be taken off. As a rule one has to cut the halyards with a knife, as they are pulled so taut on the cleats from swelling that it is impossible to loosen them. After the sails with the spars have been taken aboard the motor boat, the little craft can easily be towed. We may observe that she can be towed easiest in an upright position; for which purpose we advise lifting her bow onto the stern of the motor boat and making it fast.

A Sinking Yacht

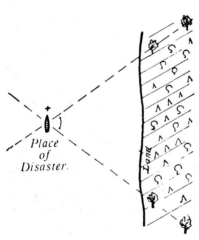

If there is danger of sinking from a leak in the planking, we should, of course, at once try to stop up the hole. It is often sufficient to put the yacht on the other tack or we may attempt by heeling her to keep the hole out of the water. But if these means fail, then we should try to reach shallow water and, if necessary, run the yacht aground.

But the case is different, when a yacht begins to sink from shipping water *in lee*. If, in spite of letting the sheets run and the crew leaning out as far to windward as possible, the yacht does not right herself, the only thing we can do is to locate the place of the disaster by *taking bearings*, in order to facilitate subsequent attempts at raising her. Bearings are taken from the yacht before she sinks or afterward from the water in the following manner: Note two objects on the shore in the same line or direction, for example two trees, one behind the other; then seek two other objects lying in a line that makes an angle of 60° to 90° with the former. The point of intersection of the two lines gives the spot sought on the water (cf. above sketch).

Collision

Let the sketches on page 292 serve as illustrations of how a collision may be averted at the last moment. The question is: How should not only the skipper of the one boat, that may not have the right of way, but also that of the other manoeuvre in order to avoid the collision?

In the case (sketch I), where the one boat A would ram her competitor B midships or farther aft, provided she continued on her course, *both boats must bear off sharply* to avoid the collision. In case II (sketch II), where boat A would strike the forward part of boat B, provided she held her course, *both boats must luff at once* to avoid fouling. Apparently very simple, but as a rule the simplest precautionary measure seldom occurs to either skipper

Sit in Front of Mast to Avoid Re-capsizing

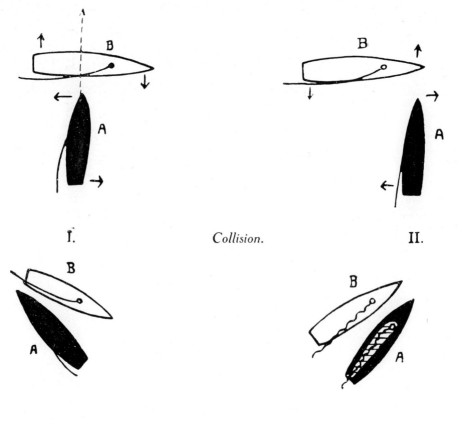

I.   *Collision.*   II.

What happens, if one manoeuvres otherwise?

at such critical moments! On the contrary, one generally acts from impulse and does just the wrong thing, unless one has foreseen the situation and manoeuvres accordingly.

The chief difficulty in such situations is that of eight possible combined actions there are only two, by which the collision may be avoided at the last moment, and then only on the assumption that both skippers manoeuvre correctly. We should, therefore, hardly be surprised that even our best skippers are not always successful in their attempts not to violate the most important racing regulation, which stipulates that in case of danger all precautionary measures should be taken by *both* skippers to avoid a collision.

E. Levick

The New York Fifty Footers Off Glen Cove in Manhassett Bay
Yacht Club Regatta, June, 1921. — What Is the Correct Manoeuvre?
(There are four boats involved!!)

Boom and Gaff on Opposite Side of Mast

This situation is indicated in the accompanying sketch. It is generally brought about by jibing in a strong wind and due to the fact that the mainsail has not been taken in *far enough* for this manoeuvre; the boom finally swings over to the other side, but the gaff is hanging off so far to leeward that it does not follow. What is to be done in this case? Should one luff — with respect to the position of boom to boat — with the hope of bringing the gaff over to the other side, or should one pull in the main sheet, bear off and jibe back again with the boom? Under no circumstances should the former attempt be made, as the gaff will swing *not back but only further off to leeward* and finally probably break under the increased pressure of the wind that is brought to bear on it in this unnatural, distorted position. The other alternative is the only correct one; upon hauling in the main sheet and bearing off, one jibes back again with the boom and thus has both the spars (with the sail) on the same side of the mast.

Breaking Mast

The Finish

We have already discussed various final struggles in the foregoing chapters, and there is but little to add thereto. In general, every sportsman should be guided by the fundamental principle that after he has begun a contest or race, he should finish it — sail the race to the finish. Except on windless days, when one is naturally inclined, after lying in a dead calm for hours, to steer a straight course for home, not to finish is equivalent to an intentional detraction from the victory of one's rivals, and therefore it is to be regarded as unsportsman-like for a competitor to abandon a race before crossing the finishing line.

We conclude the present subject with a few suggestions on the final struggle in the finish itself. First of all, we should not forget to observe, whether the line at the finish is at exactly right angles to the course or not, and to manoeuvre accordingly. If we are approaching the finish before the wind, the race may often be decided to our favor in the last few seconds by letting the spinnaker boom out as far (forward) as possible, as the time of crossing the line is taken, as soon as any part of the boat's hull or spars reaches it. Another possibility of gaining a few feet at the very last moment is to *jerk* in the mainsail just before the finish. This extremely effective manoeuvre is, however, fatal if attempted too soon. Therefore, one should measure the distance to the finishing line exactly and not resort to this means of accelerating the speed until the last moment, that is, until the last few yards before one reaches the line. This final shove forward, which, if correctly executed can amount to a yard, may be further increased in light airs, especially on a yacht, by having the crew *run* aft at the critical moment; it is determined by the physical law:

Weight of yacht $\times$ x (shove) $=$ Weight of crew $\times$ length of yacht.

For example: 1500 kg $x =$ 300 kg (4 men) 10 yds.;
hence $x =$ 2 yds.

Upon concluding the present treatise I venture to express the wish that yacht racing may develop as a more international and universal sport, quite free from all political tendencies and easily accessible to all that may choose to devote their leisure to this noblest of all sports. To effect this, more attention should be directed to international classes, less to the exclusive development of purely national types, which tend only to hinder mutual intercourse between nations and their peoples.

The Author's Successful 20 Sq. M. Racer "Aero"